Illustrated
COMPUTER
GRAPHICS
DICTIONARY

Illustrated
COMPUTER GRAPHICS
DICTIONARY

Donald D. Spencer, Ph. D.

CAMELOT PUBLISHING COMPANY
Ormond Beach, Florida

Published by
Camelot Publishing Company
P.O. Box 1357
Ormond Beach, FL 32175

This book was laser typeset in Helvetica.
Printed on acid-free paper.

TRADEMARKS
Trademarked names appear throughout this
dictionary. Rather than list the names and
entities that own the trademarks or insert a
trademark symbol with each mention of the
trademarked name, the publisher states that
it is using the names only for editorial purposes and to the benefit of the trademark
owner with no intention of infringing upon
that trademark.

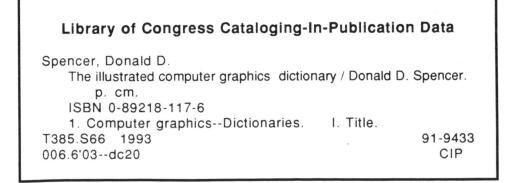

Library of Congress Cataloging-In-Publication Data

Spencer, Donald D.
   The illustrated computer graphics dictionary / Donald D. Spencer.
      p. cm.
   ISBN 0-89218-117-6
      1. Computer graphics--Dictionaries.   I. Title.
T385.S66   1993   91-9433
006.6'03--dc20   CIP

DEDICATION

To my daughter, Sherrie, who not
only typeset the book on a
Macintosh computer system,
but also produced several of the
illustrations.

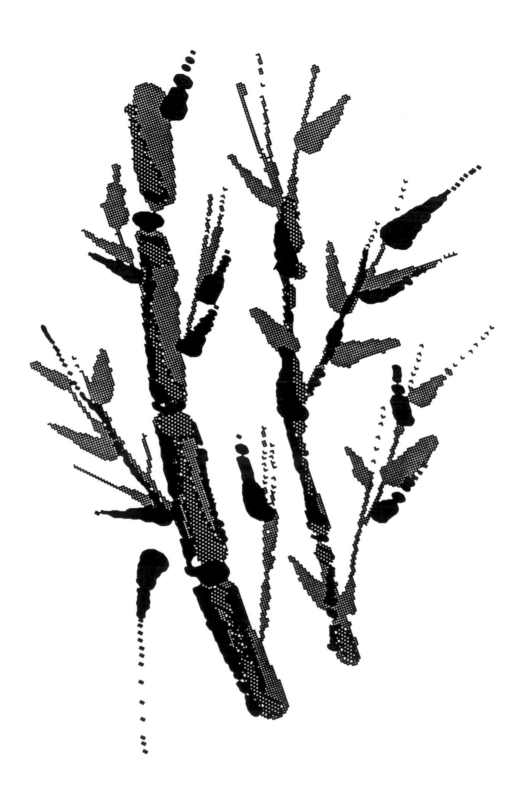

CONTENTS

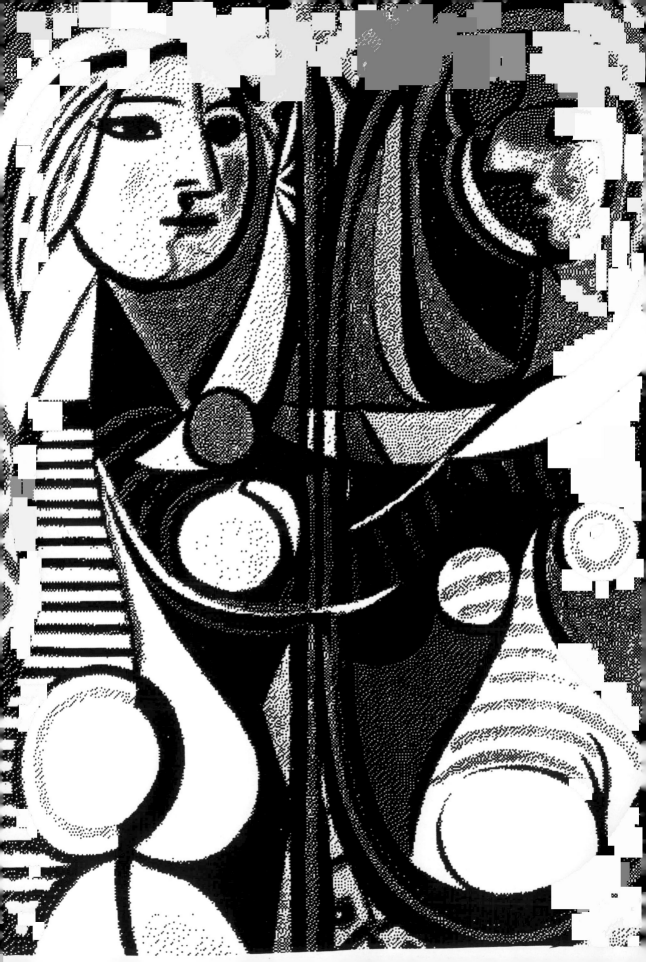

A WORD FROM THE AUTHOR

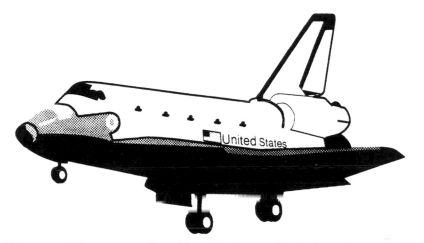

The *Illustrated Computer Graphics Dictionary* is designed to supply computer graphics artists, computer science personnel, students, teachers and others interested in computer graphics with a complete, nonspecialist reference for words and terms relating to the broad spectrum of producing images with a computer. The emphasis is on painting, drawing, and computer graphics. However, some terminology pertaining to desktop publishing, fractal geometry, computer science, graphic design, data communications, scientific visualization, computer-aided design, computer programming and business graphics is covered. The commonality of these related creative endeavors makes the inclusion of these associated terms useful and fitting.

Changing times are more evident in the computer graphic field than in almost any other. Trends toward the use of personal computers, laser printers, reproduction by scanners, optical storage, painting and drawing software, specialized graphics software, and desktop publishing have represented revolutionary changes. Computer graphics is a technology that has revolutionized the ways in which we create images.

In the *Illustrated Computer Graphics Dictionary* you will find concise, specific definitions of terms concerning processes, techniques, software, hardware and materials that are basic in the computer graphics field.

The purpose of the book is to supply everyone interested in computer graphics with accurate information covering a breadth of related material not otherwise available. If you find the dictionary useful, it will have fulfilled its purpose.

Donald D. Spencer
Ormond Beach, Florida

HOW TO USE THIS DICTIONARY

For quick reference, each term is presented as it is likely to occur in literature or conversation. "Color Monitor" can be found in the C's, not as "Monitor, Color" in the M's.

The terms normally appear in **boldface lower case** characters. Proper names and nouns are headed by an upper case letter, for example "**Mandelbrot, Benoit B.**" Acronyms are presented in **BOLDFACE CAPS** and the proper letters are amplified in the text; for example, **EPS** stands for Encapsulated PostScript. Cross-references that are important to an understanding of a term are included. If you cannot find a word, it might be listed in a slightly different form. For example, you might try looking for "graphics digitizer" and find the description under "graphics tablet." Only one definition has been included to avoid cluttering the book with the obvious.

The area from which the main word is derived, is often indicated in the definition; for example, In desktop publishing, In computer graphics, In optical scanning, In object-oriented programming, In artificial intelligence... If more than one definition is related to a main word, then the entry is itemized to reflect this and the relevant field indicated in each sub-entry.

A significant feature of this dictionary is the inclusion of over 480 illustrations. The illustrations were generated on the computer and are used to aid the reader in understanding many of the terms.

Computer Art Exhibit at the 1992 SIGGRAPH Conference

Illustrated
COMPUTER
GRAPHICS
DICTIONARY

abscissa Horizontal distance of a point from the y-axis. Contrast with ordinate.

absolute coordinates A location relative to a coordinate systems' origin. In Cartesian coordinates, a two dimensional point is identified by its distance from the origin along the x and y axis; a three-dimensional point is identified by its distance from the origin along the x, y, and z axes.

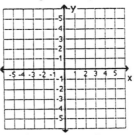

absolute coordinates

absolute value The value of the number without reference to positive or negative sign. In mathematical notation this is denoted by enclosure in vertical bars.

absolute vector In computer graphics, a vector with end points designated in absolute coordinates.

abstract art Art not primarily concerned with representation of nature. The artist or computer graphist selects and exaggerates certain aspects of reality in order to provide a visual experience by means of line, color, and form.

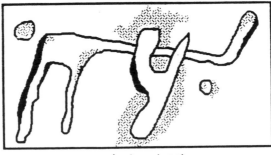

abstract art

1

accelerator A device to speed up either the computer or monitor. Typically a circuit card with an extra processing chip and/or additional RAM.

accuracy aids In CAD, pre-programmed techniques that allow a designer to achieve positioning accuracy on an interactive display, e.g. a grid constraint.

achromatic Having no color, a neutral such as black, white, or gray.

ACM See Association for Computing Machinery.

acoustic radar The use of ultra high-frequency sound waves to determine the position of an object in space. Acoustic radar techniques have been used in the design of graphic input data tablets.

acronym A word formed from the first letter (or letters) of each word in a phrase or name (e.g. VDT stands for Visual Display Terminal and IC stands for Integrated Circuit).

action lines In cartooning, extraneous lines used to suggest action.

action lines

active display A display, such as a cathode-ray tube, electroluminescent display, and plasma panel, that shows information by emitting light.

active window In a window-environment, the window in which the user is currently working.

adaptive sampling Adjusting the sampling density for a graphics calculation in response to characteristics of the object being rendered.

additive color mixing Producing colors by mixing colors of light (red, green, and blue) rather than mixing pigments (such as cyan, magenta, yellow, and black used in printing).

additive primary colors Red, blue, and green − colors that produce white when projected onto a single area.

addressable point The smallest coordinate point on the raster display screen that can be addressed; usually refers to a pixel.

Adobe Illustrator See Illustrator.

Adobe Photoshop See Photoshop.

Adobe Systems, Inc. Founded in 1982, the company has introduced several powerful software products including the postscript page image description language for text/graphics systems, Adobe Illustrator and Adobe Photoshop.

Adobe Type Manager A font generator and utility for the Apple Macintosh computer from Adobe Systems Inc.

AEC An acronym for Architecture, Engineering, and Construction, a computer graphics market requiring specialized applications that facilitate efficient planning, design, drafting, and analysis.

aesthetics A branch of philosophy having to do with the nature of beauty and art and its relation to human experience.

affine map Any transportation composed only of translations, rotations, scalings, and shears.

AIA See Automated Imaging Association.

aiming symbol A movable screen cursor on a display screen.

airbrush A fine paint spray-gun. In graphics, a term denoting a soft, diffused treatment of an image. Computer paint systems have various "brush styles" that can pick-up color from a palette to apply to the image.

Aldus PageMaker See PageMaker.

alert box A screen display, usually in a small window, which asks a question or warns the user of an impending doom of his or her next move is the wrong move. The user answers by clicking a mouse button on a choice or giving a key command.

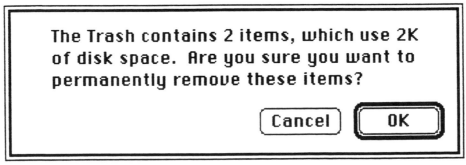

alert box

algorithm A sequence of steps designed to solve a problem or execute a process such as drawing a curve from a set of control points.

aliasing A stepped edge or "staircase" in computer generated images. Appears along lines that are not perfectly horizontal or vertical. Aliasing is especially noticeable in low-resolution monitors.

aliasing

aligning edge That edge of a form that, in conjunction with the leading edge, serves to position correctly a document to be scanned by an OCR device. Also called reference edge.

all points addressable A graphics mode in which each pixel on the display screen can be accessed directly by a program.

alphanumeric display A device that only displays letters, numbers and punctuation symbols.

Alto A personal computer designed by the Xerox Corporation in 1973. This computer pioneered the icon operating system environment and the use of a mouse. The Alto was the progenitor of the Xerox Star and the Apple Macintosh.

ambient conditions Environment conditions that surround a computer system, such as light, temperature, and humidity.

ambient light Non-directional illumination or surrounding light.

American National Standards Institute (ANSI) An association formed by industry and the U.S. government to produce and disseminate computer and computer graphics standards that are acceptable to and used by a majority of companies and the government.

Amiga Brand name for a family of microcomputers manufactured by Commodore Business Machines, Inc. The Amiga computers have been used extensively in the areas of computer graphics and animation. The Amiga personal computers are based on the Motorola 68000 microprocessor.

analogous colors Hues that are close to each other on the color wheel, such as violet-blue, blue, and blue-green.

4

analysis graphics Types of graphics programs that are designed to allow users to more clearly examine and analyze data, making it easier for them to develop conclusions about what the data itself means. The major component of business graphics, analytical graphics programs, consist basically of bar, area, line, and pie charts.

analytical graphics Traditional line graphs, pie charts, and bar charts used to illustrate and analyze data. A type of presentation graphics built into a spreadsheet, database, or word processing program.

anamorphic A change in size of an object such that it is stretched or compressed more in one dimension than another.

anchor point The starting and ending points of a Bezier curve. By moving the anchor points, the position and shape of a Bezier curve can be controlled.

animate To cause to appear lifelike and to have movement, as in animated cartoons. See computer animation.

animated graphics Moving diagrams or cartoons often found in computer-based courseware.

animation Process of making an object appear to move by rapidly displaying a series of pictures of it, each one in a slightly different position. Technique used for producing computer-generated movies. See computer animation.

animation

animator (1) In the animation production, the person who brings the designs and characters to life through animation. (2) The operator of a computer animation system.

annotation Process of inserting text or a special note or identification on a drawing, map, or diagram constructed on a graphics system. The text can be generated and positioned on the drawing using the system.

ANSI See American National Standards Institute.

antialiasing At low resolutions, diagonal lines in digitized images appear as stair-steps and are called "jaggies." This effect is called "aliasing." Antialiasing is the smoothing or removal of these "jaggies" to recreate smoother diagonal lines.

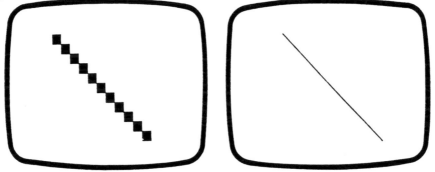

antialiasing

apothem A perpendicular line from the center to one side of a regular polygon.

Apple Computer, Inc. One of the first and certainly the most influential of the microcomputer manufacturers. Founded in 1976 by Steven P. Jobs and Stephen G. Wozniak, using the family garage as a base and $100 in capital, Apple made computers that became wildly successful. Because of excellent design principles, the early Apple II family of microcomputers is still useful, and later machines, such as the Macintosh family of microcomputers, have become extremely popular and have greatly affected the design of other machines and of software. The Macintosh computer with its innovative software is in a class by itself. Apple Computer, Inc. is a leader in high-performance personal computing.

apple key On keyboards produced by Apple Computer, Inc., a special key identified by the Apple logo symbol. The key is used by the operating system and certain applications programs.

Apple Macintosh See Macintosh.

AppleTalk A network scheme designed primarily for the Apple Macintosh computer. The system often uses the relatively slow LocalTalk hardware, but has grown in popularity because of its low cost, ease of use and installation, and general reliability. It allows computers to share files and peripherals.

Apple II A family of personal computers from Apple Computer, Inc. The first Apple II was introduced in 1977. The computer family now includes several models widely used in secondary schools, businesses and homes. The Apple II computers are based on the MOS Technology 6502 microcomputer.

application A software program specifically designed for particular user needs or the specific use of a software program. Graphics applications are usually designed to enable the user to manipulate data or images, or to create images from data or from a library of shapes or clip art.

6

application developer The person, business or organization who creates an application for a particular user need.

application programmer's interface (API) The interface to a library of language-specific subroutines (graphics library) that implement higher level graphics functions.

APT An acronym for Automatic Programmed Tool. A programming system that is used in numerical control applications for the programmed control of machine functions. The APT language allows a user to define points, lines, circles, planes, conical surfaces, and geometric surfaces.

arc A portion or section of a circle or curved line.

arcade game Computer video games popularized by coin-operated machines, characterized by high-resolution color graphics, high speed animation, and sound. Players often use joysticks to control a screen object, and the computer scores points based on the game's rules.

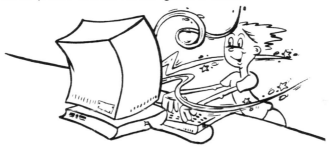
arcade game

architecture (1) The art of building with solid materials, enclosing space in a useful and pleasing way. (2) The type of computer as categorized by the microprocessor chip used in the machine; e.g. a 80386 architecture.

archival storage (1) Refers to memory (on magnetic disks, optical discs, or magnetic tape) used to store data outside of the main memory. (2) Saving digital data for future reference.

area chart Area charts are usually a combination of two line charts with the difference between the two highlighted to accentuate that difference.

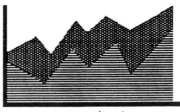
area chart

area infill In a painting system, the process of flooding a defined area of the display screen with a specific color or pattern.

area sampling The determination of a pixel's color and intensity based upon the color and intensity of the pixels surrounding it.

ART PFS First Publisher graphics format used for clip art.

artifact A visible error or oddity in a displayed image. Aliasing, for instance, is an artifact resulting from producing graphics images on a raster grid.

artificial intelligence (AI) A group of technologies that attempt to emulate certain aspects of human behavior, such as reasoning and communicating, as well as to mimic biological senses, including seeing and hearing. Specific technologies include expert systems (also called knowledge-based systems), natural language, neural networks, machine translation and speech recognition. AI is the branch of computer science that is concerned with developing computer systems capable of simulating human reasoning and sensation. AI involves using computers and software that, like the human mind, use stored knowledge to make decisions involving judgement or ambiguity.

Artline An illustrative graphics program for use with IBM-compatible microcomputers. Features include multi-layer editing, an autotrace facility, scalable fonts, 3-D shading effects, a blending function to change one image into another, and access to a large supply of clip art images.

Art Nouveau A decorative design style of the 1890s, based primarily on flowing, curvilinear plant and animal forms.

Art Nouveau

Arts & Letters Graphics Editor An illustrative graphics program which runs on Windows and OS/2. A special effect function allows text, clip art, and freeform graphics to be warped, bent, stretched and twisted by specifying the shape into which the object is to fit. A Graduated Fill function allows colorful blends and the three-dimensional illusion of depth by a variety of linear and radial fill for text and graphic art work. The program has several thousand files of clip art and an autotrace feature.

artwork (1) Visual and graphic elements on a page, such as line drawings, halftones, or solids. (2) One of the outputs of a graphics system. (3) A general term applied to any artistic production.

artwork

ascender Portion of lower-case letters that extends above the main portion of the letter, such as the tops of b, d, and h.

ascender

aspect A nongeometric property of a graphics primitive, such as its color.

aspect ratio In computer graphics, the relationship of the height and width of the video display screen frame or image area.

Association for Computing Machinery (ACM) World's largest educational and scientific society committed to the development of technical skills and professional competence of computer specialists. Founded in 1947, ACM has earned a reputation for technical excellence by publishing prestigious journals and sponsoring numerous conferences that promote an ongoing dialogue among students, educators, and practitioners. The association is dedicated to the development of information processing as a discipline, and to the responsible use of computers in an increasing diversity of applications. ACM is the parent organization of SIGGRAPH.

associative dimensioning A CAD capability that links dimension entities to geometric entities being dimensioned. This allows the value of a dimension to be automatically updated as the geometry changes.

associativity Any logical linking of geometric entities in a CAD/CAM database with their nongraphic attributes or with other geometry entities.

AT The first 80286-based personal computer, introduced by the IBM Corporation in 1984. AT stands for Advanced Technology.

Atari, Incorporated Manufacturers of a popular line of personal computer systems. Atari produced several older home computers, and in 1985 introduced the Atari ST family of microcomputers. The ST computers are high-performance personal computers with capabilities for computer graphics in color.

Atari ST A personal computer series from Atari Corporation.

attribute (1) The property of a graphic image that determines characteristics such as line type, line width, and color. (2) A nongraphic characteristic of a part, component, or entity under design on a CAD system.

autodimensioning In a drafting program, a program feature that computes and annotates the size of drawn elements.

autoflow A setting found in many page layout programs that allows for continuous placement of blocked text from page to page without operator intervention.

autofont A self-training OCR system that automatically adjusts to the type designs of different typefaces in order to read a wide range of documents quickly and accurately.

autointeractive design (AID) A combination of design automation, where the computer executes programs or routines with no operator intervention, and computer-aided design, where the operator interacts with the computer in the design process.

autoleading Automatically increasing or decreasing the space between lines of text to allow for the appropriate leading for the largest font on the lines. The space added is about 20 percent of the type size under each line of text.

automated design system (ADS) Another term for a computer-aided design system.

automated drafting system A computer-based system designed primarily to automate the process of drafting.

Automated Imaging Association (AIA) A trade group dedicated to promoting the acceptance and productive use of image processing, image analysis and machine vision technologies. The use of these technologies will include both scientific and industrial applications from all aspects of product manufacturing, physical sciences, governmental and research communities. The association's membership includes manufacturers of both related and peripheral products, integrators, end-users, consultants and research groups directly involved with these technologies. Key AIA activities include an annual financial forum, standards development, user-supplier meetings, market studies, and trade shows and conferences. AIA was founded in 1984.

automatic carriage Control mechanism for a printer that can automatically control the feeding, spacing, skipping, and ejecting of paper or preprinted forms.

automatic digitizing The automatic scanning and encoding of graphic elements contained in engineering drawings, entering their coordinate positions into computer memory.

automatic dimensioning A CAD capability that computes the dimensions in a displayed design, or in a designated section, and automatically places dimensions, dimensional lines, and arrowheads where required.

automatic hyphenation A feature that hyphenates words automatically. Often found in word processing and page layout programs.

automatic pagination A feature that automatically breaks text into pages. Often found in word processing and page layout programs.

automatic reformatting In word processing, automatic adjustment of text to accommodate changes.

auto-repeat Feature of some keyboards that allows a key to repeat automatically when held down.

auto-restart Capability of a computer to perform automatically the initialization functions necessary to resume operation following an equipment or power failure.

autoscore In word processing, an instruction that causes text to be underlined.

auto scroll On some drawing and graphics programs, a feature that appears to move a large document to make more of it visible on the screen when the mouse pointer or a tool reaches the edge of the visible region.

autotrace A feature of many drawing programs that draws lines along the edges of a bit mapped image in order to convert the image into an object-oriented one. Using the autotrace tool you can transform low-resolution graphics (72 dots per inch bit mapped image) into art that can print at substantially higher resolutions (object-oriented graphics can print at the printer's maximum resolution).

auxiliary storage Storage that supplements the main storage of a computer, such as hard disks, floppy disks, magnetic tapes, and optical discs.

Avant Garde A modern sans serif typeface design owned by the International Typeface Corporation (ITC) and included as a built-in font with many PostScript laser printers.

abcdefghijklmnopqrstuvwxyz
ABCDEFGHIJKLMNOPQRSTUVWXYZ
1234567890 .,;:'"&!?$

Avant Garde

axis One of the lines of direction on a graphics display device, or one of the reference lines of a coordinate system. Typically X is the horizontal axis, Y the vertical, and Z indicating depth.

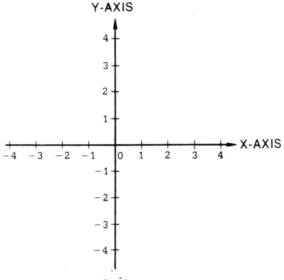

axis

axonometric view A view that shows three sides of an object to provide a three-dimensional view. Horizontal and vertical distances are drawn to scale, but diagonal lines are distorted.

axonometric view

back clipping plane (1) A specified plane that cuts across the view volume, making it finite. Graphic entities straddling this boundary are clipped in the z-axis. A plane perpendicular to the line of sight for clipping out distant objects. (2) The yon plane

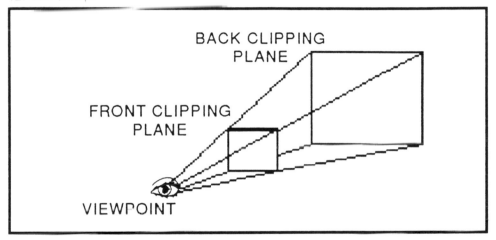

back clipping plane

back face culling Omitting the drawing of one or more backfacing polygons, thus increasing drawing speed.

background A predetermined image that provides a default image for regions in which no other graphics primitive is rendered.

background color The default color to which every pixel on the display is to be initialized.

background noise In optical scanning, electrical interference caused by such things as ink tracking or carbon offsetting.

backlight Light coming from behind a subject.

backspace Keyboard operation that moves the cursor one place to the left. Allows modification of what has already been typed before it is entered into the computer.

backup (1) Pertaining to procedures or standby equipment available for use in the event of failure or overloading of the normally used procedures or equipment. (2) To make a copy of a program or data in case the original is lost, damaged, or otherwise inaccessible.

backup copy Copy of a file or data set kept for reference in case the original file or data set is destroyed.

backup disk A duplicate copy of a floppy disk that preserves files in case of some disaster.

backwards ray tracing Ray tracing in which the computations are performed as if the rays traveled from the viewpoint to the light sources.

bad sectors During formatting of disks, all sectors are checked for usability. Unusable sectors are "flagged" as bad and are not used by the operating system. The remaining areas can then still be used. Bad sectors are sometimes used by viruses to store the code outside the reach of the users and the operating system.

balance The visual arrangement of colors, shapes, or masses to create a sense of equilibrium.

balloon (1) A box containing descriptive data (usually text) connected to a reference location in a drawing. Commonly used in cartoons. (2) A descriptive message box in some graphic user interfaces.

balloon

bar chart Widely used chart in business graphics. Used to display a time schedule. Bar charts compare adjacent pieces of data and can depict individual data items side by side, stacked on top of one another, clustered together, or positioned horizontally.

bar graph A graph made up of filled-in columns or rows that represent the change of data over time.

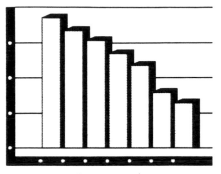

bar graph

barrel distortion Image distortion in an optical or video system, characterized by its bending of the edges of a displayed grid into a barrel shape with convex sides and compressed corners. It can be corrected by image processing techniques.

baseline An imaginary horizontal line with which the base of each character, excluding descenders, is aligned.

BASIC Acronym for Beginner's All-purpose Symbolic Instruction Code, an easy-to-learn, easy-to-use, algebraic programming language with a small repertory of commands and simple statement formats. Developed at Dartmouth College by John Kemeny and Thomas Kurtz. Widely used in programming instruction, in personal computing, and in business and industry. The language has changed over the years. Early versions are unstructured and interpreted. Later versions are structured and often compiled. Implementations of BASIC include Applesoft BASIC, BASICA, CBASIC, GW-BASIC, Turbo BASIC and QuickBASIC.

beam penetration CRT A vector display system which produces color by varying the strength of an electron beam directed at a screen coated with (typically) both red and green phosphor layers.

beam tracing A variation of ray tracing using a polygonal cone for the intersection computations rather than a single line (ray).

Bell Laboratories The research and development center of the AT & T Company and one of the most renowned scientific laboratories in the world. Many computer hardware developments and software concepts and programs were generated at Bell Laboratories.

bells and whistles Informal description of the special or extra features of a computer system, including graphics, color displays, sound, and many peripherals.

belt-bed plotter A pen plotter which uses a wide continuous belt for holding the paper.

benday A process using screens of different dot patterns to mechanically produce shading effects; named for its inventor, Benjamin Day (1838-1916). Benday screen patterns are available in almost all paint programs.

Benson, Inc. A major manufacturer in hardcopy technology, especially in electrostatic printers. Benson introduced the first electrostatic plotter in 1967.

Bezier curve A type of curve generated by an algorithm. Named after French mathematician Pierre Bezier, it is used to display nonuniform curves based upon a fitting algorithm. Bezier curves need only a few points to define a large number of shapes, hence their usefulness over other mathematical methods for approximating a given shape. Within drawing programs, Bezier curves are typically reshaped by moving the handles that appear off of the curve. Originated around 1962 for use in car body design in France.

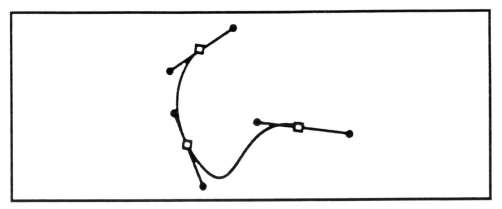

Bezier curve

Bezier patch A portion of a three-dimensional surface generated using the Bezier curve algorithm. Two-dimensional Bezier curves are drawn through selected control points, and the three-dimensional curve is interpolated between them.

biform In typography, a typeface that combines lower case and small cap characters to form the lower case alphabet.

bilinear patch A two-dimensional surface patch that can be warped into a three-dimensional surface.

bill of materials A listing of all the subassemblies, parts, materials, and quantities required to manufacture one assembled product or part, or to build a plant. A bill of materials can be generated automatically on a CAD-CAM system.

binding (1) Language-dependent code that allows a software library to be called from that computer language. (2) The association of more generally defined parameters and function with the subprogram names and formal parameters of a specific computer language.

bit The smallest unit of information that can be stored and processed by a digital computer.

bit flipping Process of inverting bits – changing 1's to 0's and vice versa. For example, in a graphics program, to invert a black-and-white bit mapped image (to change black to white and vice versa), the program could simply flip the bits that make up the bit map.

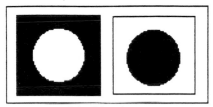

bit flipping

bit image Collection of bits stored in a computer's memory, arranged into a rectangular matrix. The computer's display screen is a bit image that is visible to the user.

bit map A data structure that describes a bit image being held in computer storage. Each picture element (pixel) is represented by bits stored in the memory. Bit mapped graphics are notorious for using lots of memory. Several million bytes of memory may be required to store a bit map for a high-resolution screen display or to store a full page scanned image.

bit map file formats See ART, CUT, GIF, IFF, IMG, MacPaint, NEO, PCX, TGA and TIFF. Contrast with object file formats.

bit mapped font A set of characters in a particular size and style, in which each character is described in a unique bit map (pattern of dots). Bit mapped screen or printer fonts represent characters with a matrix of dots. To display or print bit mapped fonts, the computer or printer must keep a full representation of each character in memory.

bit mapped graphics A method of generating screen images by creating a one-for-one correspondence between bits in memory and pixels on the screen. In color graphics, three or more bits are required in the bit map to represent the red, green, and blue values of an individual pixel. Bit mapped graphics are created by paint programs and some scanners.

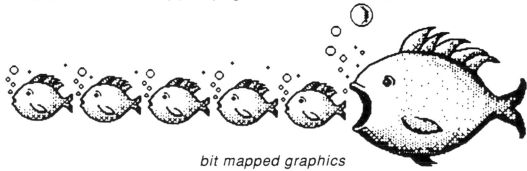

bit mapped graphics

bit plane The hypothetical two-dimensional plane containing a bit in memory for each pixel on the raster. For any raster image, there is at least one bit plane in frame buffer memory; each bit plane has a one-to-one correspondence of bits to pixels.

blanking On a display screen, not displaying a character although it is present; leaving a space.

bleed In a printed document, any element that runs off the edge of the page.

blend A feature on many digital painting programs that lets you soften the edges or mix colors where two objects or regions meet.

blinking (1) Graphics aid that makes a predefined graphic entity blink on the CRT to attract the designer's attention. (2) A means of highlighting a graphics object or text by changing the color or intensity between two values periodically.

block graphics Graphic images created by using block graphics characters. Because the block graphics characters are handled the same way as ordinary characters, the computer can display block graphics considerably faster than bit mapped graphics.

blow up (1) The changing of a smaller format picture into a larger format picture. (2) Unexpected halt to a program due to a bug or because it encounters data conditions it cannot handle.

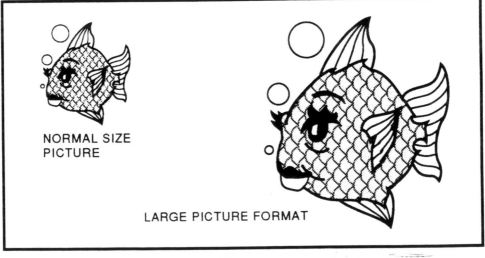

NORMAL SIZE
PICTURE

LARGE PICTURE FORMAT

blow up

blueprint style A visual style using line drawings to produce either two-dimensional or three-dimensional images and models.

blurring A technique used to model objects so they present the idea of motion to the viewing eye.

body text The type used for the body of copy, or the main text, of a document. Usually 12 points or less in size, and distinguished from headings, captions and display lettering.

boilerplate Pieces of text that get used over and over again, word for word, in different documents.

boldface A type font in which the main strokes of the letter are thicker than normal. Printed characters in darker type than the surrounding characters.

boldface font A set of type characters that are darker and heavier than normal type.

Bookman A serif typeface frequently used for body type. Bookman, a design owned by the International Typeface Corporation (ITC) and is included as a built in font with many PostScript laser printers.

abcdefghijklmnopqrstuvwxyz
ABCDEFGHIJKLMNOPQRSTUVWXYZ
1234567890 .,;:"&!?$

Bookman

boot To start up a computer. Microcomputers have a bootstrap routine in a ROM chip that is automatically executed when the computer is turned on or reset. It searches for the operating system, loads it and then passes control over to it.

bootstrapping Starting a computer system. "Cold boot" means complete restarting after switching the power on, while "Warm boot" means partial restarting under operating system control.

border (1) In on-screen windows, the edge surrounding the user's workspace. Window borders provide a visible frame around a document or graphic. (2) In printing, a decorative line or pattern along one or more edges of an illustration or page.

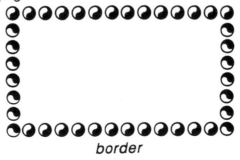

border

boundary fill Filling a region with color by switching to a new value all pixels that are bounded by other pixels having boundary values.

boundary representation One of the main methods of solid modeling, in which the object is described by its geometry and topology.

bounding box A rectangular box aligned with the axes drawn around the smallest area that entirely contains a particular polygon or object.

boxing The use of bounding boxes to select particular entities on a computer graphics display.

brightness (1) In the HSB color model, one of the three characteristics used to describe a color. Brightness refers to the color's percentage of black. (2) In computer graphics, the relative presence or absence of shading (whiteness to grayness to blackness). (3) On some CRT terminals, the ability to vary the intensity of the screen display. Especially useful in highlighting selected segments. (4) The perceived amount of light emitted or reflected by an object. (5) The amount of lighter shades in an image relative to the amount of darker shades. In this context, a preponderance of lighter shades corresponds to a brighter image.

brilliant Having both high color value and high color saturation.

brush In computer paint programs, a tool used to produce brushstrokes of varying width, and in some cases calligraphic or shadowing effects.

brush

B-spline curve A sequence of parametric polynomial curves (typically quadratic or cubic polynomials) forming a smooth fit between a sequence of points in three-dimensional space. The curve is defined by a series of control points. The control points define a series of continuous Bezier curves. The piece-wise defined curve maintains a level of mathematical continuity dependent upon the polynomial degree chosen. It is used extensively in mechanical design applications in the automotive and aerospace industries.

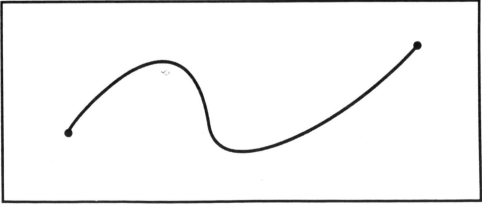

B-spline curve

bubble memory See magnetic bubble memory.

bug A flaw in the design or implementation of a software program or hardware design which causes erroneous results or malfunctions.

built-in font A printer font encoded permanently in the printer's read-only memory (ROM).

bulk annotation A graphics feature which enables the designer to automatically enter repetitive text or other annotation at multiple locations on a drawing or design.

bullet An open or closed circle used to set off items in a list.

bulletin board service A service that permits individuals who have personal computers to communicate with others who have similar interests. Individuals who subscribe to the service can retrieve information from a common database. Called BBS.

business graphics (1) Pie charts, bar charts, scattergrams, graphs, and other visual representations of the operational or strategic aspects of a business, such as sales vs. costs, sales by department, comparative product performance, and stock prices. (2) Applications programs that allow the user to display data as visual presentations.

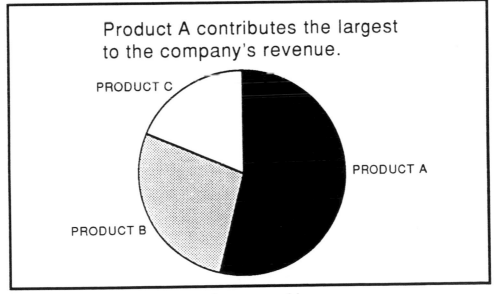

business graphics

button box Keyboard function keys that can provide additional programmable features to a system.

byte (1) Eight binary bits of data grouped together to represent a character, digit or other value.

C Full name of a programming language designed for use on microcomputers. Combines high-level statements with low-level machine control to deliver software that is both easy to use and highly efficient. It is very popular with system programmers because of its transportability between computer systems. C was developed by Dennis Ritchie at Bell Laboratories in the early 1970s. The language is closely associated with the Unix operating system, now widely used by professional programmers. The language is capable of providing especially concise and efficient code.

```
float radians_to_degrees(float degrees)
{
    float angle;

    while (degrees >= 360)
        degrees -= 360;
    while (degrees < 0)
        degrees += 360;
    angle = rad_per_degree*degrees;
    return angle;
}
```

C

C++ An object-oriented version of the C programming language, developed by Bjarne Stroustrup in the early 1980s at Bell Laboratories. The language has been chosen by several large software publishers for major development projects. The term C++ means "more than C."

© Copyright symbol indicating the exclusive right granted by law to sell, distribute, or reproduce a graphic image or document.

C4 Represents CAD, CAM, CAE, CIM; the disciplines related to the use of computers and computer graphics to automatic design and production processes.

cabling diagram A diagram showing connections and physical locations of system or unit cables, and used to facilitate field installation and repair of wiring systems. Can be generated by computer-aided design.

CAD Acronym for Computer-Aided Design, a term applied to programs and computer systems used in designing engineering, architecture and scientific models. The process involves direct, real-time communication between a designer and a computer, generally by the use of a CRT display and a light pen, mouse or graphics tablet. Some CAD applications create objects in two or three dimensions, presenting the result as wire-frame "skeletons", as models with shaded surfaces, or as solid objects.

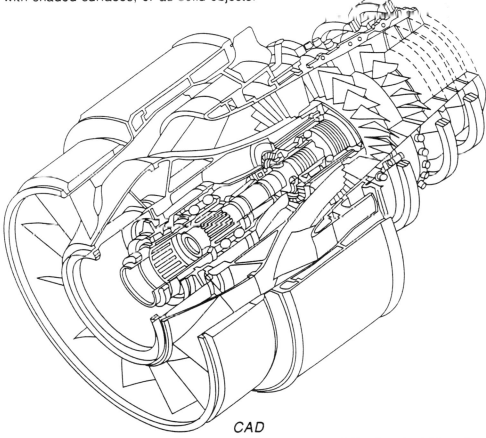

CAD

CADAM Acronym for Computer graphics Augmented Design And Manufacturing, the process of or methods for using computer systems as tools in design and manufacturing applications.

CAD/CAM Acronym for Computer-Aided Design/Computer-Aided Manufacturing.

CADD See Computer-Aided Design and Drafting.

CAE Computer-Aided Engineering; analyzes a design for basic error-checking, or to optimize manufacturability, performance, and economy. Information drawn from the CAD/CAM design database is used to analyze the functional characteristics of a part, product, or system under design, and to simulate its performance under various conditions.

CalComp Short for California Computer Products. One of the first pen plotter manufacturers and an early leader and supporter of computer graphics. Almost all of the early (1960s) hardcopy computer graphic images were drawn on CalComp plotters. Today the company has grown to become one of the most versatile companies in the business offering displays, plotters, digitizers and other equipment.

calligraphic graphics Method of forming an image from scan lines oriented in arbitrary directions and drawn in an arbitrary order. Expensive electronics are required, but spatial antialiasing is not. Typical of this style of graphics are the "wire-frame" models that were considered synonymous with computer graphics in the early days.

calligraphy (1) The art of beautiful writing, or controlled, flowing line used in a decorative manner. Oriental characters that are written with a brush. (2) The art of handwriting.

Calma Company A pioneer of computer graphics hardware for CAD/CAM applications since 1964. Owned by the General Electric Company.

CAM Acronym for Computer-Aided Manufacturing. The use of computers to assist in any or all phases of manufacturing.

cameo type Typeface in which characters are reversed white out of a solid or shaded ground.

camera cone A device which allows a user of a graphics system to take a "snapshot" directly off a CRT monitor by shielding the display from incident light.

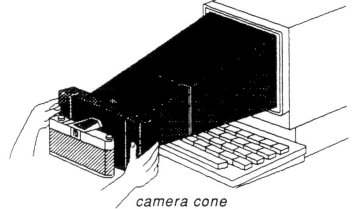

camera cone

camera-ready In publishing, final copy that is photographed to create a printed copy.

CAMM Acronym for Computer-Aided Maintenance Management. Using computers to reduce the time to find and correct the causes of breakdowns in automated manufacturing systems.

canned software Programs prepared by computer manufacturers or software developers and provided to a user in ready-to-use form. General enough to be used by many businesses and individuals. Contrast with custom software.

Canon engine The internal mechanism of a Canon office photocopier, used in many laser printers.

Canvas A power-packed multi-purpose drawing and painting program for the Apple Macintosh computer. With 24-bit color, unlimited layers, Bezier curves, precision tools, bit mapped editing at high resolutions, a spelling checker and full color separation, it combines color capabilities and powerful object-editing options with a friendly interface and ease of use. Other features include fractional leading and kerning, tab support within a text block, text wrapping around irregular objects and binding text to any curve/shape. It also includes object blending from one shape to another, splitting/combining of objects, custom gradient color fills, the ability to edit multiple Bezier curve anchor points simultaneously and EPSF, CGM, and Illustrator import/export translators.

CAP Acronym for Computer-Aided Publishing.

cap height The height of a capital letter from the baseline.

cap line In desktop publishing, the hypothetical line that connects the tops of capital letters.

caps Capital letters. All caps means that all letters are capitalized; initial caps means the capitalization of the first letter of each significant word. ALL CAPS WOULD LOOK LIKE THIS.

caption (1) A title or subtitle identifying what is being displayed on the screen. (2) Text associated with a cartoon.

ALL MY DREAMS ARE IN PASCAL.

caption

carbon ribbon Ribbon used with printers to produce extremely sharp characters with excellent definition.

caricature An amusing distortion or exaggeration of something so familiar it would be recognized even in the distortion. A caricature captures the likeness of a person but exaggerates and distorts various features of that person. Used to create a humorous or satirical likeness.

caricature

carriage Control mechanism for a printer that automatically feeds, skips spaces, and ejects paper forms.

carriage return (CR) In a character printer the operation that causes the next character to be printed at the left margin.

Cartesian coordinate system System named for French mathematician Rene Descartes whereby, in a flat plane, a point can be located by its distances from two intersecting straight lines, called the axes, the distance from one axis being measured along a parallel to the other axis. The numbers associated with the point are called the coordinates of the point.

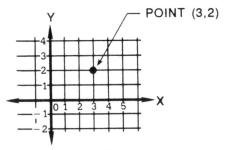

Cartesian coordinate system

cartoon (1) A drawing, usually humorous, that stands by itself as a work of art. It is an art form designed for publication. Today, cartoons can be prepared using a computer and a drawing software package. Computer produced cartoons are beginning to appear in publications. A cartoon is generally accompanied by a caption. (2) An animated film, usually with various characters and a set story line. (3) A satirical drawing or caricature. (4) A comic strip.

THIS ONE IS A FAKE! IT WAS DONE WITH
A COMPUTER-CONTROLLED PLOTTER!

cartoon

cartridge A generic term that can refer to any of several devices that are self-contained, usually in some kind of plastic housing. For example, ROM cartridge, disk cartridge, toner cartridge, memory cartridge, tape cartridge, or font cartridge.

cartridge font A series of typefaces contained in ROM chips mounted within a plastic module called a cartridge. The cartridge is placed in a compatible laser printer to allow it to use the typefaces.

cast (1) A tint or overemphasis of one color in a color image, particularly an unintended one. (2) In some animation programs, the elements that can be moved around the screen.

catalog Ordered compilation of item descriptions and sufficient information to afford access to the items, such as a listing of programs or data file names that are stored on a diskette. To catalog a disk is to instruct the computer to print out a list of all of the files on the disk.

cathode ray tube (CRT) Electronic tube with a screen upon which information may be displayed.

cathode ray tube (CRT)

cavalier projection A type of oblique projection in which the direction of projection is at 45 degrees to the projection plane.

C-curve A type of line fractal, made by applying a fractal generator to a line.

CD Acronym for Compact Disc, a 4-5/8-inch silver platter used for audio recordings. Compact, durable, and capable of extraordinary fidelity, the CD is an excellent long-lasting recording medium. See CD-ROM.

CDR A Corel Draw object file format.

28

CD-ROM An acronym for compact disc read-only memory, a type of optical disc that uses the same basic technology as do the popular CD audio discs. Although a CD-ROM drive can only read data (the data is permanently stamped onto the disc during manufacturing), the discs are inexpensive to make and can each hold about 650 megabytes of data. Contents are typically an entire encyclopedia on a single CD, a set of reference works, a clip-art library, a collection of fine art, or any other publication which is for reading only.

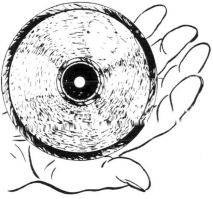

CD-ROM

cel (1) Conventional animation is painted upon thin sheets of clear acetate called cel (or cell). Computer graphics systems are now used to produce cels. (2) In computer animation, a single-frame image. (3) In computer graphics, a pattern of an image including both color and transparency values for each pixel that is mapped as a texture into a scene.

cel animation An animation technique in which a background painting is held stationary while animated images are moved over the painting, producing the illusion of movement. Animation programs are available that perform cel animation.

cel animation

cell (1) A rectangular display screen element. (2) In an alphanumeric display, a block of pixels, each in a fixed position, in which a character or symbol may be displayed.

centering Word processing feature that places a line of text midway between the left and right margins.

center of perspective The position at which an image subtends the same angle to the viewer as the object subtended to the camera (in photography) or to the "synthetic camera" (in computer graphics).

central processing unit (CPU) Major component of a computer system with the circuitry to control the interpretation and execution of instructions.

central structure store (CSS) An editable hierarchy of structures composed of attributes, elements, and transformations. CSS attributes are qualities such as color and style. CSS elements are drawing primitives such as lines and polygons.

Centronics interface A de facto standard for parallel data exchange paths between computers and peripherals. Centronics Corporation was one of the original printer manufacturers to use the parallel scheme for communications between computers and printers. The 36-pin parallel interface was introduced in 1970.

CG An acronym for Computer Graphics, any graphical element created with the aid of a computer.

CGA Acronym for Color Graphics Adapter. The original low-resolution color standard for IBM Corporation in 1981. The CGA is capable of several character and graphics modes. CGA has been superseded by EGA and VGA.

CGI (1) Acronym for Computer Generated Imager, images generated using computer graphics techniques. (2) Acronym for Computer Graphics Interface, a standard for direct communication of drawing primitives to graphics devices.

CGM Acronym for Computer Graphics Metafile. A standard object-oriented graphics file format. CGM stores images primarily in vector graphics, but also provides a raster format.

chamfer A beveled edge between two intersecting lines.

CHAMFER

chamfer

chaos A topic that has connections with fractal geometry. Chaotic systems have the appearance of unpredictability but are actually determined by precise deterministic laws, just like many fractal images. The rise of chaos has been meteoric. During the 1980s it received widespread prominence, and some scientists have even placed it alongside two other great revolutions of physical theory in the twentieth century – relativity and quantum mechanics. The growth of chaos is linked with the rapid development of powerful computers. Within the last fifteen years, successful innovation in computer graphics is one of the factors which has enabled scientists and mathematicians to make progress in nonlinear systems from which chaos is derived.

character (1) Any symbol, digit, letter, or punctuation mark – including the blank character – stored or processed by computing equipment. (2) In animation, any person or animal who plays a part in an animated film.

character graphics A set of special symbols that are placed together to create simple graphic images.

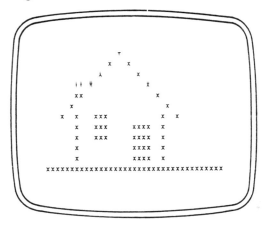

character graphics

character pitch In a line of text, the number of characters per inch.

character recognition Technology of using machines to identify human-readable symbols automatically, and then to express their identities in machine-readable codes. This operation of transforming numbers and letters into a form directly suitable for electronic data processing is an important method of introducing information into computing systems.

character set All of the numbers, letters, and symbols associated with a given device or coding system. All of the characters recognized by a computer system.

characters per inch Method of expressing the output from dot matrix and daisy wheel printers as determined by type size and style. Abbreviated cpi.

chart Visual representation of quantatative information – such as a bar graph, in which the information is made visual by heavy horizontal or vertical lines, or a circle graph or pie chart, in which the information is pictured as slices of an imaginary pie.

chartbook In business and presentation graphics, a collection of chart formats from which a user may select an appropriate format for his or her application.

check plot A pen plot generated automatically by a CAD system for visual verification and editing prior to final output generation.

chiaroscuro Shading.

chip Small component that contains a large amount of electronic circuitry. Thin silicon wafer on which electronic components are deposited in the form of integrated circuits. Chips are the building blocks of a computer and perform various functions, such as doing arithmetic, serving as the computer's memory, or controlling other chips.

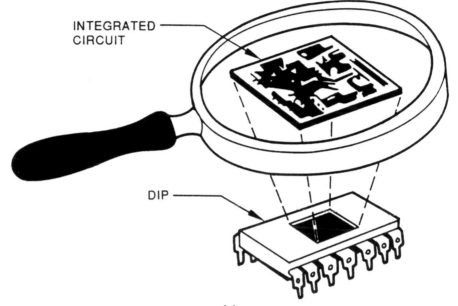

INTEGRATED CIRCUIT

DIP

chip

chooser In the Apple Macintosh environment, a desktop accessory that allows the user to select a device driver to be used by the system.

chroma (1) Color attributes, such as saturation, shade, and hue. (2) The intensity, strength, or saturation of color, distinguishing the chromatic colors from black and white.

chromaticity Dominant wavelength and purity of a color as objectively measured; corresponds to hue and saturation of the color without regard to brightness.

chrominance Portions of composite video signal controlling color.

CIM Acronym for Computer Integrated Manufacturing. The total integration of all computerized tools, including CAD/CAM and others for a controlled manufacturing process or plant operation.

circle A collection of points equally distant from a fixed point, the center. See conic sections.

circular graph A graph in which the values are plotted from a central point along radiating axes.

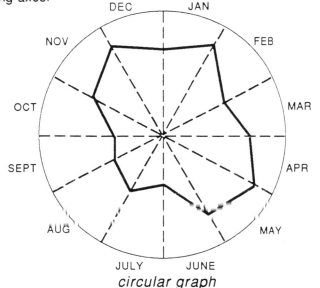

circular graph

Claris CAD A full-featured, easy-to-use two-dimensional computer-aided design program for the Apple Macintosh computer from Claris Corporation. Claris CAD gives one the power to create accurate, professional illustrations and drawings.

class A collection of graphics objects having the same type of attributes as to which the same types of operators apply.

clear (1) Keyboard function that removes the contents from the display screen. (2) Same as zap.

click Means to point the mouse pointer at a word or icon on the screen, press the mouse button, and then release it quickly. Clicking is usually performed to select or deselect an item or to activate a program or program feature.

click art Clip art on a diskette or CD-ROM. A floppy disk or CD-ROM of professional drawn pictures that are ready to copy and use in computer produced documents.

clicking The term used to describe the pressing of a button on the top of a mouse.

client (1) Any computer using the services of a computer network. (2) Any process that accesses either a graphics library or a graphics server.

clip To select a part of a graphic to show on the screen or place into a document. Clipping is used to select a region of interest rather than scaling the entire image.

clip art Collections of pictures and design elements (such as borders, symbols, drawings, etc.) The collections may be in printed form or stored on diskettes or CD-ROM. This pre-drawn artwork can be used in designing newsletters, brochures, flyers, books, magazines and incorporated into other documents.

clip art

clipboard A temporary holding place that facilitates the cutting and pasting of text and graphics. Clipboard information is held in memory only while the computer is turned on. A clipboard allows information to be transferred from one program to another. A clipboard stores a copy of the last information that was "copied" or "cut." A "paste" operation passes data from the clipboard to the current program.

clip boundary The defining boundary of display space, outside of which display elements will not be visible.

clipping Removing portions of an image that are outside the boundaries of the edge of a window or display screen. Certain graphics programs also support clipping as a means of masking everything but a certain object so that painting tools, for example, can be applied to the object alone.

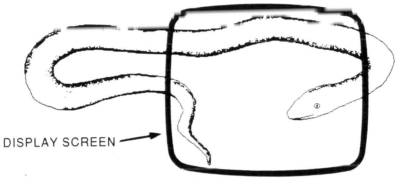

DISPLAY SCREEN

clipping

clipping path An outline, in a graphics program, which is used to select a portion of an object to be manipulated.

clipping plane In graphics programs, a plane perpendicular to the line of sight that can be applied anywhere between the viewer's position and the target so it blocks whatever is behind or in front of it. The clipping plane is employed to constrain the amount of memory required by a drawing. Any object, or portion of an object, occurring beyond the clipping plane is discarded. Often, there is both a front clipping plane and a back clipping plane.

clone In nonbiological terms, a product or idea that is an exact duplicate or copy of another. A computer or a software program that duplicates another program exactly. (e.g., a personal computer that closely imitates the operation and architecture of the IBM PS/2 computer.)

close box A small box at the upper left-hand corner of a window used to close the window.

closed architecture Personal computer design that limits add-ons to those that can be plugged into the back of the machine.

closed broken line A figure formed when the starting point of the broken line intersects its endpoint.

closed plane figure A figure that starts at a point and comes back to the point.

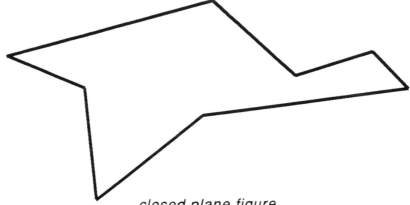

closed plane figure

closed surface A solid surface with no holes such that none of the interior is visible.

CMY Abbreviation for Cyan, Magenta, Yellow. Color mixing system used to print colors.

CMYK Abbreviation for Cyan, Magenta, Yellow, Key/Black. The color model used in the printing color separation process. The colors of this model are also known as process colors, and are based on the three main tones of printing inks used in much color reproduction.

collage A composition of flat objects, such as paper and cloth, pasted together on a surface and often combined with drawings and colors for artistic effect. A similar effect can be created with computers using images input via a digitizer. The combination of graphics and/or effects; or producing images with a mixture of media and textures, typography and/or photography.

collage

color graphics

color graphics

color The hue perceived for different wavelengths in the portion of the electromagnetic spectrum to which the human eye responds. It is possible to create almost all visible colors using two systems of primary colors. Transmitted colors use red, green and blue (RGB), and reflected colors use cyan, magenta, and yellow (CMY). Color displays use RGB and color printers use CMY. What we perceive when our eyes sense the waves of visible light reflected from a surface. As the light hits the object, our eyes absorb certain colored rays, while others are reflected. These reflected rays cause us to see the hue of that wave, such as red, yellow, or blue. Color is also formed by coating a surface with a pigment that reflects certain rays.

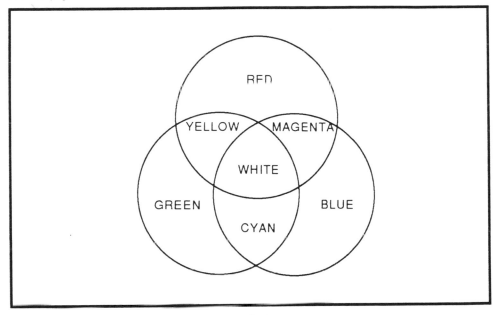

color

color bits A predetermined number of adjacent bits assigned to each displayable pixel that determines its color when it is shown on a display screen. For example, 2 color bits are required for 4 colors, 4 color bits are required for 16 colors, 6 color bits are required for 64 colors, 8 color bits for 256 colors, 10 bits for 1024 colors, 12 bits for 4096 colors, 24 bits for 16.7 million colors, 30 bits for 1 billion colors, 36 color bits for 68 billion colors, and 64 color bits for 281.5 trillion colors.

color burst signal Signal present in composite video output that provides color information. Sometimes turning off the color burst signal improves the quality of pictures on black-and-white monitors.

color correction The process of changing the color balance of an image to more closely approach the desired values.

color graphics Any type of computer graphic in which the images displayed on a visual display screen, printed copy, or other type of display are shown in more than one color.

colorizing (1) The capacity of certain computers and software programs to modify the colors in images. (2) Pseudocoloring. (3) Adding color to a black-and-white graphic image.

color look-up table A small section of computer memory which contains color content values.

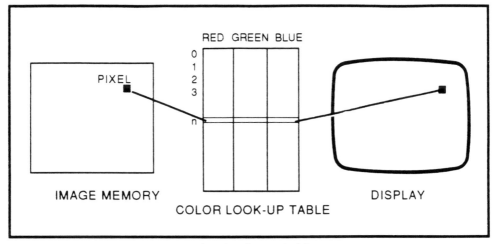

color look-up table

color map The color options in a graphics system, arranged by index number. Same as color look-up table.

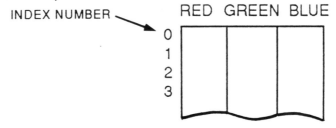

color map

color map animation An animation method in which the object or character does not actually move but is made to appear as if it is moving. The consecutive images are drawn on subsets of the bit planes in the frame buffer in a different stage of movement. All the bit planes are visible simultaneously; the color map is used to cycle through the animation sequence on the bit planes, illuminating just one of the duplicate images at a time in the object color and the remainder of the objects in the background color. This is an advantageous method, because it is faster to change the colors in the color map than it is to redraw the image again and again.

color model Any method for representing color in graphic arts and printing areas, colors are often specified with the Pantone system. In computer graphics, colors can be described using any of several different color systems: RGB (red, green, blue), CMY (cyan, magenta, and yellow), and HSB (hue, saturation, and brightness).

color monitor A computer display designed to work with a video card or adapter to produce text or graphics image in color. A color monitor has a screen coated internally with three phosphors – one each for red, green and blue. To light the phosphor and produce a spot of color, such a monitor also usually contains three electron guns – again, one for each of the three colors.

color monitor

color printer Output device that can produce text, charts, graphics, and art-work in several colors. Dot matrix, ink-jet, thermal-transfer and laser printers can print full-color output.

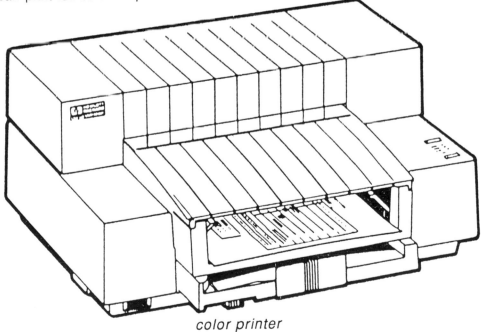

color printer

ColoRIX A draw/paint program for IBM-compatible microcomputers. In addition to the usual draw/paint tools, the program includes several scalable bit mapped fonts, a printing/screen capture feature, a presentation slide show, an application/language independent screen loader and sophisticated animation effects.

color resolution The number of different colors or gray-scale values a system can produce or work with. A value is usually given in bits.

color saturation The amount of a hue contained in a color; the more saturation, the more intense the color.

color scanning The analysis of full color images into the subtractive primary colors (cyan, magenta, and yellow) and black.

color separation The creation of a multicolor graphic by creating several layers, with each layer corresponding to one of the colors that will be printed when the graphic is reproduced by a commercial printer.

color space An imaginary area or volume containing all the points whose positions represent the available colors in a system when those points are graphed on a set of axes.

color spectrum The range of colors available on a particular device or system, usually presented in the same order as the colors in the normal visible spectrum.

ColorStudio An Apple Macintosh 24-bit true color imaging program for graphics arts professionals. It allows for merging high-resolution color photos, video captures, pixel artwork and PostScript type. Features include powerful paint and retouching tools, a full density gray scale mask and six pressure tools: airbrush, charcoal, paintbrush, pencil, waterdrop and fingertip. Painting and selection tools can be customized for photo-retouching, masking and special effects. It allows for precise calibrating its own color balance as well as that of other applications.

COMDEX COMputer Dealer's EXposition. The largest computer trade show in the world. Held in the United States and in other locations throughout the world.

COMDEX

comic strip A popular art form, generally found in newspapers, characterized by having continuing characters, a number of panels, and dialogue presented in balloons. Comic strips can be prepared with either pen and ink or computer graphics systems.

comic strip

commercial art Art that is created to serve a specific business purpose, such as selling a product, advertising illustration, fashion illustration, etc.

commercial art

Commodore 64/128 The Commodore 64 is a home computer introduced in 1982 by Commodore Business Machines, Inc. Over 10 million of these machines have been sold worldwide. The Commodore 128 was an upgraded Commodore 64 that was introduced in 1986.

Commodore Business Machines, Inc. Manufacturer of the Amiga family of microcomputers and several older microcomputers including the popular Commodore 64.

compact disc An optical disc, a nonmagnetic, shiny metal disk used to store digital information.

Compaq Computer Corporation A manufacturer of IBM-compatible microcomputers. Founded in 1982, Compaq has become an industry leader and is known for producing reliable computers.

compart Computer art.

compatible (1) Pertains to the degree of interworking possible between two devices or systems. If an element in a system is fully compatible with the functional and physical characteristics of a system, it can be incorporated into the system without modification. (2) Personal computer that can run software designed for the IBM PC and/or IBM PS/2 computers.

compatible software Programs that can be run on different computers without modification.

compiler A program that converts or translates symbolic commands into instructions that can be executed by a computer.

complementary colors The hues that appear opposite each other on the color wheel, such as orange and blue, red and green, yellow and violet. When mixed in equal amounts, these hues form a neutral gray.

composite Type of video signal in which all three primary video color signals (red, green, blue) are combined, which limits the sharpness of the monitor image. Used in some monitors and TV sets that use only one electron gun to generate the three primary colors.

composite map A single map created on a graphics system from a mosaic of individual adjacent map sheets.

composite curve A series of curves grouped together as a single entity so that they appear to be a single curve.

composite video Color output from a computer color display described in terms of its hue and its brightness and encoded in a single video signal. The color control signal is a single data stream that must be decoded into three colors (red, green, and blue). Inexpensive color monitors, called composite monitors, use composite video and produce a slightly better picture than a TV set but not the high quality of RGB monitors.

composition (1) The arrangement of elements in a visual field so as to please the eye or obtain an intended effect. In computer graphics it is frequently necessary, or more convenient, to generate the various elements of a picture separately and merge them together afterwards. (2) The combining of two or more separately prepared images into one.

composition

Composition And Make-up (CAM) terminal A CRT display device capable of showing and changing exact point sizes and character widths. Used for computer phototypesetting.

compute-bound Pertaining to a program or computer system that is restricted or limited by the speed of the central processing unit. Same as processor bound.

computer Device capable of solving problems or manipulating data by accepting data, performing prescribed operations (mathematical or logical) on the data, and supplying the results of these operations.

computer

computer accessories The equipment that can be attached to a computer, such as mouse, disk drive, visual display device, keyboard, or printer.

computer-aided choreography The use of computers, particularly computer graphics, to devise and score choreographic movements in ballet.

computer-aided design (CAD) Computer systems and programs used in designing tools, automobiles, buildings, aircraft, molecules, farm equipment, integrated circuits, and thousands of other products. Computer-aided has become a mainstay in a variety of design related fields, such as architecture, mechanical engineering, interior design, civil engineering and electrical engineering. CAD applications are graphic and calculation-intensive, requiring fast computers and high-resolution video displays. Computer-aided design workstations are used to design a tremendous range of things, including cars, engine parts, airplanes, farm equipment, and complex computer circuitry.

computer-aided design

computer-aided design and drafting (CADD) Drafting is the producing of drawings; design is the ordering of intentions. Drafting is the most common way of giving form to designs, much as typing is the most common way of giving form to writing. CADD systems are graphics systems that permit automatic drafting and design functions. These systems are used widely in numerical control, robotics, manufacturing resources planning and computer-aided process planning.

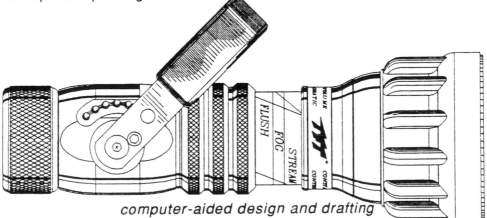

computer-aided design and drafting

47

computer-aided design/computer-aided manufacturing (CAD/CAM) Efforts to automate design and manufacturing operations, a rapidly-growing branch of computer graphics, currently relying primarily on calligraphic graphics but branching out to incorporate raster graphics. Wide-ranging uses include designing auto parts, buildings, and integrated circuits.

Computer-aided Publishing (CAP) The use of software packages to facilitate the layout of text and graphics in publishing applications.

computer animation Animation produced with the use of a software program and a computer. Computer animations makes possible an added dimension in which there are no rules for time and space, light and color, or for obeying the laws of Physics as known to Newton or Einstein. No other medium has given artists such complete control and achieved such stunning results. Computer animation can take either two-dimensional or three-dimensional form. Two-dimensional animation uses flat images for creating characters and/or backgrounds. Three-dimensional animation requires modeling or model design. Geometric models are stored in a computer and can be rotated, translated and scaled as needed to create and manipulate images. More sophisticated three-dimensional animation systems allow the design and manipulation of complex scenes and characters for film making. Most three-dimensional animation is used in advertising.

computer animation

computer art A broad term that can refer either to art created on a computer or to art generated by the computer, the difference being whether the artist is human or electronic. When created by human beings, computer art is done with painting and drawing programs that offer a range of drawing tools, brushes, pencils, patterns, shapes, and colors. The artist can dream lovely images and use the computer to bring them to vivid reality. In the arts, computer graphics is dramatically changing visual media as we know it.

computer art

49

computer artist Person who uses computers as tools in producing art. See computer graphics artist.

computer artist

computer classifications Digital computers are broken down into three classifications: mainframes (which includes supercomputers), minicomputers and microcomputers.

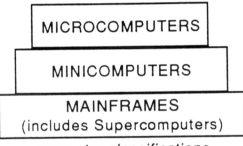

computer classifications

computer drawing A specific image prepared by a computer output device, usually drawn by a graphics printer or plotter, or a visual display representation reproduced as a 35 mm slide or instant photograph.

computerese Jargon and other specialized vocabulary of people working with computers and information processing systems.

computerese

computer family A term commonly used to indicate a group of computers that are built around the same central processing unit, same microprocessor, or around a series of related microprocessors and that share significant design features. For example, the IBM PC and IBM PS/2 models represent a family designed by IBM Corporation around the Intel 80x86 series of microprocessors (80286, 80386 and 80486).

computer flicks Movies made by a computer.

computer game Interactive software or firmware in which the input data consists of the human player's actions and the output is an interactive graphics display.

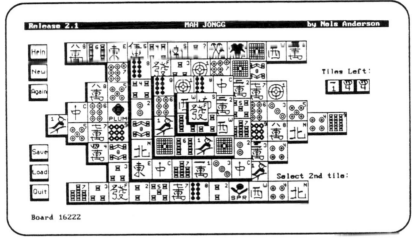

computer game

computer generated animation Animation produced by using a computer to control the movements of an animation stand or camera. Makes possible a greater degree of accuracy, repeatability, sophistication, and speed of operation.

computer generated surface Computer graphics image representing a plot of three-dimensional data.

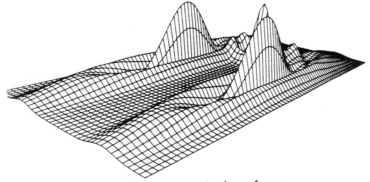

computer generated surface

computer graphicist Specialist who uses computer graphics systems to produce graphs, charts, animated diagrams, art forms, and graphics designs.

computer graphics General term meaning the appearance of pictures or diagrams, as distinct from letters and numbers, on the display screen or hard-copy output devices. The term computer graphics encompasses different methods of generating, displaying, and storing information.

computer graphics

computer graphics artist A person who uses computers as tools in producing fine art and commercial art. One of the 15 hottest careers of the 1990s, reports a survey conducted by Money magazine. The career of computer graphics artist appeared third on a list of the 15 most fast-growing, lucrative, challenging, and prestigious professions for the next decade.

computer graphics magazines Magazines that focus specifically on computer graphics and its applications are useful sources of obtaining the latest information on computer graphics hardware, software and uses. Some of the popular computer graphics periodicals are: Computer Graphics World, Computer Pictures, IEEE Computer Graphics and Applications, and ACM SIGGRAPH Newsletter, Computer Artist and MacArtist.

computer graphics metafile (CGM) An international device-independent file format for storage of object-oriented graphics images. CGM files can be exchanged among users of different systems and different programs.

computer graphics peripherals External devices added to a computer system to provide a graphics capability: for example, visual displays, graphics printers, plotters and film recorders.

computer jargon Technical vocabulary associated with the computer field. See computerese.

computer letter Personalized form letter produced by a word processing system or a special form-letter program.

Computer Museum Archive for computer history, located in Boston, Massachusetts, whose collection contains many early computer systems and taped presentations of computer pioneers.

computer network An interconnected complex of two or more computer systems.

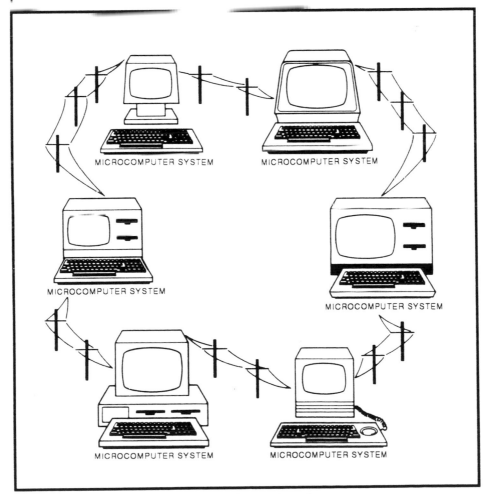

computer network

computer program A specific set of software commands in a form acceptable to a computer and used to achieve a desired result.

computer program

computer programmer Person whose job is to design, write, and test programs that cause a computer to do a specific job.

computer science Field of knowledge embracing all aspects of the design and use of computers. Aspects of computer science range from programming and computer graphics to artificial intelligence and robotics. Offered as a degree program in many colleges and universities.

computer store Retail store where customers can select, from the shelf or the floor, a full computer system or just a few accessories. These stores typically sell software, books, supplies, and periodicals. In a broad-based computer store, one can examine and operate several types of microcomputer systems.

computer store

computer system System that includes computer hardware, software, and people. Used to process data into useful information.

computer typesetting The use of a special-purpose computer to process an input medium resulting in a justified, hyphenated, and formatted output medium. See desktop publishing.

computer user Any person who uses a computer system or its output.

computer user

computer users group Group whose members share the knowledge they have gained and the programs they have developed on a computer or class of computers of a certain manufacturer. Most groups hold meetings and distribute newsletters to exchange information, trade equipment, and share computer programs.

computer vendor Organization that manufacturers, sells, or services computer equipment.

computer virus A program that attaches itself to other programs or data. A virus' typical purpose is to disrupt the processing of information on an infected system. When an infected program is executed, the virus reproduces and spreads by searching for other software that is not infected, and then attaching itself to previously "clean" software.

computer vision (1) The processing of visual information by a computer. (2) Technology concerned with the perception of images and identifying objects.

Computerworld A weekly publication that provides articles and advertisements regarding topics of interest, such as word processing, robotics, office automation, and programming languages.

computing Act of using computing equipment for processing data. Art or science of getting the computer to do what the user wants.

computing power The relative speed of computing. One computer is described as being more powerful than another if it can handle more work at a faster speed.

concave Pertaining to a region or shape, such as a polygon, for which at least one straight line segment between two points of the region is not entirely contained within the region. Contrast with convex.

concave polygon A polygon having at least one interior angle greater than 180 degrees.

conceptual art A work of art or an event that depends primarily upon an intellectual concept conceived by the artist.

condensed type Type narrowed in width so that more characters will fit into a linear inch

ABCDEFGHIJKLMNOPQRSTUVWXYZ&ab
cdefghijklmnopqrstuvwxyz$¢1234567

condensed type

cone A device used to eliminate reflections when photographing a display screen.

configuration (1) A particular arrangement of computer equipment, including a computer, peripherals, and interfaces, all of which will work efficiently together. (2) Layout or design of elements in a hardware or computer graphics system.

conic generator A function generator capable of drawing any conic section, i.e., any ellipse, hyperbola, or parabola.

conic sections Curves formed by the intersection of a plane and a right circular cone. Depending on where the plane cuts through, the conic section may be a circle, an ellipse, a parabola, or a hyperbola.

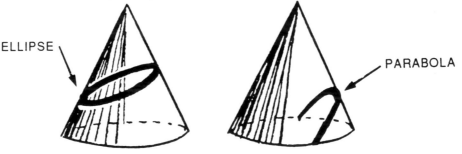

ELLIPSE

PARABOLA

conic sections

connect mode In computer-aided design, an attachment point for lines or text.

contiguous graphics Making diagrams with certain characters that touch each other.

contiguous graphics

continuous line A drawing produced by not removing the drawing tool from the drawing surface until the image is complete.

continuous line

continuous scrolling Moving text, line by line, forward or backward, through a window.

continuous shading A smoothly varying shaded surface.

continuous tone Any photograph or art work that is not yet screened for printing. A very close look at a photograph or piece of artwork reveals the colors or grays blending smoothly into one another. A newspaper photo shows the image made of various-sized dots, called a line screen. This must be done to all photographs, black-and-white or color, before they are printed. Magazines and books use a finer screen and it is harder to see the individual dots.

continuous-tone image Color or black-and-white image formed of combinations of separate areas made up of different color tones or gray tones.

contour (1) A single closed-loop boundary which encloses an area, as on a contour map. The contours on a map are the curves of equal elevation of the terrain. (2) The outer limit of an object. (3) An outline.

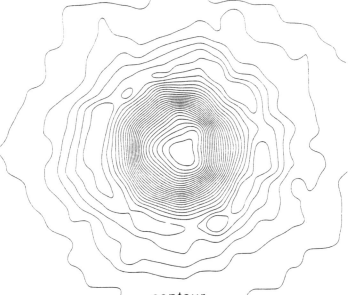

contour

contour characters Letters having a continuous, even-weight line drawn around the outside of the character, but not touching it.

contour characters

contour drawing A line drawing using one continuing line or as few lines as possible.

contour map A map that describes geographic terrain in the form of closed contours that define a three-dimensional path in space at a constant height.

contouring (1) In computer graphics, the creation of the outline of a body, mass, or figure. For example, in a CAD model, the representation of the surface of an object – its bumps and crannies. (2) In image processing, contouring refers to the loss of detail that occurs in a shaded image when two few gradations of gray are used to reproduce a graphic such as a photograph.

contrast A difference between two visual elements (such as dark and light or dull and bright) to generate emphasis and display. High contrast is desirable in computer displays and printed text, but excessive contrast causes eyestrain. For pictorial and graphic matter, two little contrast causes the picture to look dull or flat, while too much makes the picture seem stark and overexposed.

contrast enhancement Improvement of light-to-dark distinctions. A real digitizing process typically involves some kind of nonlinear detector that destroys the·light-to-dark relationships of the object scanned. Correct contrast can be reintroduced if the characteristics of the detector are known. Contrast can even be heightened if desired.

control points The points that control the shape of a curve or curved surface.

convention A formula, rule, or practice developed by artists to create a usage or mode that is individual to the artist, yet communicable to the culture of which he or she partakes.

convex Pertaining to a region or shape, such as a polygon, for which a straight line segment between any two points of the region is entirely contained within the region. Contrast with concavo.

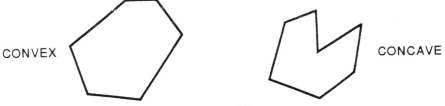

CONVEX   CONCAVE

convex

convolutions Filtering techniques used to sharpen, or soften an image for purposes of image enhancement.

cool Referring to color images, ones that have a bluish tint. Those that are more red are referred to as "warm."

coordinate dimensioning A system of dimensioning where points are defined as a specified dimension and direction from a reference point measured with respect to defined axes.

coordinate graph A graph in which two variable quantities (in two-dimensional graphs) or three variable quantities (in three-dimensional graphs) are plotted as a series of points along coordinate axes.

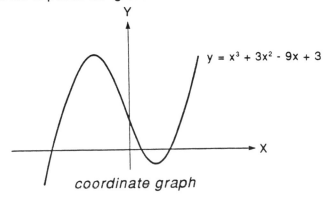

$y = x^3 + 3x^2 - 9x + 3$

coordinate graph

coordinate paper Continuous-feed graph paper used for graphs or diagrams produced on a digital plotter.

coordinate points Points in a Cartesian coordinate system at which axes converge. Specific coordinates can be selected by referring to the numbered points along the axes of the particular coordinate system. For instance, the coordinates (2,5) in a two-dimensional coordinate system denote a coordinate point that is 2 points to the right of the origin along the X-axis and 5 points up the Y-axis. The coordinates (4,5,6) in a three-dimensional coordinate system denote a coordinate point that is 4 points along X, 5 points along Y, and 6 points along Z.

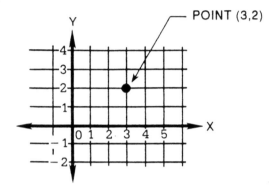

coordinate points

coordinates (1) Ordered set of absolute or relative data values that specify a location in a Cartesian coordinate system. (2) Two numbers used to position the cursor, or pointer, on the screen.

coplanar (1) A technique for building three-dimensional models from two-dimensional blueprints by using two coplanar views, a plan view and an elevation. (2) With respect to two or more points, lines, line segments, or polygons, lying in the same plane.

coprocessor A device that performs specialized processing in conjunction with the main microprocessor of a system. It works in tandem with another central processing unit to increase the computing power of a system. An extra microprocessor to handle some things faster than the main processor, i.e. a math coprocessor or a graphics coprocessor.

copy (1) To reproduce data in a new location or other destination, leaving the source data unchanged, although the physical form of the result may differ from that of the source; for example, to make a duplicate of all the programs or data on a disk, or to copy a graphic screen image to a printer. (2) A duplicate of a graphic image.

copyfit To get text to fit within the available area.

copy program (1) A program designed to duplicate one or more files to another disk. (2) A program that circumvents the copy-protection device on a computer program so that the software can be copied to another disk.

copy-protection Methods used by software developers to prevent any copying of their programs. To protect against illegal copying of software, many software developers build copy-protection routines into their programs. Now that hard disks are common to many microcomputer systems, copy protection has been abolished.

copyright Recognized ownership of creative work; protection against unauthorized use of work.

copyright notice A notification of copyright that is part of a program and is often printed on the display screen at the start of the program. It reminds the user that the program has a copyright, and that making copies for any purpose other than for backup is illegal.

copyrighted software Software that costs money and must not be copied without permission from the software developer.

Corel Draw An illustrative graphics program which runs on Windows. It has an advanced autotracing feature that quickly and easily builds a vector-based image from an entire bit mapped black-and-white, gray scale, or color clip art, paint program or scanned image file. It was introduced in 1989 by Corel Systems Corporation. Corel Draw includes over 100 precision fonts and is known for its speed and ease of use.

courier Monospaced typeface which resembles typewriter text. Commonly a built-in font on laser printers.

crawl Text characters moving at an easily readable rate across the display screen, usually horizontally or vertically.

Cray Research, Inc. A manufacturer of supercomputers founded in 1972 by Seymour Cray, a leading designer of mainframes at Control Data Corporation. In 1976, Cray Research sold its first supercomputer, the Cray 1, to Los Alamos National Laboratories. Other supercomputers manufactured by Cray Research include the Cray X-MP, the Cray 2, and the Cray Y-MP. The Cray Y-MP, introduced in 1988, costs 20 million dollars and can perform over a billion calculations per second.

creative designer In desktop publishing, the individual who lays out and designs a page.

creeping A type of scrolling in which text moves horizontally across the screen like a news wire moving along the bottom of a television program.

Creative Draw An object-oriented PostScript drawing program from Computer Associates International Inc. The program offers extensive Bezier tools, object-to-Bezier path conversion and comprehensive text manipulation.

Cricket Stylist A popular object-oriented drawing program for the Apple Macintosh computer. Using Cricket Stylist you can create drawings using the familiar line, rectangle, and oval tools. The program offers black-and-white, gray scale and full color support. A full set of drawing tools is provided, including a novel starburst tool to create starburst objects.

crop To trim a graphics image for a better fit or to eliminate unwanted portions. In preparing an illustration for traditional printing, cropping is used to clean up a graphic for placement in a document.

crop marks Marks or indications on graphic images to be reproduced that give instructions where to crop or cut.

crop marks

cross hairs On an input device, two intersecting lines – one horizontal and one vertical – whose intersection marks the active cursor position of a graphics system.

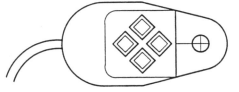

cross hairs

crosshatching In computer graphics, the shading of some portion of a drawing with a pattern of intersecting lines or figures repeated across the area being shaded. Crosshatching is one of several methods for filling in areas of a graphic.

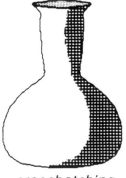

crosshatching

cross-section view A two-dimensional view that you would see if you were to slice through an object and look at the area thus revealed. By using several cross-sectional views of the same object, you can even show three-dimensional construction.

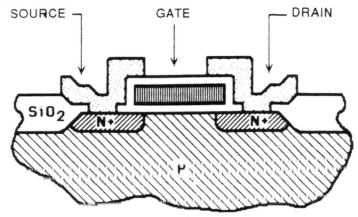

SOURCE ─┐   GATE   ┌─ DRAIN

SiO₂   N·   N·

P

cross-section view

CRT Acronym for Cathode Ray Tube, the picture tube of the standard computer display screen. A CRT display is built around a vacuum tube containing one or more electron guns whose electron beams rapidly sweep horizontally across the inside of the front surface of the tube, which is coated with a material that glows when irradiated.

CRT

CRT plot Computer-generated drawing or graph projected onto the screen of a cathode ray tube.

CRT terminal (1) Visual display unit (VDU). (2) Display device with keyboard as used by an operator to communicate with a computer. As the operator types a message or text on the keyboard, the characters are displayed on the screen.

Crystal Paint A drawing and graphic design tool for the Apple Macintosh microcomputer. Can be used to produce intricate and ornate designs produced by repeating patterns.

Crystal Paint drawing

CSG Acronym for Constructive Solid Geometry. One of the chief methods of solid modeling, using solid primitives and Boolean operators to construct complex solids.

CSS See central structure store.

cube A six-sided object in three-dimensional screen space.

cube

culling The removal of unwanted representations in an image.

current page box In desktop publishing programs, an area that displays the current page being worked on.

cursive scanning Scanning technique used with video display terminals in which the electrons being sent toward the screen are deflected to form the outlines of the picture one line at a time in the same way an artist might draw the same image.

cursor (1) Moving, sliding, or blinking symbol on a CRT screen that indicates where the next character will appear. (2) Position indicator used on a video display terminal to indicate a character to be corrected or a position in which data is to be entered. (3) On graphic systems, it can take any shape (arrow, square, paintbrush, etc.) and is used to mark where the next graphic action is to take place. (4) A cursor is guided by an electronic or light pen, mouse, track ball, joystick, keyboard, data tablet, etc., and follows every movement of the input device.

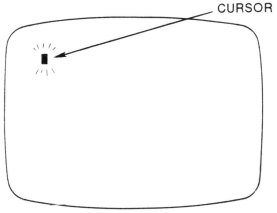

cursor

cursor control Ability to move a video display prompt character to any position on the screen.

cursor control keys Keys that, when pressed, move the cursor in a designated direction. Cursor movement keys generally have directional arrows on their keytops.

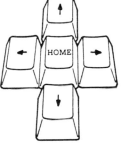

cursor control keys

cursor tracking Positioning a cursor on a display screen by moving a stylus on a graphics tablet connected to the computer.

cursor tracking

curve fitting Mathematical technique for finding a formula that best represents a collection of data points. Usually the formula is used to plot the best-fit line through the points.

curvilinear Composed of curved lines.

customized form letters Personalized form letters produced by word processing systems and special form-letter programs.

cut Act of removing text or graphics from a document. Compare paste.

CUT A bitmap format used by Dr. Halo and a few other graphic programs.

cut and paste Method employed by some systems to move graphics and/or text from one location to another. Such systems usually permit the performance of other operations between the cut and the paste steps. Cut and paste enables compatible programs to share text and graphics.

cutout (1) An image extracted from its original image for use in making up another image. (2) An area deleted from a background image to allow for the printing of an overlay color.

cut plane (1) A capability of graphics systems that enables the designer to define and intersect a plane with two-dimensional entities of three-dimensional objects in order to derive sectional location points. (2) A plane that intersects a three-dimensional object at a specific point, yielding a cross section of the object.

cut-sheet feeder Device that feeds sheets of paper to the printer, one at a time. Usually a friction-feed device.

cutter path The path of a cutting tool through a part. The optimal cutter path can be defined automatically by a CAD/CAM system and formatted into a numerical control tape to guide the tool.

cyan A blue-green color, containing no red component. It is one of the three primaries used in subtractive color mixing.

cycle A series of animation drawings that begin and end with the same position.

cycle overlap The arrangement of a set of graphics objects so that they cannot be placed in priority order where higher priority objects strictly occlude lower priority objects.

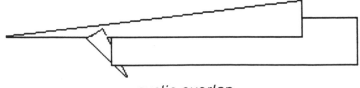

cyclic overlap

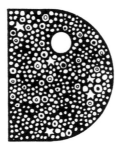

daisy wheel printer Printer that uses a metal or plastic disk with printed characters along its edge. The disk rotates until the required character is brought before a hammer that strikes it against a ribbon. Popular letter-quality printer used with personal computers.

dark bulb Type of cathode ray tube, almost black in appearance when turned off, that gives good contrast to video displays.

darkness Intensity, especially low intensity or limited brightness.

dash pattern The sequence of dots or line segments and spaces that make up a dashed line (- - - - - - -).

database Most generally, any clearly identified collection of data, such as a telephone book or the card catalog at a library. In theory, a database should contain all its information in one central store or file, each record in the file containing roughly the same type of information – such as name, address, city, state, zip code, area code, and telephone number. Each of these categories is called a field, while a record consists of a set of fields pertaining to one person or item. The database file is made up of a number of related records. Some people differentiate between a data base (two words), meaning an underlying collection of data in the real world, and a database (single word) as a coherent system. As applied to data in the computer, it particularly means data organized so that various programs can access and update the information.

data tablet Manual input device for graphic display consoles.

decision support graphics Business graphics that aid senior business managers in making financial and marketing decisions based on information contained in them.

decluttering Selective erasure of display items.

deep Having high color saturation and low color value.

de facto standard A programming language, product, design or program that has become so widely used and imitated that it has little competition but those whose status has not officially been declared by a recognized standard establishing organization. For example, the enhanced 101/102-key keyboard

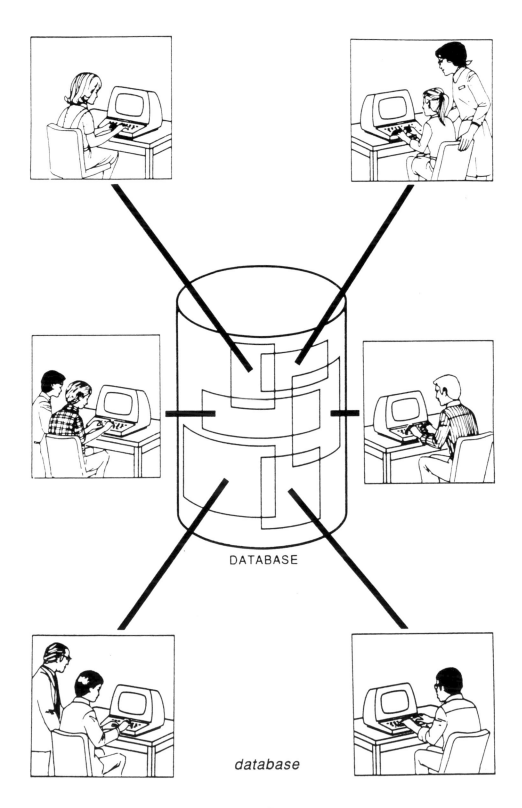

DATABASE

database

introduced by IBM partway through the life of the IBM PC/AT computer has become the de facto standard keyboard for most newer IBM-compatible microcomputers.

default Assumption made by a system or language translator when no specific choice is given by the program or the user. A choice that has been pre-set for you. You can override it or simply accept the setting which the manufacturer or developer has deemed most likely appropriate.

deformation In computer animation, changes in the geometry of an object to give the illusion of creating action.

dejagging See antialiasing.

DEGAS A color paint program for the Atari ST microcomputer. Developed by programmer Tom Hudson.

delete (1) To remove or eliminate. To erase data from a field or to eliminate a record from a file. (2) Method of erasing data.

deletion record New record that will replace or remove an existing record of a master file.

DeluxePaint A popular paint program for IBM-compatible and Commodore Amiga microcomputers.

demo A demonstration program designed to emulate some of the functions of an application program for advertising and marketing purposes.

depth buffer See Z-buffer.

depth clipping Clipping at the back clipping plane when this plane cuts through the object being displayed.

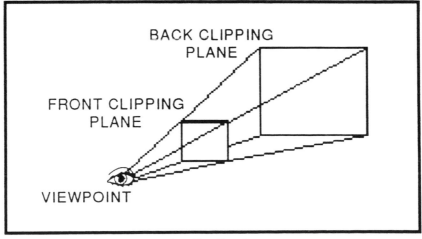

depth clipping

depth-cueing In three-dimensional graphics, the process of reducing the intensity of the lines or surfaces of an object as it recedes from the viewer. This fading technique helps establish visual order in objects that might otherwise appear confusing or flat, and it improves a scene's visual depth.

descender Portion of lower-case letters (g, j, p, q, and y) that extends below the baseline of other characters.

g, j, p, q, y ____ BASELINE

descender

descender line In desktop publishing, a hypothetical line that connects the bottoms of descender letters.

descriptive art Art that is realistic or representative of actual things.

descriptive art

design A comprehensive scheme, plan, or conception.

design automation (DA) The technique of using a computer to automate portions of the design process and reduce human intervention.

Designer An illustrative graphic program for IBM compatible microcomputer systems. Features include color bit mapping, text wrapping, autotracing, Bezier curve controls, slideshow, scalable fonts, color separations, several fill patterns, and a large clip art library.

desk accessory (DA) In a graphical user interface, helpful utilities (e.g. calculator, notepad, thesaurus, paint program, word processor, etc.) that you can open when you're in the middle of any program. Desk accessories are accessed by selecting them from a special pull-down menu. Desk accessories are conveniences that can be activated when needed and then either put away or moved to a small part of the display screen.

DeskPaint/DeskDraw An Apple Macintosh paint/draw application in desk accessory form. The application features a full set of paint and draw tools that allow creation or editing black-and-white, gray scale and color images and work with MacPaint, PICT and TIFF file formats. Users can convert from one pixel depth to another, auto-trace black-and-white bit maps and create graduated fills.

desktop (1) Screen display containing icons that represent programs, files or resources available to the user. (2) Small enough to fit on the top of an office desk, particularly a computer system.

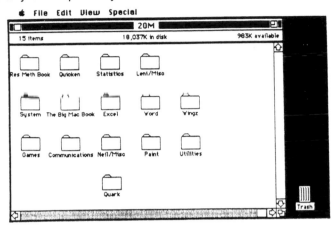

desktop

desktop computer A computer that will fit on the top of a standard size office desk. Most personal computers and lap computers can be considered desktop computers. A desktop computer is equipped with sufficient internal memory and auxiliary storage to perform business computing tasks.

desktop computer

71

desktop computer animation The production of computer animation and graphics using a stand-alone microcomputer system, configured with appropriate graphics and video boards, peripherals, and a turn-key animation/graphics software package.

desktop presentation Presenting text, video, and graphics on the computer for display to others.

desktop publishing This is when printed pieces including words and pictures (ads, newsletters, magazines, brochures, books) are created almost entirely on a computer. Desktop publishing programs convert normal text into professional quality documents that can be printed on laser printers or imagesetters. The term "desktop publishing" was coined by Paul Brainerd, president of Aldus Corporation, the developer of PageMaker.

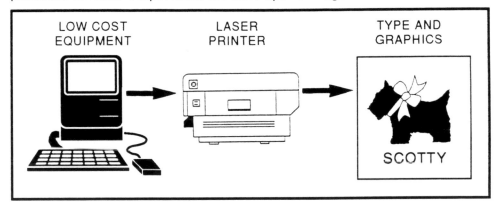

LOW COST EQUIPMENT LASER PRINTER TYPE AND GRAPHICS

SCOTTY

desktop publishing

desktop publishing template Already prepared page layouts stored on disk.

desktop video Using a computer to create and edit video images.

distort To deform, elongate, misshape, twist, or exaggerate.

detachable keyboard Keyboard not built into the same case as the video display or desk unit. Connects to the system with a cable and allows greater flexibility in positioning of the keyboard display—one result of ergonomics.

detachable keyboard

detail Small section of a larger file or graphics picture.

detail drawing The drawing of a single part design containing all the dimensions, annotations, etc., necessary to give a definition complete enough for manufacturing.

device coordinates The coordinates in the coordinate system that describe the physical units by which the computer screen is defined.

device dependent Software that has been written for a specific computer device, and runs on that device exclusively. Software that can run only on a specific vendor's computer hardware is known as vendor-dependent.

DGS Paints A professional PC-based program for doing painting, composition, image retouching and image processing. The program is intuitive, designed to let the user build and customize on-screen functionality by choosing from a vast number of effects and tools. Up to seven brushes paint in 32-bits. Other features include multiple masks and stencils, digital compositing with pixel-by-pixel manipulation, patterns, texture mapping, and an extensive set of image processing functions including edge detection.

dialog box Interactive message box. A temporary window on the screen that contains a set of choices whenever the executing program needs to collect information from the user.

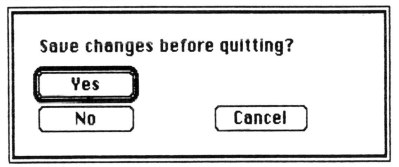

dialog box

Dicomed Corporation A major developer and manufacturer of sophisticated computer graphics systems for computer graphics designers. The company was founded in 1969 by two former Univac engineers.

diffuse highlight Object highlights that result when a light source interacts with a non-reflective surface.

digital computer A computer that operates on discrete data. A device that performs arithmetic, logical, and comparative functions upon information represented in digital form and that operates under control of an internal program. Digital means that the computer uses data in the form of discrete numbers; for example, binary ones and zeros. Most computers used today (mainframes, minicomputers and microcomputers), are digital. Contrast with analog computer.

digital computer animation A computer graphics system that generates and animates graphics. The digital signal is understood by the computer as discrete units of data.

Digital Darkroom An image processing program from Silicon Beach Software that acts as a computerized darkroom to compose images. The program uses computer processing techniques to edit and enhance scanned images.

digital image (1) An image that has been converted into an array of pixels. (2) A generic term that can apply to all computer graphics images.

digital mapping The digitizing of geographic information for a geographic information system.

digital picture library A disk (floppy or hard disk) or optical disc based system for storing and retrieving graphic images, and provides the user with a method of rapid retrieval.

digital plotter Output device that uses an ink pen (or pens) to draw graphs, line drawings, and other illustrations.

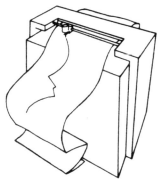

digital plotter

digital tracer A special hinged arm which can be used to trace over drawings and graphs and which sends the information to the computer.

digitization The assignment of a numerical value to each point of an image, indicating color or gray tone. Photographs can be digitized by an optical scanner and then combined indistinguishably with computer generated imagery.

digitize To register a visual image or real object in a format that can be processed by the computer. Digitized data are read into the system with graphics input devices. It includes scanning an image, tracing a picture on a graphics tablet or converting camera images into the computer. Also, to convert an analog signal (voltage or temperature) into a digital value.

digitized image An image put into a computer that can then be manipulated for various purposes.

digitized type Type stored in computer readable form as a collection of dots or line elements.

digitizer (1) A device which converts pictorial information to its digital equivalent. Often used for devices obtaining input from a plotting surface and providing coordinates as output, such as a digitizing tablet (graphics tablet). (2) Digitizers are often used to convert images viewed by a video camera to pictorial (dot-by-dot) images in a computer's memory. These digitized images may be shown on a display screen or printed on paper by a graphics printer. (3) Digitizing is used in mapping and in space exploration to allow data to be sent over long distances by radio-like transmissions.

digitizing Process of converting graphic representations, such as pictures and drawings, into digital data that can be processed by a computer system.

digitizing camera A camera coupled with a processor used for encoding highly detailed images such as pictures or three-dimensional objects into digital data.

digitizing resolution The fineness of detail that a scanner can distinguish.

digitizing tablet A graphics input device that allows the user to create images. It has a special stylus that can be used to draw or trace images, which are then converted to digital data that can be processed by the computer.

digitizing tablet

dimmed command A command in a pull-down menu that is grayed-black. A dimmed command means that that choice is not currently available to you; perhaps because another function needs to be accomplished before that selection can be made.

dimmed icon A grayed-black icon indicates that the object it represents, such as a disk, or a folder, or document on a disk, has either been opened or been ejected from the disk drive.

dingbats Small graphical elements used for decorative purposes in a document. Some fonts, such as Zapf Dingbats, are designed to present sets of dingbats.

dingbats

direct color Same as 24-bit color.

directed beam A technique for displaying information on a CRT that directs the beam from point to point on the display screen of the CRT. The beam traces only the points required to display the desired information.

direction The line of movement of some aspect of an image. These directions are sometimes known as vectors.

directional light Light emanating from a light source that is virtually infinite, such as the sun. Contrast with ambient light.

directory (1) In a partition by software into several distinct files, a directory is maintained on a device to locate these files. (2) Index file containing the names and locations of all the files contained on a storage medium. (3) Major section of a hard disk drive. You can name as many directories as you like, and create sub-directories within them. As you create files, then, you will store the files in the directories.

disc A round, flat circular piece of nonmagnetic, polished metal designed to be read from and written to by optical (laser) technology. Optical discs uses the disc spelling. Floppy disks and hard disks are spelled disk.

disclaimer Clause associated with many software products that states the vendor is not responsible for any business losses incurred due to the use of the product.

> Every effort has been made to supply complete and accurate information. However, the publisher assumes no responsibility for its use, nor for any infringements of patents or other rights of third parties which would result.

disclaimer

disk Magnetic device for storing information and programs accessible by a computer. Can be either a rigid platter (hard disk) or a sheet of flexible plastic (floppy disk). Disks have tracks where data is stored.

FLOPPY DISK

HARD DISK

disk

disk drive Device that reads data from a magnetic disk and copies it into the computer's memory so it can be used by the computer, and that writes data from the computer's memory onto a disk so it can be stored.

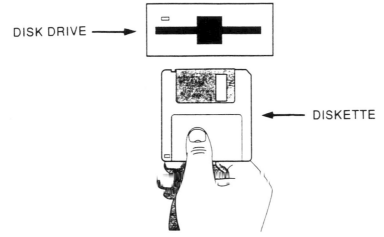

DISK DRIVE ⟶

◄── DISKETTE

disk drive

diskette A single magnetic disk on which data is recorded as magnetic spots. Available in both 3.5-inch format and 5.25-inch format.

disk operating system (DOS) A collection of software stored on disk that controls the operation of the computer system. A computer cannot function unless it has access to its own operating system. Typically, it keeps track of files, saves and retrieves files, allocates storage space, and manages other control functions associated with disk storage.

display (1) Physical representation of data, as on a screen or display. (2) Lights or indicators on computer consoles. (3) Process of creating a visual representative of graphic data on an output device.

display

display adapter Adapter board that electronically links the computer to a display screen and determines its capabilities, such as degree of resolution, color vs. monochrmone, and graphics vs. no graphics.

display background That part of displayed graphic data that is not part of the image being processed and is not subject to change by the user. Used to highlight the image part of the display, called the display foreground.

display composition In desktop publishing, lines of type that are in bold, ornamental, or contrasting typefaces; used to attract attention.

display console Input/output device consisting of a display screen and an input keyboard.

display cycle Time it takes a visual display screen to be completely refreshed.

display device Device capable of producing a visual representation of data, such as a graphics printer, digital plotter, and video display terminal.

display face A typeface suitable for titles and headings in a document, distinguished by its ability to stand out from other text on the page. Display (or decorative) type styles can be either serif or sans serif. Display type styles are used when you want to create a dramatic effect in headings, logos, and product names. They are rarely used in long passages of text since they are typically difficult to read.

VAG Rounded Bold
TRAJAN
Bodoni Poster
Hobo
COTTONWOOD
Freestyle Script

display face

display font The font as it appears on the display screen. Ideally, it closely represents the printer font of the same name and size specification.

display foreground That part of graphic data being displayed on a visual display device that is subject to alteration by the user. Contrast with display background.

display frame One image in an animation sequence.

display highlighting Ways of emphasizing information on a display screen by using such enhancers as blinking, boldface, high contrast, reverse video, underlining, or different colors.

display image That portion of a displayed graphics file that is currently visible on the display device.

display list In computer graphics, a collection of vectors that make up a graphics image. A description of the desired image via a list of primitives and attributes. Display lists provide an intermediate picture storage for quick image redraw.

display list processor A graphics peripheral board used to speed up the processing of vector graphics information.

display menu Onscreen series of program options that allows the user to choose the next function or course of action to be executed, such as to print the contents of the visual display or to save a graphic display on a disk.

display menu

display PostScript (DPS) A display language from Adobe Corporation that translates elementary commands in an application program to graphics and text elements on screen. The screen counterpart of the PostScript printer language. See PostScript.

display screen The part of a display unit on which images and text are shown.

display segment In computer graphics, a collection of graphics primitives that can be manipulated as a single element.

display space The portion of image space which can be viewed at any one time on the display.

display surface (1) Medium upon which a visual representation of graphic data is made, such as a visual display screen, printer paper, plotter paper, or film.

display terminal Any output device capable of producing a visual representation of graphic data.

display tolerance Measure of accuracy with which graphic data can be output.

display type (1) Technology of the display, such as cathode ray tube (CRT), light-emitting diode (LED), and liquid crustal display (LCD). (2) In desktop publishing, type which is greater than 14 points.

DISPLAY TYPE
display type

display unit Device that provides a visual representation of data.

DisplayWrite A full-featured word processing program for IBM microcomputer systems.

dissolve A visual transition between two pictures in which the whole area of the first gradually disappears as it is replaced by the second.

dissolve

dithering The creation of additional colors or shades of gray to create special effects or to make "hard edges" softer. Dithering takes advantage of the eye's tendency to blur spots of different colors by averaging their effects and merging them into a single perceived shade or color. Dithering is used to add realism to computer graphics, and to create a wide variety of patterns for use as backgrounds, fills and shading.

dither pattern For a scanner, a pattern of dots used to simulate gray tones or intermediate colors.

document (1) Handwritten, typewritten, or printed sheet or sheets of paper containing data. (2) Any representation or collection of information or text, whether human-readable or machine-readable.

door swing The rotation of an image on any screen axis.

DOS Operating system for IBM-compatible microcomputers. DOS is available in both generic MS-DOS and IBM-specific PC DOS versions. DOS is an acronym for Disk Operating System.

dot A small mark. Computers generate dots (on visual displays) that are called pixels. Printers use dots to form letters and other visual material. The typical dot-matrix printer generates 75 dots per inch in contrast to the laser printer, which produces 300 or more dots per inch.

dot chart A scatter graph, showing the distribution of quantities as a collection of dots.

dot command A command that consists of a period followed by letters. Used in some older types of word processing programs for embedded commands.

dot density The number of dots per unit of measure in printing, e.g. 24 dots per character (dot matrix printers) or 300 dots per inch (laser printers).

dot matrix Techniques for representing characters by composing them out of selected dots from within a rectangular matrix of dots.

dot matrix printer Printer that creates text characters and graphs with a series of closely spaced dots. Uses tiny hammers to strike a needle mechanism against the paper at precise moments as the print head moves across the page. Some produce dot patterns fine enough to approach the print quality of a daisy wheel printer.

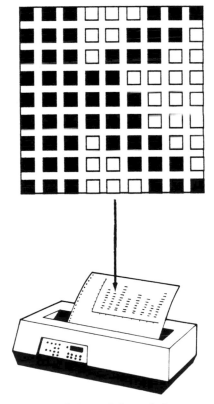

dot matrix printer

dot pitch The resolution of a dot matrix. (1) For display screens, it is expressed as the width of an individual dot; for example, a .28 dot pitch refers to a dot that is 28/100 ths of a millimeter in diameter. The smaller the number, the higher the resolution. (2) For printers, it is expressed as the number of dots per linear inch; for example, a desktop laser printer prints at least 300 dpi. The larger the number, the higher the resolution.

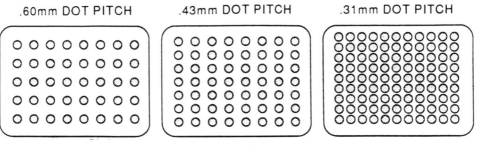

dot pitch

dots/mm Short for dots per millimeter, a unit of measure for the digitizing resolution of scanners and other graphics systems.

dots per inch (1) a linear measure of the number of dots a printer can print in an inch. For example, a 300 dpi laser printer can print up to 300 dots for each horizontal or vertical inch on the paper. (2) A measure of screen resolution that counts the dots that the device can produce per linear inch.

double buffering The process of using two frame buffers for smooth animation. Graphical contents of one frame buffer are displayed while updates occur on the other buffer.

double-click Method to invoke a command by using the mouse button. The pointer or cursor is placed in the correct position on a display screen and the mouse button is pressed twice in rapid succession. A double-click is used to open a file, disk, or folder.

double click

double density Having twice the storage capacity of a normal disk or tape. Ability to store twice as much data in a given area on a disk or tape as single density. In IBM compatible microcomputers, a double-density 5.25-inch disk has a capacity of 360K, while the double density 3.5-inch disk has a capacity of 720K.

double quote Another name for the quote mark (").

double-sided disk Magnetic disk capable of storing information on both of its surfaces. Contrast with single-sided disk.

download (1) Process of transferring data (files) from a large computer to a smaller one. (2) To transfer information to a laser printer from a computer. Opposite of upload.

downloadable font A set of characters of the same typeface and size stored on disk and sent (downloaded) to a printer's memory when needed for printing a document.

downtime Length of time a computer system is inoperative due to a malfunction.

dpi Acronym for dots per inch. The density of a printer's output; determines the overall appearance/quality of printed output. Laser printers offer 300 dpi and up. True typesetting starts at 1000 dpi. Dot matrix printers, on the low end, range from 72 to 150 dpi.

draft quality Measure of quality for printed output. Usually refers to the result of top-speed printing and therefore not the most precisely defined or fully filled-in characters. Considered acceptable for working copies but not final work. Contrast with letter quality.

drag Action of moving the mouse while holding the button down; used to move or manipulate objects on a computer's display screen.

dragging An interactive technique for repositioning an image on a display screen.

dragon curve The dragon curve vaguely resembles a sea dragon paddling with its clawed feet, his curved snout and coiled tail just above an imaginary waterline. The dragon curve can be generated in several different ways and is an excellent example of a self-similar fractal. One method of generating the dragon curve follows. Begin with a line segment. Replace the line segment with a right angle in such a way that the old line segment would have been the hypotenuse of an isosceles right triangle with the new line segments as legs. Continue this procedure, replacing each new segment formed at the last stage with a right angle. A resulting dragon will be traced out in an infinite number of stages.

dragon curve

DRAM Short for dynamic memory, meaning a type of memory chip that keeps its contents only if supplied with regular clock pulses and a chance to periodically refresh the data internally. DRAM is far less expensive than static RAM (which needs no refreshing) and is the type found in most personal computers.

DRAW A graphics instruction in many versions of the BASIC programming language, which is useful for high-resolution graphics.

drawing Process of creating a graphic image with an object-oriented drawing program.

drawing program A program for creating and manipulating object-oriented graphics, as opposed to creating and manipulating pixel images. For example, in a drawing program the user can manipulate an element such as a triangle, or a block of text as an independent object simply by selecting the object and moving it.

DrawPerfect A drawing program for IBM-compatible microcomputers. This charting, drawing and presentation program provides 256 colors. It creates two-dimensional bar, pie, and graph charts.

Dr. Halo A paint program for IBM-compatible microcomputers.

drop cap An initial letter of a chapter or paragraph enlarged and positioned so that the top of the character is even with the top of the first line and the rest of the character descends into the second and subsequent lines.

drop-down menu A type of menu that drops from the menu bar when requested and remains open without further action until the user chooses it or chooses a menu item. Same as pull-down menu.

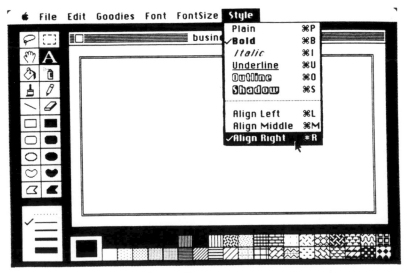

drop-down menu

drop in Character that appears erroneously – on a display screen, on a printout, or in a file – because the disk drive or tape drive misstored or misread one or more bits.

drop out (1) In data transmission, a momentary loss in signal, usually due to the effect of noise or system malfunction. (2) Character that vanishes from a display, printout, or file because the disk drive or tape drive misstored or misread one or more bits.

dropshadow A shadow placed behind an image, slightly off-set horizontally and vertically, that creates the illusion that the topmost image has been lifted off the surface of the page. Drop shadow is very difficult to draw manually, but can be generated by computer graphics instantly. The dropshadow is a feature found in many paint programs.

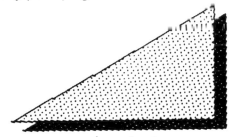

dropshadow

drum plotter Output device that draws schematics, graphs, pictures, and so forth on paper with automatically controlled pens. The paper is wrapped around a cylindrical drum that turns forward and backward at various speeds under one or more pens that slide to and fro, marking the paper.

drum plotter

drum printer Printing device that uses a drum embossed with alphanumeric characters. Type of line printer, that can print several thousand lines per minute. Each print position has a complete set of characters around the circumference of the drum.

DTP See desktop publishing.

dual disk drive Floppy disk system that contains two disk drives, providing an increased storage capacity.

dual y-axis graph In presentation graphics, a graph that uses two Y-axes when comparing two data series with different measurement scales. Useful when comparing two different data series that must be measured with two different values axes.

dumb terminal Video display terminal with minimal I/O capabilities and no processing capability.

duplex printing Printing a document on both sides of the sheet, so that the verso (left) and recto (right) pages face each other after the document is bound.

duplicate To copy so that the result remains in the same physical form as the source, such as to make a new diskette with the same information and in the same format as an original diskette. Contrast with copy.

Durer's pentagon fractal Albrecht Durer (1471-1528) was an early artist who generated a fractal object based on regular pentagons. His basic figure was a pentagon surrounded by five identical pentagons. Further subdividing this figure results in a truly fractal object.

Durer's pentagon fractal

Dvorak keyboard Keyboard arrangement designed by August Dvorak. Provides increased speed and comfort and reduces the rate of errors by placing the most frequently used letters in the center for use by the strongest fingers. In this fashion, finger motions and awkward strokes are reduced by over 90 percent in comparison with the familiar QWERTY keyboard. The Dvorak system, although patented in 1936, did not really become popular until its approval by ANSI in 1982. The Dvorak keyboard puts the five vowel keys, AEIOU, together under the left hand in the center row, and the five most frequently used consonants, DHTNS, under the fingers of the right hand.

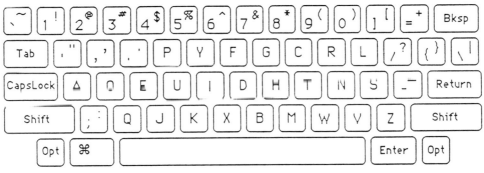

Dvorak keyboard

DVT Acronym for Digital Video Interactive; use of compact disk with a drive that allows for, not only visual, audio and text information, but also full motion video.

DVST Acronym for Direct View Storage Tube. A vector CRT device in which the image is held in a storage grid in the display device.

DXF Acronym for Drawing Interchange Format. AutoCAD's format for two-dimensional and three-dimensional drawings.

dynamic graphics option Technique used in some storage tube products to combine refresh and stored information on the same display. This allows operation in the dynamic mode of the refreshed display while maintaining the advantages of the storage tube.

dynamic RAM (DRAM) The most common type of computer memory; the computer must refresh DRAM at frequent intervals. Contrast with static RAM, which is usually faster and does not require refresh circuitry.

earth colors Paint colors derived from natural, colored earths. Usually browns, reds, and yellows.

Easy Color Paint An Apple Macintosh graphics program designed for non-professionals. It emphasizes "simplicity, economy and fun." Simply pick a color and pattern, choose a tool, and start printing.

ECAD Acronym for Electronic Computer Aided Design. CAD for electronic design.

echo To provide visual feedback to the designer during graphic input to the system.

edge (1) In computer graphics, the straight line segment which is the intersection of two planes' faces of a solid, such as the edges of a cube. (2) Connection between two nodes in a graph. (3) In image processing, a set of values determined to be the dividing line between one image and another or an image and background.

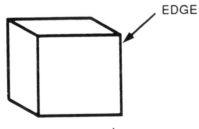

EDGE

edge

edge cutter/trimmer Device for removing the sprocketed margin from continuous-form printer paper.

edge detection An image processing technique in which edge pixels are identified by examining their neighboring pixels.

edge enhancement An image enhancement technique in which edges are sharpened by increasing the contrast between the lighter and darker pixels on opposite sides of the edge.

edge sharpening Process of sharpening the edges of a digitized picture.

edit To modify, refine, or update an emerging design or text on a graphics system.

edit mode An input mode that allows the editing of previously entered information.

EGA Acronym for Enhanced Graphics Adapter, a video display adapter introduced by IBM in 1984. Video display standard for IBM compatible microcomputers featuring 640- by 350-pixel resolution. EGA can display no more than 16 colors at once. EGA has been superseded by VGA.

eight-bit color The color range possible with an eight-bit graphics system. Each pixel in an eight-bit system can display one of 256 colors at any given time.

elastic banding In computer graphics, the movement of a line drawn from a specified point can be moved around the screen by using a mouse, and the line length will expand or contract as if the line were made of elastic material. This makes alteration of diagrams much easier than it would be if lines had to be rubbed out and redrawn, so elastic banding is much used in computer-aided design programs. Also called rubber banding.

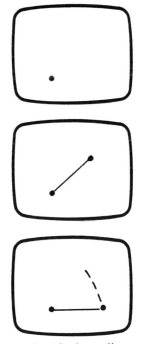

elastic banding

electroluminescent A type of flat display.

electron beam The beam of electrons produced by the electron gun. The electron beam illuminates the phosphors of the monitor to display the pixels on the raster grid in a selected pattern.

electron gun The device within the computer CRT that produces an electron beam.

Electronic Computer Aided Design (ECAD) CAD for electronic design.

electronic halftoning To simulate shades of gray by using patterns of black and white dots.

electronic magazine Magazine published in a floppy disk, video disc or video tape format. A type of electronic publishing.

electronic pen Pen-like stylus commonly used in conjunction with a cathode ray tube for inputting or changing information under program control. Often called light pen.

electronic publishing (1) Technology encompassing a variety of activities that contain or convey information with a high editorial and value-added content in a form other than print. Includes educational software disks, CD-ROM, online databases, electronic mail videotext, teletext, videotape cassettes, and video discs. (2) Use of a personal computer, special software, and a laser printer to produce very high-quality documents that combine text and graphics. Also called desktop publishing.

electrophotographic A printing process where light is used to create a latent image on a photoconductive intermediary. The latent image is rendered visible by liquid or powder toner, transferred to a paper and fixed by heat, cold, pressure, chemical vapors or a combination of these. Printers using this process often are referred to by the source of light used to create the image – laser, liquid-crystal shutter (LCS), light-emitting diode (LED), etc.

electrostatic plotter Output device that draws graphic data on paper by using static electrical energy. Generally faster than a pen plotter.

electrostataic printer/plotter Output device that delivers raster images by depositing patterns of negative charges on plain paper surfaces. The patterns are then coated with postively-charged toner.

electrothermal printer High-speed printer that uses heated elements to create characters as matrices of small dots on heat-sensitive paper.

elements of a microcomputer Components of a microcomputer, include a microprocessor for the central processing unit, program and data storage, input/output circuitry, and clock generators.

elite type Size of type that fits twelve characters into each inch of type. Contrast with pica.

ellipse The conic section that is formed when a plane intersects all of the elements of a cone but is not perpendicular to the axis.

em A unit of measure equal to the width of the capital M in a particular font.

embedded command (1) One or more codes inserted into a document that do not print but direct the application program or printer to control printing and change formats. (2) Low-level assembly level instructions that are inserted within a program written in a high-level language. Embedded code is used to make a program more efficient or to produce a capability not available in the high-level language.

embossing The effect of letters being raised from their background.

em dash A dash (—) that is one em wide.

employment, computer graphics The computer graphics artist is one of the 15 hottest careers of the 1990s, reports a survey conducted by Money magazine. The career of computer graphics artists appeared third on a list of the 15 most fast-growing, lucrative, challenging, and prestigious professions for the next decade.

employment, computer graphics

emulate (1) To imitate one hardware system with another, by means of an electronic attachment, such that the imitating system accepts the same data, executes the same programs, and achieves the same results as the imitated system. (2) To have a program simulate the function of another software or hardware product. Printers often have emulation options so that you can specify a brand name in configuration or setup, even though you don't have that brand.

en One half the width of the em.

encapsulated PostScript (EPS) A file format developed to facilitate the exchange of PostScript graphics files between applications. Like all PostScript files, EPS files are resolution independent and can be printed by a PostScript printer.

en dash A dash (–) that is one en wide. A punctuation mark.

end color One of two colors at either end of a range of colors.

endpoints In vector graphics, the points that specify each end of a line segment.

end user Person who buys and uses computer software or who has contact with computers.

engineering drawing sizes
A – 8.5 in x 11 in
B – 11 in x 17 in
C – 17 in x 22 in
D – 22 in x 34 in
E – 34 in x 44 in

Enhanced Graphics Adapter See EGA.

enhanced keyboard A standard keyboard for newer IBM personal computers. It has become the de facto standard for most IBM-compatible keyboards.

enhancements Hardware or software improvements, additions, or updates to a computer or a software system.

enlargement A proportional copy of an image that is larger than the original.

ORIGINAL   200% ENLARGEMENT

enlargement

ENTER key Special key on some keyboards that means "execute a command." Same as RETURN key on some keyboards. Often used interchangeably with carriage return.

environment In a computing context, this is more likely to refer to the mode of operation, such as a network environment, than to physical conditions of temperature, humidity, and so forth. With respect to personal computers, everything surrounding the PC, including peripherals and software.

EP Acronym for Electronic Presentations. A process where a user creates a presentation using a desktop computer system. The diskette (containing the presentation) is then inserted into an EP player, which can produce an animated video presentation.

EPS Acronym for Encapsulated PostScript. A directly printable PostScript file; the output of a PostScript compatible printer driver captured in a file instead of being sent to a printer. The typical filename extension for encapsulated PostScript files is EPS.

EPS graphics

EPSF Acronym for Encapsulated PostScript Format. See EPS.

Epson A well-established make of dot matrix printers which can print graphics as well as text.

equalization A process by which the range of gray shades in an image is expanded to make the image more attractive.

equipment Part of a computer system.

erasable optical disc An optical disc on which data can be stored, moved, changed, and erased, just as on magnetic media. Erasable drives perform much like large, interchangeable hard disks. Erasable drives use two lasers rather than one; one laser melts the surface of the media to an amorphous state, effectively erasing any information stored there – the other laser writes or reads information.

erase In a computer paint program, a tool that deletes part of an image by switching pixels to the background color.

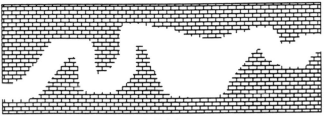

erase

ergonomics Study of the physical relationships between people and their work environment. Adapting machines to the convenience of operators, with the general aim of maximum efficiency and physical well-being. Numeric keypads on standard keyboards, detachable keyboards, and tilting display screens are tangible results. The word, comes from ergo (work) and nomics (law or management).

ergonomics

94

ESCAPE key Standard control key available on most computer keyboards. Used to take control of the computer away from a program, to escape from a specific program, or to stop a program. Abbreviated ESC.

Escher drawing Dutch artist Maurits Escher (1902-1972) created several tilings of plane figures that have a fractal form.

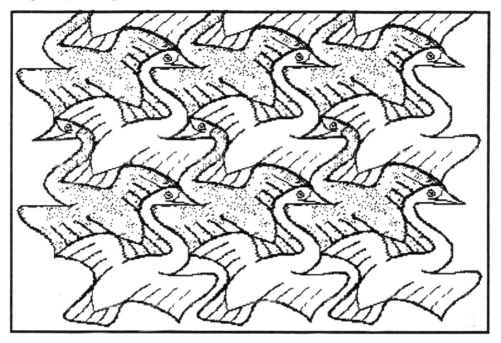

Escher drawing

Evans & Sutherland, Inc. A manufacturer of graphics workstation equipment and flight simulations visual systems. One of the pioneering companies in computer graphics.

evocative typeface A display type design intended to evoke an era or place.

expanded type Type that has been increased laterally so that fewer characters are contained per linear inch.

ABCDEFGHIJKLMN
OPQRSTUVWXYZ

expanded type

expansion A means of increasing the capabilities of a computer by adding hardware designed to perform a task that is not built into the basic system.

expansion card A circuit board that plugs into a computer and gives it additional specialized functions (e.g. enhanced graphics, expanded memory, modem).

exploded pie graph A pie graph in which one or more of the slices has been offset slightly from the others.

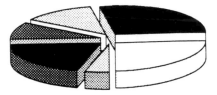

exploded pie graph

exploded view Illustration of a solid construction showings its parts separately, but in positions that indicate their relationships to the whole.

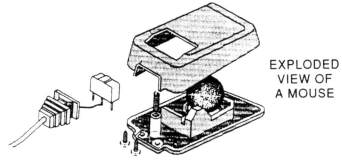

EXPLODED
VIEW OF
A MOUSE

exploded view

expression Having to do with those factors of form and subject that together give the work of art its content and meaning.

extents Lines, rectangles or solids that separate or surround individual polygons or segments. They are not displayed on the screen, but are devices used by graphic programmers.

external CD-ROM An optical disc equipped with its own case, cables, and power supply.

external drive A disk drive that sits in its own case, rather than being mounted in the chassis of the main computer. Often, external drives include their own power supply.

extrusion An interactive modeling technique in which a further dimension can be added to an existing definition, e.g. a line can be extruded from a point, a plane from a line, and a solid from a plane.

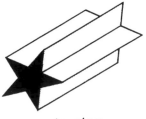

extrusion

96

fabric design Textiles are basic to contemporary living, yet are rooted in fiber arts of the past. Today, computers and graphics are frequently involved in textile design. Where precise repetition of pattern is essential, few artists can operate with the speed and efficiency of a machine. Color combinations can be unlimited when the operation is computerized.

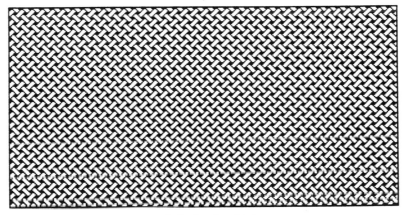

fabric design

face (1) In computer graphics or geometry, one side of a solid object, such as a cube. A cube has six faces. (2) In printing and typography, a shortened form of typeface.

FACES OF A CUBE

face

face list The list of faces and their vertices that make up the surface shape of a model.

facets In three-dimensional modeling, polygons that comprise the surface of a computer generated object. Flat surfaces, usually convex polygons, forming a surface.

facing pages The two pages of a bound document that face each other when the document is open. The even-numbered page (verso) is on the left, and the odd-numbered page (recto) is on the right.

VERSO  RECTO

facing pages

facsimile The use of computer technology to send digitized text, graphics, and charts from one facsimile machine to another. Abbreviated FAX.

fair use A situation in which limited copying of copyright material is legal.

false color Color which is added to monochrome images by transforming intensity values into color values.

family (1) In computer science, a compatible series of computers, i.e. Apple Macintosh Classic, Macintosh LC, and Macintosh IIsi all constitute a family of microcomputers. (2) In desktop publishing, a family of type, i.e. Helvetica, Helvetica Italic, Helvetica Bold, and Helvetica Bold Italic all constitute a family of type.

fan (1) The cooling mechanism built into computer cabinets, laser printers and other devices to prevent malfunction due to heat buildup. (2) To flip through a stack of laser printer paper to ensure that the pages are loose and will not stick together or jam the printer.

fanfold paper One long continuous sheet of paper perforated at regular intervals to mark page boundaries and folded fan-style into a stack. Fanfold paper is available with vertical perforations, so the sprocket hold strip can be removed. The paper can be divided on the perforations thus enabling the paper to be separated into sheets.

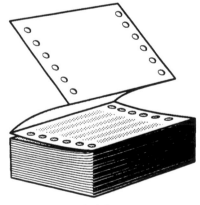

fanfold paper

fantasy (1) Art that is irrational, mystic, or "make-believe." (2) A product of the imagination; an artwork produced from the imagination.

fantasy

fat bits Selection on a painting and drawing program that enlarges a portion of the screen to allow precise manipulation of individual screen elements. Useful for precision work or font designing.

fat bits

fax (1) Facsimile. (2) Equipment configuration that facilitates the transmission of images over a common carrier network. (3) A fax machine sends an image to another fax, over standard telephone networks. Imagine the process as similar to making a photocopy; reproduction quality of fax is typically lower, though.

feather To blend or smooth the edge of a region or shape into a background or other object.

feathering Adding an even amount of space between each line on a page or column to force vertical justification.

feature Something special accomplished in a program or hardware device, such as the ability of a paint program to create animation cells, or a word processing program to check the spelling of words.

feature extraction Selection of dominant characteristics for pattern recognition. Enables a computer-controlled video camera to recognize objects by such features as shapes and edges.

field In raster graphics, one complete scan of the picture image from top to bottom.

field of view In computer graphics, the limits of what a simulated camera can see, usually expressed as a horizontal angle centered at the camera. For simplicity of computation, computer graphicists assume that what a camera sees lies within a pyramid – rather than a cone – with the apex at the camera.

field upgradable Hardware capable of being enhanced in the field (in one's office or at a local repair center or computer store).

fifth-generation computer The next generation of computers. A term describing new forms of computer systems involving artificial intelligence, parallel processing, natural language, and expert systems. Fifth generation computer systems are expected to appear in the mid 1990s and will represent the next quantum leap in computer technology.

file A collection of related information in the system which may be accessed by a unique name. May be stored on a disk, tape, or other storage media.

fill (1) To place a pattern or color in a defined region. (2) A color or pattern occupying a region.

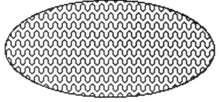

fill

fill algorithm An algorithm that fills polygons with a color, gray scale shade, or pattern.

filled Refers to objects in computer images. If they are filled, they appear as shaded solids.

fillet The representation of a filled-in or rounded intersection of two lines or curves.

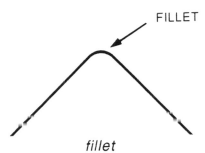

FILLET

fillet

filling In computer graphics, a software function that allows the interior of a defined area to be filled with a color, shading, or hatching of the operator's choosing.

fill line A line that indicates one boundary of an area to be filled.

fill point A point that indicates the radial center of an area to be filled.

film recorder An output device that takes a 35mm slide picture from a graphics file which has been created using a graphics program. Widely used in producing presentation-quality hardcopy. Film recorders offer both high resolution (up to 2000 dots per inch) and a true color reproduction capability (up to 68 million simultaneous colors). Lines show perfectly smooth edges, and colors blend imperceptibly in film recorder images.

film recorder

filtering An image-processing technique that reduces unwanted features or colors in an image.

find and replace See search and replace.

finder A system program that provides the "desktop" metaphor you encounter when a Macintosh microcomputer is booted up. The finder presents icons (little pictures) depicting applications, documents, file folders, and a garbage can that can be used to discard unwanted files. This highly visual interface program keeps the user from having to type commands directly to the operating system.

fine art (1) Art whose primary concern is aesthetics. (2) Art primarily produced for the artists' satisfaction rather than for direct commercial purposes.

fine art

fine tune To make small adjustments in order to get best results.

finite elements Discrete mathematical sub-elements of a complex part that are more easily evaluated than the parts as a whole.

firmware Software that has been copied on integrated circuits, usually ROMs. Since it is on ROM, which cannot be altered, it is neither completely soft nor hard and therefore referred to as firm.

first generation computers First commercially available computers, introduced with UNIVAC I in 1951 and terminated with the development of fully transistorized computers in 1959. Characterized by their use of vacuum tubes, they are now museum pieces. Compare second generation computers, third generation computers, fourth generation computers, and fifth generation computers.

fitting In computer graphics, the calculation of a curve, surface, or line that fits most accurately to a set of data points and design criteria. Compare curve fitting.

flashing The blinking on and off of characters on a display screen; used to call attention to something on the screen. The intermittent display of a graphic entity.

flatbed plotter Digital plotter using plotting heads that move over a flat surface in both vertical and horizontal directions. The size of the bed determines the maximum size sheet of paper than can be drawn. A pair of arms attached to a trolley and controlled by a computer can place the trolley at any part of the paper. A pen attached to the trolley can be raised or lowered to contact the paper. Then, under computer control, this device can draw pictures. If several pens of different colors can be controlled, then pictures can be drawn in color.

flatbed scanner A scanner with a glass surface upon which you place material to be scanned. Because the original never moves during the scanning process, flatbeds produce more precise results than sheetfed scanners. The scanner can transform a full-page (8.5- by 11-inch) graphic into a digitized file.

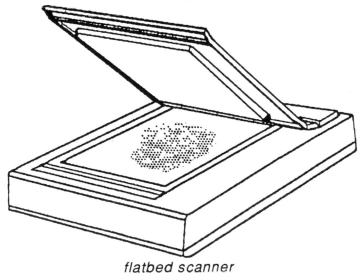

flatbed scanner

flat panel display Thin-screened peripheral device upon which information may be displayed, such as electroluminescent, liquid crystal, and plasma displays.

flat screen Thin panel screen, such as those found on flat panel displays.

flat shading A shading method that applies a lighting model to only one point on each polygon face. Each face is rendered in a single color that represents the amount of light interacting with that face. This tends to give the object a faceted look, like a diamond. Uniform shading.

flicker Undesirable, unsteady lighting of a display due to inadequate refresh rate and/or fast persistence. Occurs whenever the refresh speed is not fast enough to compensate for natural luminance delay on the screen.

flight simulator (1) Computer-controlled simulator used by airline companies to train pilots on new aircraft. Some are so realistic that they are acceptable to the FAA for use in renewal of pilot licenses. (2) Flight simulator software running on personal computers provides entertainment and practice in instrument reading and navigation.

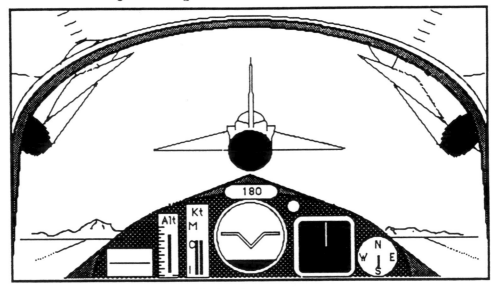

flight simulator

flip To reverse an image side to side (to flip horizontally) or top to bottom (to flip vertically).

floppy disk Floppy disks are a form of computer storage medium consisting of a thin flexible disk covered with magnetic oxide held inside a protective sleeve within which it can be rotated. They are lightweight, cheap and portable. The first floppy disks were 8-inch disks (which meant that the whole package was 8 inches square), but these earlier disks are now superseded by 5.25 and 3.5 inch versions. The 3.5 inch version is much improved over its predecessors by having a hard, rather than flexible, casing and a protective "door" over its access holes, which mean that its reliability is likely to be much greater. Storage capacities on disks have increased greatly during development. Early disks offered only about 100K byte on an 8-inch disk. Recent drives offer up to 2M byte on a standard 3.5 inch disk. Floppy disks are standard equipment on vertically every personal computer.

floppy disk

floppy disk unit Peripheral storage device in which data are recorded on magnetized floppy disks.

focus The clarity or sharpness of an image. Soft focus generates images that are not precise and clear and produces a dream-like effect.

focusing Sharpening a blurred image on a display screen.

folder A collection of files. You can place files into folders. To access a file that has been placed in a folder, double-click on the folder's icon.

folio (1) A page number. (2) To number pages consecutively.

font A complete assortment or set of all the characters (letters, numbers, punctuation and symbols) of a particular typeface, all of one size and style (e.g. 12 pt. Bookman, 18 pt. Helvetica, 36 pt. Cooper Black, 8 pt. Times Roman). Two types of fonts exist: bit mapped fonts and outline fonts. Each comes in two versions, screen fonts and printer fonts.

ABCDEEFFGHIJKLMNOPQ
RSTUVWXYZ&abcdefghij
klmnopqrstuvwxyz$¢123
4567890.,:;-!?'""()%

font

font cartridge A set of bit mapped or outline fonts for one or more typefaces contained in a module that plugs into a slot in a printer. The fonts are stored in a ROM chip within the cartridge.

font family A set of fonts in several sizes and weights that share the same typeface.

font generator A program that converts an outline font into the precise patterns of dots required for a particular size of font.

font groups Fonts are often divided into three groups: Serif groups have additional strokes (serifs) at the top and bottom of each letter. Type styles in the Sans Serif groups do not have serifs. Display (or decorative) type styles can be either serif or sans serif. Type styles in this group are used when you want to create a dramatic effect in headings, logos, and product names. They are rarely used in long passages of text since they are typically difficult to read.

font size The size of a character font in points. The size most often used for text is 10-12 points. Point size is a vertical measurement; horizontal measurement is not taken into consideration.

8pt
9pt
10pt
11pt
12pt
14pt
16pt
18pt
20pt
22pt
24pt
30pt
36pt
45pt
72pt

font size

font substitution Substituting an outline font for printing in place of a bit mapped screen font. In some systems, the laser printer driver substitutes an outline font for a specific bit mapped screen font.

font weight Weight refers to the heft and/or slant of a font. Most fonts are available in four weights: Medium (or Roman or Book or Normal), Italic, Bold and Bold Italic (or Bold Oblique). Some decorative fonts (e.g. Zapf Chancery Medium Italic) are only available in one weight. A few fonts (e.g. Helvetica) are available in many more weights than the four listed above.

Helvetica Roman 12

Helvetica bold 12

Helvetica italic 12

Helvetica bold italic 12

font weight

footer Information printed at the bottom of a page, such as page numbers.

Wild Animals — HEADER

KANGAROO

Of Australia's roughly 200 species of marsupials (mammals whose young develop further in their mothers' abdominal pouches after birth), the 40-odd species of kangaroos are the best known. The **red kangaroo** *(Macropus rufus)* is the largest of all marsupials, with a head-and-body length of about 65 inches and a weight of about 180 pounds. It can jump up to 8 feet high, up to 14 feet in distance. At birth the joey (young kangaroo) has a weight $\frac{1}{30,000}$th of its mother's; it remains in her pouch for $7\frac{1}{2}$ months. The red kangaroo, which is red, gray or a mix, lives in large groups, cropping vegetation mainly at night.

Page 1 — FOOTER

footer

footnote In a page layout or word processing program, a note positioned at the bottom of the page.

forced page break A page break inserted by the user.

formalism Art prescribed by rules of color, design, or other specific intent.

format code A word processing code that describes how text will be printed or formatted.

formatting Preparing a diskette for use so that the operating system can route information on it. Formatting erases any previous information there.

form feed (FF) (1) Physical transport of continuous paper to the beginning of a new line or page. (2) Standard ASCII character that causes a form feed to occur.

form letter program Program that can be designed to send out "personalized" letters that look like letters produced on a typewriter.

FORTRAN Acronym for FORmula TRANslation, a scientific programming language used by many businesses and organizations in the past to develop computer graphics software.

four-color printing Another term for process color, in which cyan, magenta, yellow, and black colors are used to reproduce all the hues of the spectrum.

fourth-generation computers A computer that is made up almost entirely of chips with limited amounts of discrete components. Fourth generation computers are currently being manufactured and sold.

fractal The term fractal was coined in 1975 by Benoit B. Mandelbrot from the Latin adjective fractus, meaning irregular or broken, to describe a new class of mathematical functions that mimic the irregular curves, shapes, and patterns found in natural phenomena such as coastlines, cloud patterns, and the aggregation of galaxies. Aside from those fractals which imitate natural phenomena, however, others believe the relative simplicity of the recursive algorithms from which they derive. A geometric fractal is generated by the repetitive application of a mathematical formula to a line or a set of points. Natural fractals are produced when randomness is introduced in the repetition of a fractal formula. In either case, the complexity of the resultant shape is uniquely characterized by a number called the fractal dimension. The fractal dimension is always larger than the corresponding topological or Euclidean dimension. The fractal curve, for example, by definition has infinite length and a fractal dimension between one and two. Fractals often exhibit self-similarity; successively smaller pieces retain a geometric similarity to the shape of the whole. If a fractal curve were examined under increasing magnification, it would continue to show the same level of detail. Computer graphics has played a central role in the development of fractals. Simple sets of directions or mathematical recipes, called algorithms, can direct computers to draw various shapes and curves with amazing speed. Fractals can be used for stunning graphic effects. Fractals can be used to create images of great beauty and are a constant source of inspiration to some computer artists.

fractal dimension A feature of fractals that measures their geometry in relation to familiar Euclidean elements which have integer topological dimensions of zero, one, two, and three. A point has dimension zero; a line, whether straight or curved, has dimension one. Points on a plane or any

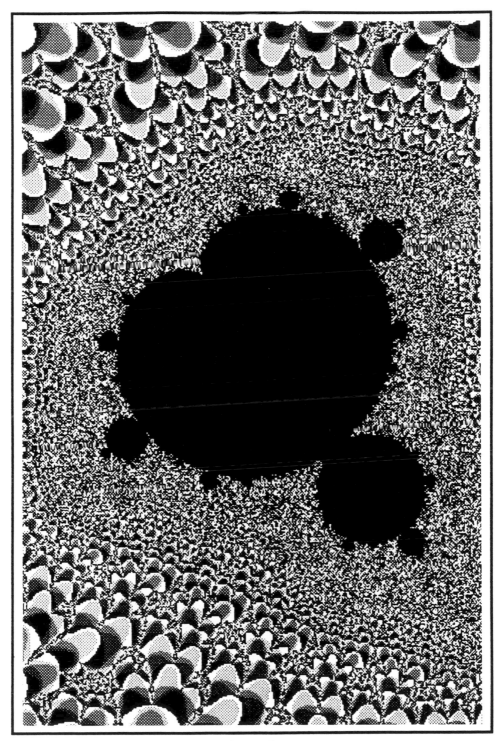

fractal

109

normal curved surface has a dimension of two. A three-dimensional object has a dimension of three. A fractal dimension (D) of a shape can be obtained from the formula $D = \ln(N)/\ln(1/S)$, where N is the number of equal subdivisions that could be made on a curve or surface and S is the scale factor associated with each subdivision.

fractal geometry Associated with the modeling of forms exhibiting the properties of fractals. Fractal geometry and computer graphics are inextricably linked. Computer graphics provides a convenient way of picturing and exploring fractal objects, and fractal geometry is a useful tool for creating computer images. The simple, repeated operations that go into the construction of a fractal are ideally suited to the way a computer functions. The computer patiently performs the same set of operations over and over again to generate a particular fractal object.

fractal surface A surface exhibiting fractal properties. These surfaces have been used to model natural phenomena such as mountain ranges, seascapes and clouds.

fractal surface

fractal trees Start with a stem. At its end branch off in two directions and draw two branches. Repeat this process at the end of each new branch. The result is a fractal tree. Mathematical formulas are a nice way of generating tree curves, however, a real tree is much more complex, and much more interesting.

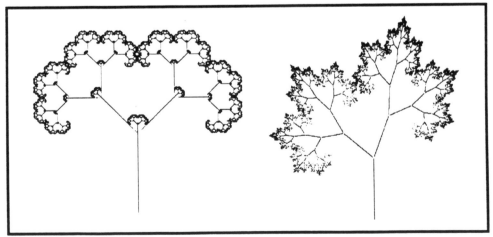

fractal trees

110

frame (1) Video image produced by one complete scan of the screen of a raster-scan display unit. (2) In computer animation, a frame is a single picture. (3) Area, one recording position long, extending across the width of magnetic tape perpendicular to its movement. (4) In computer graphics, an outline or a boundary of some type.

frame buffer In computer graphics, a special area of RAM memory that holds the contents of a screen display. Frame buffers are composed of arrays of bit values that correspond to the display's pixels. The number of bits per pixel in the frame buffer determines the complexity of images that can be displayed. Sometimes used interchangably with the term "bit map."

frame grabber A device used to capture a still video image for storage or processing in a computer.

frame rate (1) The speed at which screen images are transmitted to, and displayed by, a raster-scan monitor. It is measured in hertz and is about 60 times per second (60 Hz) on a monitor in which each pixel on the screen is refreshed. (2) In animation, a measurement of the number of individual pictures that are displayed for each second of action.

frames per second In animation, a measurement of the number of individual pictures that are displayed for each second of action.

free-form windows A method of presenting windows on the screen that allows them to overlap one another.

Freehand A professional design/illustration program for the Apple Macintosh computer. Completely integrated, it combines basic shape and advanced drawing tools, text handling capability, full color support and special effects. Features include movable on-screen palettes for color, graphic styles and layers; fast "flicker-free" screen redraw and editing; automatic text on an ellipse; vertical text; and the ability to convert characters into editable outlines. Included are WYSIWYG text effects (zoom, shadow and outline, for example), the ability to make transparent holes in objects or fill words with fills or TIFF images, and the ability to view, separate and print 32-bit color TIFF images. Time-saving tools include automatic reblending of blended objects and colors, snap-to-print feature and built-in arrowheads. A full Pantonic color palette is provided enabling users to perform color separations for process colors (CMYK), spot color or a combination of both. Paint, EPS and PICT files can be imported as well as black-and-white, gray scale and color TIFF images.

freeware Software provided by a vendor at no charge. Freeware developers often retain all rights to their software thus preventing users from copying it or distributing it further.

freeze frame The capacity of computers using certain software programs to capture an image and keep it immobile.

friction-feed Paper-feed system that operates by clamping a sheet of paper between two rollers. As the rollers rotate, the paper is drawn into the printing device. Many printers use this method, which is effective for single-sheet feeding.

frob To fiddle with a picking device, such as a joystick or mouse.

frustum of vision The three-dimensional space within which graphics objects are viewed. The space is enclosed by left, right, top and bottom planes plus near and far clipping planes.

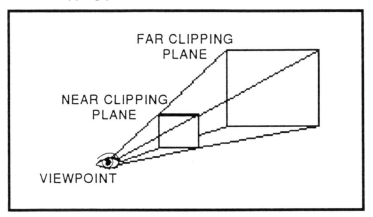

frustum of vision

full color Same as 24-bit color.

full frame Process by which a display image is scaled to use the entire viewing area of a display device.

full page display A monitor that allows viewing an entire page (8 1/2" x 11" vertical page) at actual size. Makes for greater flexibility and ease in desktop publishing or word processing applications.

full page display

full screen Condition in which the entire face of the video screen is used for display.

full screen editing Ability to move the cursor over the entire screen to alter text or graphic images.

112

functional art Any art that fills a utilitarian need and is aesthetically satisfying.

functional art

function codes Special codes that help control functions of peripheral devices. "Clear display screen" would be a function code.

function keys Specially designed keys that, when pressed, initiates some function on a computer keyboard, word processor, or graphics terminal. Most software assign function keys (F1, F2, etc.) for common tasks, but not universally. For example, in one word processor, F4 might mean "save file," while in a different word processor, F4 might mean "increase size of character." These special keys are programmed to execute commonly used commands.

function keys

futurism A style of drawing that represents and interprets modern machines and technology. An attempt to represent movement and speed with nonmoving materials.

Gallery Effects A collection of image-editing filters that may be used to enhance graphics stored in PICT or TIFF formats.

game paddle A hand-held input device used to move the cursor on the screen through the use of a dial. Game paddles are commonly used in video games.

gamma correction The intensity of the luminescent phosphor on the raster display when struck by the electron beam is non-linear. Gamma correction is an adjustment to the color map to make up for this inherent nonlinearity, and results in a truer mix of colors when objects are displayed.

gamut Total range of colors that can be produced on a computer display or output device.

Gantt chart A scheduling chart primarily used by business executives and managers to devise project schedules from beginning to end. Gantt charts are especially effective for complex projects, since they clearly illustrate at a glance critical tasks and milestones that must be completed before a succeeding task can be begun. Named after its developer, Henry Gantt.

gasket A piece of material from which sections have been removed. Mathematical gaskets, such as Sierpinski gaskets, can be generated by removing sections of a region according to some rule. Usually the process of removing leaves pieces which are similar to the initial region; thus the gasket may be defined recursively.

gasket

gas plasma display An output device that works on a principle similar to that of neon signs; a narrow gap filled with neon and argon gas separates two glass plates. An alternating-current voltage applied between closely spaced row-and-column electrodes ionizes the gases between the electrodes, causing them to glow. Once initiated, the glow continues at a reduced voltage. Gas plasma screens are easier to read than liquid crystal display (LCD) screens, but they are more expensive and consume more power.

GCR Acronym for Gray Component Replacement, a technique for reducing the amount of cyan, magenta, or yellow not only in a neutral area but also in a colored area and replacing it with an appropriate level of black.

GEM Acronym for Graphics Environment Manager. A graphics-based operating environment designed by Digital Research. Used primarily on IBM compatible microcomputers and Atari microcomputers. A program used with the operating system which creates and manages all the icons and graphics features of the computer.

GEM file format An object file format commonly used by programs that were designed to run under GEM. Ventura Publisher is the most notable example.

generation A level of mainframe computer development. The first generation of computers used vacuum tubes, the second generation used transistors, the third generation used early types of integrated circuits, the fourth generation uses large scale integrated circuits. The next generation of computers, the fifth generation, is expected to appear in the mid 1990s and will represent the next quantum leap in computer technology.

genre art The casual representation of everyday life and surroundings.

geodesic dome A dome first devised by R. Buckminster Fuller, composed of small modules based on the triangle.

geographic information system (GIS) A graphics application using a database of specialized information, such as demographic and geographical data.

geographic mapping An application for graphics systems used for a variety of projects that require meaningful mapping information.

geometric abstraction The use of geometric shapes – lines, squares, triangles, rectangles, circles, polygons – to design a composition.

geometric abstraction

geometric design rules User-defined design constraints aimed at ensuring a functional, reliable product.

geometric modeling A complete, geometrically accurate three-dimensional or two-dimensional representation of a shape, a part, a geographic area, a plant or any part of it, designed on a graphics system and stored in the database. A mathematical or analytic model of a physical system used to determine the response of that system to a stimulus or load.

geometric model

116

geometric object A two- or three-dimensional shape.

geometric primitive One of a set of mathematically defined shapes specified for rendering by a graphics system, e.g. points, lines, triangles, rectangles, polygons, etc.

geometry Branch of mathematics that deals with the relationships, properties, and measurements of solids, surfaces, lines, and angles. Considers spatial relationships, the theory of space, and figures in space. In computer graphics, refers to the specific physical arrangement of lines that make up the shape of a specific entity. Geometry is an essential part of computer graphics programs. See fractal geometry.

CIRCULAR PLANE SECTION
FORMED BY INTERSECTION
OF CONE WITH A PLANE
PARALLEL TO ITS BASE.

geometry

ghost A faint second image that appears close to the primary image on a display or printout.

ghost icon An outline of an icon or window used to show the current position of the icon or window as it is being dragged to a new location on the desktop.

GIF A graphics format often used for pictures that are transmitted by modem. Especially popular with computer bulletin boards and information services such as CompuServe. Acronym for Graphic Interchange Format.

GIS Acronym for Geographic Information System.

GKS Acronym for Graphical Kernal System.

glare Reflection from the surface of a display screen.

glare filter A fine mesh screen that is placed over a CRT screen to reduce glare from overhead and ambient light.

golden section A canon of proportion marked out in the first century BC to establish architectural standards, and used since in painting and sculpture as well as in architecture. The proportions considered to be ideal are those in which the shorter is to the taller, as the taller is to the whole: approximately 5 units to 8 units.

good enough color A phrase used for color printing that does not require an exact color match. Relatively easy to produce with desktop color systems.

Gouraud shading A sophisticated shading method capable of producing realistic results.

grabber (1) A device for capturing data, i.e. a video digitizer. (2) A computer program that takes a "snapshot" of the currently displayed screen image by transferring a portion of video memory to a file on disk. (3) Fixture on the end of a test equipment lead wire with a spring-actuated hook and claw designed to connect the measuring instrument to a pin of an integrated circuit, socket, transistor, and so forth.

grabber hand In graphics programs, an on-screen image of a hand that you can position with the mouse to move selected units of graphics or text from place to place on-screen.

grabber hand

gradient fill A feature on some graphics programs that adds color or a shade of gray to a region, varying the color or shade smoothly in a defined direction. Sometimes called a graduated fill.

graftal A class of graphics objects sharing some of the properties of fractals in which the rules for generation permit local modification of properties.

graft (1) Diagram showing the relationship of two or more variable quantities. A mathematical graph is usually in the form of a curve drawn in a frame of reference formed by the two axes of coordinate geometry. (2) A method of displaying number relationships visually.

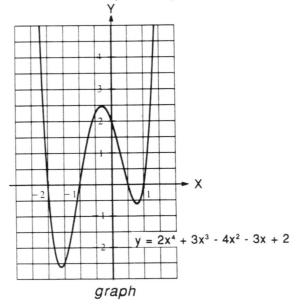

$y = 2x^4 + 3x^3 - 4x^2 - 3x + 2$

graph

graphical kernel system (GKS) An internationally accepted standard for computer graphics. GKS is an interface that provides computer users with standardized methods of describing, manipulating, storing, and transferring graphical images. GKS is designed to free the programmer of many of the low-level programming tasks involved in creating and manipulating graphics on a terminal.

graphical terminal Visual display terminal that has a screen to display a drawing as well as textual information.

graphical user interface (GUI) A type of display format that enables the user to choose commands, start programs, and see lists of files and other options by pointing to pictorial representations (icons) and lists of menu items on the screen. Graphical user interfaces are used on the Apple Macintosh microcomputer, by the Microsoft Windows program for IBM-compatible microcomputers, and other systems.

graphic character Any ASCII character that is represented by a visible symbol and can be printed; includes letters and digits.

graphic data structure Logical arrangement of digital data representing graphic display.

graphic digitizer Input device that converts graphic and pictorial data into binary inputs for use in a computer. See digitizer.

graphic display mode Mode of operation that allows the computer to print graphics on a special (graphics) screen.

graphic display resolution Number of lines and characters per line able to be shown on a video screen.

graphic display terminal Computer terminal that displays information on a screen, usually a cathode ray tube, TV terminal, or video monitor.

graphics display terminal

graphic input device Any device, such as a digitizer, that gives the computer the points that make up an image in such a way that the image can be stored, reconstructed, displayed, or manipulated.

graphic limits (1) The boundary of a graphical display screen image in a graphics software program. (2) Plotting area of a graphics device, such as a digital plotter, as defined by its mechanical limits, such as the size of the drum or platen.

graphic output Computer-generated output in the form of visual displays, printouts, or plots.

graphic output device Device used to display or record an image. A display screen is an output device for soft copy; hard copy output devices produce paper, film, or transparencies of the image.

graphic primitive See primitive.

graphics Any computer-generated picture produced on a screen, paper, or film. Graphics range from simple line or bar graphs to colorful and detailed images. All computers have some amount of graphics capability, but nowdays most feature high-resolution graphics, in which the detail of the diagrams can be considerably finer than was possible in early systems. Modern microcomputers feature high-resolution graphics in color, and printed pictures can also be produced in color.

graphics

graphics

121

graphics

122

graphics accelerator A hardware device dedicated to increasing the speed and performance of graphics. Graphics accelerators calculate pixel values, and write them into the frame buffer, freeing up the central processing unit for other operations.

graphics adapters CGA-EGA-VGA adapters that must be matched with compatible monitors. Note the alphabetical order – it happens to match their order of age and sophistication. CGA was first. EGA was the new standard for a long while. VGA is now the popular standard for color presentations. VGA has high resolution modes and sharper text and image quality.

graphics based The display of text and pictures as graphics images, for example, a bit mapped image.

graphics character A character that can be combined to create simple graphics.

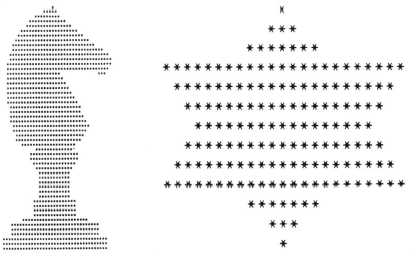

graphics character

graphics coprocessor A special microprocessor chip, mounted on some video adapters, that can generate graphical images, thereby freeing the computer for other work.

graphics device interface (GDI) A collection of Microsoft Windows routines that allows you to display information without concern for the specific hardware used.

graphics display Any output device that can present an image of graphic data derived from a computer system.

graphics editor A program for editing pictures. Typical operators include drawing, moving, rotating, and enlarging items on the screen.

graphics engine Specialized hardware that performs graphics processing independently of the main central processing unit.

graphics file format In a graphics program, the way in which information needed to display the graphic is arranged and stored on disk.

graphics input hardware Peripherals used to put graphics information in the computer, such as a graphics tablet, mouse, and light pen.

graphics language A set of instructions that let a programmer express a graphics image in a high-level language. The language is translated into graphics images by software or specialized hardware.

graphics library A collection of standard, often-used symbols, components, shapes, or parts stored in the graphics database as templates or building blocks to speed up future design work on the system. Generally an organization of files under a common library name. The graphics library usually includes a defined set of primitives and function calls that enable the programmer to bypass many low-level programming tasks.

graphics mode Resolution of the image together with the number of colors a particular video system can display. For example EGA and VGA are considered different graphic modes.

graphic output hardware Peripherals on which the computer displays graphics, such as a display screen, a film recorder, or a laser printer.

graphic output hardware

graphics package A program that helps depict ideas through graphs and other types of drawings.

graphics processor An extension of a compiler which permits the syntax of an existing language to be augmented by new graphics commands.

graphics primitive In computer graphics, a graphical building block, such as a triangle, circle, line, or arc. A graphics primitive is drawn and manipulated as a single unit.

graphics printer Output devices that can produce text, charts, graphics, and artwork.

graphics program A computer program that aids computer users in producing computer generated images. Pictures can be entered into the computer using input devices such as mice, graphics tablets or light pens, and existing pictures on paper can be scanned into the computer using digitized scanners. Once stored in the computers memory, pictures can be manipulated in a variety of ways and printed on paper, display screen or film. Popular graphics programs are Adobe Illustrator, Deluxe Paint, MacDraw, MacPaint, PC Paintbrush, Studio 1/8/32, SuperPaint, and UltraPaint. See business graphics.

graphics resolution Measure of the detail in which graphics can be drawn by output hardware. High-resolution pictures have greater detail than low-resolution pictures. See resolution.

HIGH-RESOLUTION   LOW-RESOLUTION

graphics resolution

graphics routine A collection of code in a computer program that draws graphical objects.

graphics scanner A graphics input device that transforms a picture into an image displayed on-screen.

graphics screen Screen that displays graphics information.

graphics simulation Graphics simulation is different from ordinary computer simulation, although they may overlap somewhat. While computer simulation may use computer graphics, graphics is not the primary tool. For example, a simulation of automobiles on a busy highway is a statistical study rather than a visual one, although computer graphics is used to show models of cars on the road. Graphics simulation has come to mean the use of computer graphics to represent any form of dynamic physical phenomenon. As an example, a supercomputer may be used to simulate the collision of galaxies and generate a set of data.

graphics spreadsheet A spreadsheet program that displays the worksheet on-screen, using bit mapped graphics instead of relying on the computer's built-in character set.

graphics standards Agreed specifications which define the common interfaces between computer graphics systems or subsystems. See Initial Graphics Exchange Specification and International Standards Organization.

graphics tablet Input device that converts graphic and pictorial data into binary inputs for use in a computer. Provides an efficient method of converting object shapes into computer-storable information. Utilizes a flat tablet and a stylus for graphic input. See digitizer.

graphics tablet

graphics terminal A "smart" terminal capable of displaying graphics; usually interpret graphics control codes to render images on the display screen.

graphics utilities Computer programs designed to assist graphics processing in such functions as copying, saving, compress, etc.

Graphics Workshop A color paint program for the Commodore Amiga computer. Features include 10-brush library, true antialiasing, true polygons, rays, 4-point curves, color replacement, pattern draw, automatic shadows, animation option and the ability to convert cell animation into page animation.

gray-map editor A function found in many imaging programs that allows the user to change the way gray shades are displayed.

gray scale A strip of standard gray tones, ranging from white to black. (1) When used with scanners, it refers to the device's ability to capture more than simple black and white. (2) When used with monochromatic displays, variations in brightness level (gray scale) are used to enhance the contrast among various design elements. The larger the gray scales, the better the picture quality. (3) It refers to the many levels of gray supported by a scanner or a monitor. 8 and 16 levels were early standards; now the standard is 256 levels.

gray-scale manipulation An image enhancement technique in which the appearance of a digital image is improved by adjusting its gray levels.

grayscale mode A scanner setting for digitizing an image made up of grays or intermediate colors by assigning more than 1 bit of data to each point.

gray value A number that determines the level of gray in a particular pixel. A pixel that is 80 percent gray is darker than a pixel that's 20 percent gray.

greeked text In desktop publishing, unreadable letters or characters that simulate a typeset line.

green-bar paper Computer paper with green bands.

grid (1) Network of uniformly spaced points or crosshatched lines displayed on a visual display screen or digitizer and used for exactly locating a position, inputting components to assist in the creation of a design layout, or constructing precise diagrams. For example, coordinate data supplied by digitizers is automatically calculated by the computer from the closest grid point. The grid determines the minimum accuracy with which design entities are described or connected. (2) Display of an electronic spreadsheet model composed of columns and rows. (3) Horizontal and vertical lines on a chart to aid the viewer in determining the value of a point. (4) On a pie chart, the grid is an implied set of lines radiating out from the center, representing the degrees of a circle.

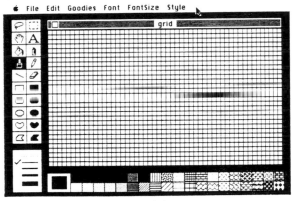

grid

grid constraint An accuracy aid that causes the screen cursor to jump to the nearest grid intersection whenever a point is entered.

gridding Graphic image construction constraint that requires all line endpoints to fall on grid points.

grouping A feature of drawing and page layout applications in which two or more objects are combined so that they are treated as one object.

group technology A CAM system of classifying drawings and parts according to similarities of design and manufacturing.

GUI Acronym for Graphical User Interface.

gun Group of electrodes constituting the electron beam emitter in a cathode ray tube.

gutter (1) The margin at the binding edge of a page. (2) White space between a multiple-column page layout.

hairline A very fine or delicate line.

half-height drive A disk drive that occupies only half the vertical space of earlier disk drives.

halftone A continuous-tone image, e.g. a photograph shot through a screen and reproduced as an array of tiny dots. A halftone is a printed reproduction of these tiny dots which the naked eye sees as various tones of gray shading into one another.

halftone

halftone cell A halftone dot created on a laser printer or imagesetter. The cell is created by grouping printer dots into a grid. The more dots present in the grid, the larger the cell appears.

halved line A line drawn continuous, while lines intersection it are drawn with gaps around the potential points of intersection.

hand cursor A hand-held device (often called a "puck") for inputting coordinate data. It has "cross-hairs" to identify exact locations and is used with a data tablet.

hand-held scanner An optical scanner that is operated by manually running a scanning head over an image. Small rollers on the bottom of the scanning head serve to guide the hand movement.

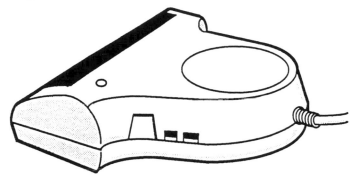

hand-held scanner

handle (1) In computer graphics, a small square associated with a graphical object that can be used to move or reshape the image. (2) A number that can be used to uniquely identify an object. (3) In programming, a pointer to a pointer. In other words, a variable that contains the address of another variable, which in turn contains the address of yet another variable.

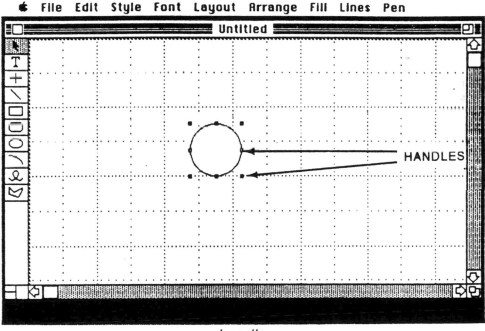

handle

hanging indent A paragraphing style with a full-measure first line and indented succeeding lines (called turnover lines).

hard clip area Limits beyond which lines cannot be drawn on a digital plotter.

hardcopy Computer output onto a tangible substrate, such as paper or film.

hard disk Fast auxiliary storage device either mounted in its own case or permanently mounted inside a computer. A single hard disk has storage capacity of several million characters or bytes of information. This storage media makes computers usable in the real world. Contrast with floppy disk.

hard hyphen Hyphen required by spelling and always printed, such as in three-dimensional. Contrast with soft hyphen.

hardware Physical equipment, such as electronic, magnetic, and mechanical devices. The components of a computer graphics system responsible for user input, display, and mathematical processing. Contrast with software.

Harvard Graphics A business graphics program for IBM-compatible microcomputer systems from Software Publishing Corporation. It is a versatile and easy-to-use program for producing business related presentation graphics. The program requires little knowledge of graphics presentation principles because it guides the user through each step of the process and produces output that meets high standards of aesthetics and professional graphics.

hash Visual static on the screen.

hatching Drawing close parallel lines on a surface to produce a dart tone and thereby simulate the appearance of shadows. Shading in overlapping directions is crosshatching.

hatching

header (1) First part of a message, containing all the necessary information for directing the message to its destination(s). (2) Top margin of a page, usually the title of the book, the name of the chapter, the page number, and so on.

helix A spiral-shaped space curve. A cylindrical helix lies on a cylinder. A conical helix lies on a cone. For example, the shape of the thread on a screw is a helix.

helix

helmet mounted display A display device in which the display is attached to a head-tracked helmet worn by the user.

help (1) Handy function available on many systems. Supplies the user with additional information on how the system or program works. (2) On screen reference material providing assistance with the program.

help

help balloon An operating system and application program user help aid that tags a desired object on screen with a comic book style "balloon" full of information on how to use that object.

help balloon

help screen A display screen full of information displayed by a program that has a help facility.

Helvetica A popular sans serif typeface developed in the 1950s. It is one of the most widely used fonts in the world and is included as a built-in font with many laser printers.

ABCDEFGHIJK
Helvetica

Hercules Graphics Card (HGC) A monochrome video adapter introduced by Hercules Computer Technology in 1982. HGC provides a monochrome graphics mode for IBM PC graphics with a screen size of 720 by 348 pixels.

Hewlett-Packard Company (HP) A major manufacturer of computer equipment; founded in 1939 by William Hewlett and David Packard in a garage behind Packard's California home. HP has introduced several computer series, workstations, laser printers, and many other electronic products.

Hewlett-Packard Graphics Language (HPGL) A language devised by Hewlett-Packard for storing graphical images.

hexagon A polygon with six sides.

hidden line (1) When displaying a three-dimensional object, any line that would normally be obscured from the viewer's sight by the mass of the object itself, visible as a result of the projection. (2) Lines that have been drawn on the screen in background color and will not become visible until the colors are switched. (3) Lines of a diagram that are invisible.

HIDDEN LINES

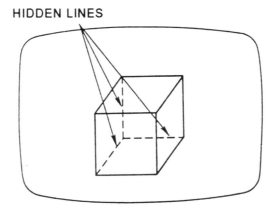

hidden line

hidden line removal Process of deleting line segments from a drawing when they would be obscured were the object displayed as a solid three-dimensional figure. This method reduces the potential of ambiguity in an object's appearance. Many types of computer graphics software and hardware can remove such hidden lines automatically.

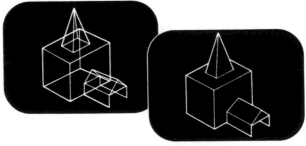

hidden line removed

132

hidden objects Distinct graphic entities that would be obscured from view by other entities if they were displayed as solids.

hidden surface Entire surface or plane that would be obscured from view if the graphics figure were displayed as a three-dimensional solid.

hierarchical data structures In a Programmer's Hierarchical Interactive Graphics System, objects are defined in hierarchical relationship to one another. The hierarchical data organization enables structures to inherit the attributes of other structures, which enables the programmer to manipulate objects efficiently.

high-density disk A floppy disk that holds more information than a double-density disk. 5.25-inch and 3.5-inch high-density disks hold 1.44 megabytes.

highlight In graphics, this refers to a user's ability to somehow enhance a graph or drawing, by, for example, creating three dimensional images, superimposing one image over another, "exploding" or pulling out a pie slice, using color, or screening an image.

highlighting (1) Process of making a display segment stand out by causing blinking, brightening, underlining, by reversing the background and the character images, such as dark characters on a light background, or creating a color combination that draws attention to it. (2) Highlighting is often used in word processing and page design programs as a means of selecting characters that are to be deleted, copied, or otherwise acted upon.

high-persistence phosphor Phosphor coating used on some display monitor screens that holds an image much longer than the coating used on standard display screens.

high-resolution (1) Pertaining to the quality and accuracy of detail that can be represented by a graphics display. Resolution quality depends upon the number of basic image-forming units (pixels) within a picture image—the greater the number, the higher the resolution. High-resolution pictures,

HIGH-RESOLUTION   LOW-RESOLUTION

high-resolution

133

produced by a large number of pixels, are sharper than low-resolution pictures. For microcomputer system color displays, 800 x 600 or 1024 x 768 pixels may represent high resolution. For workstations, 1600 x 1280 pixels is typically high resolution. For film recorders, 4000 x 4000 pixels may be considered high resolution. (2) In printing, resolution is defined as the number of dots per inch (dpi) that are printed. In general, laser printing is about 300 dpi; typesetters and imagesetters can produce output at 1000 dpi, 2000 dpi, or more.

high-resolution graphics (HRG) A high-quality image on a display screen or printed form.

high-speed printer (HSP) Any printer capable of printing from 300 to 3,000 lines per minute. See line printer.

hinting In desktop publishing, the reduction of the weight of a typeface so that small-size fonts print without blurring or losing detail on 300-dpi laser printers.

hi-res graphics Abbreviation of high-resolution graphics, a smooth and realistic picture on a display screen produced by a large number of pixels. Contrast with low-res graphics.

histogram Vertical bar chart often used to graph statistical information. Column widths represent interval ranges; lengths indicate frequencies.

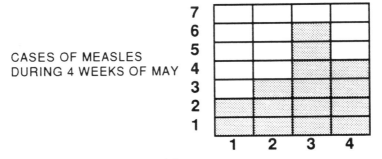

histogram

hither plane The front clipping plane that defines a finite view volume.

hologram An image which gives an impressive illusion of being three-dimensional, in such a way that it appears to exist in real space.

holography Method of storing data by making a multidimensional photograph on a storage medium.

home Starting position for the cursor on a display screen. Usually in the top left-hand corner.

home computer A personal computer designed and priced for use in the home.

homegrown software Software developed at home rather than in software development businesses. Many public-domain software, freeware and shareware are created in the home.

home key Keyboard function that directs the cursor to its home position, usually in the top left portion of the display screen.

horizontal Going from left to right.

horizontal axis The X-axis in a Cartesian coordinate system.

horizontal scrolling Moving of horizontal blocks of data or text, allowing users to view more data than can fit on the screen at one time.

horizontal software Programs designed to serve a wide range of users, who must tailor the programs to their own needs. Examples include paint and draw programs, and word processing programs.

hot As applied to images, very bright or excessively bright.

hot spot The position in a mouse pointer that marks the exact display screen location that will be affected by a mouse action such as a button press. The mouse pointer's hot spot is a single pixel in size.

hot zone On some word processors, a user-defined region beginning at the right margin of a page and extending about seven spaces to the left. If a word ends in the hot zone, the system automatically places the next character entered at the beginning of the next line.

Houston Instrument A major manufacturer of pen plotters, digitizers and graphic recorders. Many of the early hardcopy graphic images of the late 1960s and 1970s were drawn on plotters made by this company.

HPC A Hewlett-Packard LaserJet graphics file format.

HPGL Acronym for Hewlett-Packard Graphics Language. An object file format originally developed to drive plotters. Now used to store graphical images.

HSB (Hue, Saturation, Brightness) A type of color system. Hue refers to pure color, that is, light of a distinct wave length – red, green, violet, etc. Saturation refers to the degree of white it contains. Brightness refers to the color's percentage of black. HSB is used in computer graphics for describing color.

HSV (Hue, Saturation, Value) A color model used in some graphics programs. HSV has to be translated into another model for colored printing or for actually forming screen colors.

hue (1) In the HSB color model, one of the three characteristics used to describe a color. Hue refers to pure color, that is, light of a distinct wave length – red, green, etc. (2) The apparent color of an object.

hyperbola See conic sections.

HyperCard An implementation of a hypertext system for the Apple Macintosh family of computers. A HyperCard document consists of a series of cards collected together in a stack; each card can contain text, graphics and sound. Items on the cards can be linked together in a variety of different ways.

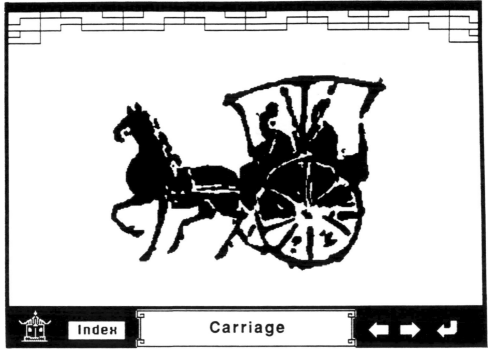

HyperCard

hypermedia A term describing hypertext-based systems that combine text, graphics, sound, and video with traditional data. In a hypertext system, you select a word or phrase and give a command to see related text. In a hypermedia system, such a command reveals related graphics images, sounds, and even snippets of animation or video. Hypercard is an example of a hypermedia application.

hypertext An approach to information management of not only text, but video and audio as well.

hyphenation In page layout and word processing programs, an automatic operation that hyphenates words on certain lines to improve word spacing.

hysteresis A tendency for a display element to stay in either the on or off condition once it has been switched. With hysteresis, for example, a sustaining voltage can be applied to a display to keep all lighted pixels glowing without lighting any that are supposed to be off.

I-beam pointer In a graphical user interface, a special pointer shaped like a capital "I" that indicates the insertion point for text editing.

IBM-compatible microcomputer A personal computer that is compatible with the IBM Personal Computer and PS/2.

IBM Corporation The International Business Machines Corporation is the world's largest computer company. It started in New York City in 1911 when the Computing-Tabulating-Recording (CTR) Company was formed by a merger of four companies. Thomas J. Watson, Sr. became the general manager in 1914. Over the next decade, Watson turned CTR into an international enterprise. In 1924 the company was renamed IBM. IBM started making computers in 1953 and have since introduced computers of all sizes – from personal computers to supercomputers. A few models produced by IBM include the 650, 701, 702, 703, 704, 705, 709, 1401, 1410, 1620, 1790 and 1794. In April 1964, IBM introduced the third generation of computers with the introduction of the System 360 family of computers. Throughout the 1970s, IBM introduced several minicomputer systems: System/3, System/34, System/38, Series 1 and 8100. In 1981, IBM introduced the IBM Personal Computer. In 1987, IBM introduced the PS/2 series of personal computers. Today, product lines of the IBM Corporation span personal computers to large mainframes.

IBM draw/paint programs See Art & Letters Graphics Editor, Artline, ColoRIX, Corel Draw, DeLuxePaint, Designer, DGS Paint, Dr. Halo, Lumena, Painting Effects, PC Paintbrush, Portfolio, Rio-Sable, Tempra, TIPS, Water Color.

IBM PC clone A popular term for personal computers that adhere closely to the appearance and functionality of personal computers in the IBM PC family. Often manufactured abroad, these computers are generally reliable and inexpensive.

IBM PC compatible A term for personal computers that adhere closely to the functionality of personal computers in the IBM PC family. PC compatibles, as opposed to "clones", have never necessarily had to look like standard IBM PC designs, and some manufacturers have insisted on incorporating proprietary, non-standard features in their "compatibles" even while maintaining general compatibility with the MS-DOS, Intel-based features of the IBM PC family.

IBM Personal Computer August 12, 1981, came and went, but nothing would ever be the same again. That day, the IBM Corporation introduced a Personal Computer based on the Intel 8088 microprocessor. The machine went on to become the most significant technology to hit the world since the telephone. Although the IBM PC was not the first, it legitimized the machines in the computer market. It has transformed the way millions of people work, spawned new industries and made computer technology less mysterious. The PC created the home computer movement, allowing people to work out of their living room and "commute" by sending reports to the office over the phone. IBM set the stage for clones when it announced the PC by deciding not to block other companies from providing software or accessories for its PC. It reasoned that if the technology was "open", or non-proprietary, the market for the machines would grow faster. But that decision soon led to the creation of clones of the entire computer. Today, every nation from Hong Kong to Hungary has a local industry cranking out inexpensive PC clones. There are three machines in the PC line: IBM PC, IBM PC-XT and IBM PC-AT.

IBM Personal Computer

IBM Personal Computer AT A personal computer, based on the Intel 80286 microprocessor, that was introduced by the IBM Corporation in 1984. The 80286 chip was "upwardly compatible" with the Intel 8088 in the sense that it could run all the PC software written for the 8088-based PCs which preceded it. It also came standard with a hard disk drive, a feature many users were still not accustomed to having at their disposal.

IBM Personal Computer XT A personal computer, based on the Intel 8088 microprocessor and including a hard disk, that was introduced by the IBM Corporation in 1983. The XT type computer occupies a prominent and useful place on desktops throughout the business world.

IBM Personal System/1 (PS/1) A home computer from IBM Corporation introduced in 1990. The PS/1 computer uses an Intel 80286 microprocessor and comes in a small attractive case, with a color VGA display and a 2400 band modem built in. The computer contains about everything an ordinary computer user is likely to need.

IBM Personal System/2 (PS/2) A series of personal computers from IBM Corporation introduced in 1987. These computers were designed to replace the IBM Personal Computer line: IBM PC, IBM PC-XT, IBM PC-AT. The PS/2 machines are based on the Intel 8086, 80286, 80386, and 80486 microprocessors. The IBM PS/2 runs all or almost all the software developed for the IBM Personal Computer.

IBM PS/2

icon A tiny on-screen pictorial representation of a software function. A symbol used on the display screen to represent some feature of the program. For example, in one program, an icon representing a waste-paper basket is selected if you want to erase information. Many workstations in a networking environment, for instance, use a mailbox icon to symbolize an electronic mail-reading utility. Non-technical people find symbols easier to understand than technical words.

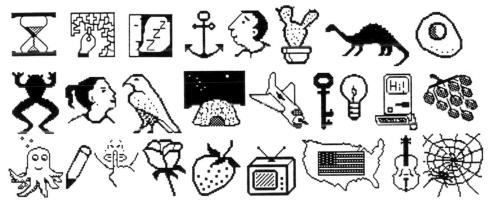

icon

iconic interface A user interface that displays objects on the screen as tiny pictures that the user can point to and select via a mouse.

iconography (1) The visual imagery used to convey the meaning of a work of art, and the conventions governing such imagery. (2) The study of various forms of meaning to be found in pictorial representations.

ideal line The make-believe line between two points that we approximate with fixed-resolution display systems.

IEEE See Institute of Electrical and Electronic Engineers.

IEEE Computer Society A section of the Institute of Electrical and Electronics Engineers. Publishes a monthly periodical on computer graphics and applications.

IFF A graphics format designed for the Commodore Amiga and common to almost all Amiga paint, draw and animation programs.

IGES Acronym for Initial Graphics Exchange Specification. A standard 2-D and 3-D format for exchanging data between different vendor CAD/CAM systems.

illuminance The amount of light falling on a surface area.

illuminate To increase the brightness or luminosity of graphical output at a display screen.

illustration A picture that tells a story or is used to support and accompany a written text.

Illustrator A PostScript-based, Apple Macintosh drawing program with powerful capabilities. A complete set of tools for drawing, blending, grouping and transforming objects enables users to create very sophisticated graphics. Text can be created and modified in any fashion desired with every aspect of typographic formatting controllable, including outline fonts. A graph module enables users to create publication quality graphs. Any color and percentage of tint can be applied to both text and objects. Color models supported are CMYK and Pantone Color Matching System. Designs can be previewed on-screen in 8- and 24-bit color and black-and-white. Color separations can be printed using Adobe Separator. In effect, this professional level program is an illustration, page layout, type manipulation and graphing application all rolled into one. Adobe Illustrator was introduced in 1987 by Adobe Systems Incorporated.

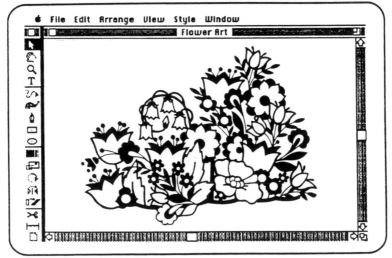

illustrator

image (1) Exact logical duplicate stored in a different medium. If the computer user displays the contents of memory on a display screen, he or she will see an image of memory. (2) In computer graphics, the output form of graphics data, such as a drawn representation of a graphics file. (3) A visual representation of an object, figure, or event in any visual art.

image

image analysis The process of extracting useful information from images, such as estimating types of surface ground cover from satellite photographs.

image averaging The averaging of a small area of an image to reduce picture resolution.

image compression As applied to graphics computer systems and scanners, encoding the data describing an image in a more compact form to reduce storage requirements or transmission time.

image enhancement The process of improving the appearance of all or part of a graphics image through such techniques as coloring, shading, highlighting, edge enhancement, gray-scale manipulation, zooming, reverse video, blinking, smoothing, or sharpening.

image processing Method for processing pictorial information by a computer system. Involves inputting graphic information into a computer system, storing it, working with it, and outputting it to an output device. Once a photograph has been digitized into binary data, the computer can process the data in any way the user wishes in order to enhance the contrast of an image, blend images, change shapes, change colors, and so on. Typical image processing techniques include filtering and thresholding. Once the computer manipulations are complete, the processed image may be displayed on a display screen, a printer, or any other suitable device. Image processing is used to extract information from images and to sharpen images for presentation. It is a special subfield of the wider engineering area of signal processing.

image reconstruction An imaging technology used in a variety of industries, including medical imaging. Image data are gathered through one of several methods, including CAT-scan and magnetic resonance imaging. These data are processed (reconstructed) into viewable two- or three-dimensional images.

image restoration The process of returning an image to its original condition by reversing the effects of degradations.

imagery The art of making images, or pictures, as in drawing or painting, to represent or evoke a particular thing.

141

imagesetter A typesetting device that can transfer output of a desktop publishing system directly to paper or film. Imagesetters commonly print at high resolution (from 1200 dpi to over 3000 dpi). Imagesetters are professional typesetting machines that use chemical photo-reproduction techniques to produce high resolution output.

imagesetters service bureau A company that specializes in the sale of PostScript output, usually at the per page or per color charge. Some bureaus specialize in type-only output, others in film.

Image Studio A powerful gray-scale painting program for Apple Macintosh computers. The program includes a selection of brush and paint tools.

image synthesis The creation of two- and three-dimensional images from mathematical models with the aid of computers.

image understanding Image processing and image synthesis combined with artificial intelligence.

Imagewriter A dot matrix printer used with Apple Macintosh and Apple II microcomputers.

imaging (1) The process involved in the capture, storage, display, and printing of graphical two-or three-dimensional images. (2) The area of graphics involved with creation of continuous tone pictures rather than line drawings or graphs. (3) The broad category of image-related computer technologies that includes computer graphics, image processing, and image reconstruction.

imaging model The method of representing output on a display screen. In a graphical user interface, the goal is to use a unified imaging model, so that the text displayed on-screen closely resembles the text printed.

IMG Commonly, though not always, a bit mapped GEM file. Used by GEM Paint, Ventura Publisher, and other programs written to run under GEM.

impact printer Data printout device that imprints by momentary pressure of raised type against paper, using ink or ribbon as a color medium.

import To bring information from one system or program into another. PageMaker, for example, can import MacPaint files created by SuperPaint.

in-betweens In computer animation, the frames that come "in-between" the key frames and which smooth the movements of the cartoon figure being animated.

in-betweens

inches per second (IPS) Measure of the speed of a device (i.e. the speed of a pen plotter).

incident light Light falling on an object. The color of an object is perceived as a function of the wavelengths of incident light reflected or absorbed by it.

increment (1) Amount added to a value or variable. Contrast with decrement. (2) Distance between any two adjacent addressable points on a graphics input/output device.

incremental plotter Digital plotter that outputs graphic data in discrete movements of the plotting head.

indent To begin, or move, text a specified number of positions from the left edge or right edge of a page.

indentation White space found at the beginning of a line of text; often denotes the beginning of a paragraph.

indexed color A limited set of colors, selected from a much larger color palette, are indexed in a color lookup table or color map, and the application accesses them by their index numbers.

industry standard Parts of a computer system hardware or software subsystem that have been standardized and adopted by the industry at large. Standards enable application developers to write software applications using a standard set of tools.

initial In desktop publishing, an enlarged letter at the beginning of a paragraph or chapter. Initials set down within the copy are drop caps. Initials raised above the top of the text are stickup caps.

initial

Initial Graphics Exchange Specification (IGES) A standard file format for computer graphics that is particularly suitable for describing models created with computer-aided design programs. IGES offers methods for describing and annotating drawings and engineering diagrams. IGES is an ANSI-approved standard file format for representation of three-dimensional wire frame models.

initialization Process of formatting a diskette so that it is ready for use. Initialization erases any previous information that happens to be on the diskette.

ink jet printer A printer that sprays ink from jet nozzles onto the paper. A nozzle emits a continuous stream of ink droplets that are selectively guided either to the paper or to a gutter where they may be recycled for re-use or sent into a discard container. Ink jet printers produce high-quality printouts.

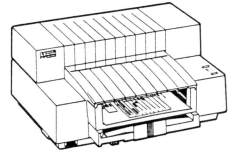

ink jet printer

input Introduction of data from an external storage medium into a computer's internal storage unit. Contrast with output.

input device A hardware device that enables the user to communicate with a computer system. Examples of input devices are keyboard, mouse, light pen, track ball, or graphics tablet. Contrast with output device.

input/output device Unit used to get data from the human user into the central processing unit, and to transfer data from the computer's internal storage to some storage or output device. Examples are digitizers, graphics tablets, printers and display devices.

inscribe To draw a figure inside another with maximum number of contact points.

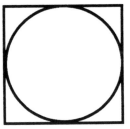

inscribe

insert To create and place entities, figures, or information on a CRT or into an emerging design on the display.

insert mode In word processing, a text input mode in which text is inserted at the current cursor position without overwriting any text already in the document.

install program A program that prepares a software program to run in the computer. It customizes elements of the new program so a specific computer system can use it.

installation (1) A program provided with an application program that assists you in installing the program on a hard disk and configuring the program for use. (2) General term for a particular computer system.

installer A program that adds software to a computer system and prepares it for subsequent execution.

Institute of Electrical and Electronic Engineers (IEEE) A professional engineering organization founded in 1963 for the furthering of education, research, and standards in the electronics and electrical fields. IEEE has a strong interest in computer technology. It sponsors many educational opportunities and publications for members.

Institute of Electrical and Electronics Engineers Computer Society (IEEECS) Computer specialty group within the IEEE. One of the leading professional associations in advancing the theory and practice of computer and information processing technology.

integrated circuit (IC) An electronic circuit etched on a tiny germanium or silicon chip. Integrated circuits are categorized by the number of elements (transistors, resistors, etc.) they hold. The categories of IC's are small-scale integration (SSI), medium-scale integration (MSI), large-scale integration (LSI), very large-scale integration (VLSI), super large-scale integration (SLSI), and ultra large-scale integration (ULSI). Integrated circuits were invented in the late 1950s by Jack Kilby (an engineer at Texas Instrument) and Robert Noyce (an engineer at Fairchild Semiconductor).

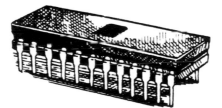

integrated circuit

integrated software An applications software package containing programs to perform more than one function. The package typically includes related word processing, spreadsheet, database, and graphics programs. Since the information from the electronic spreadsheet may be shared with the database manager and the word processor (and vice versa), this software is called integrated. Some integrated programs, for instance, split the screen into windows and allow the operator to work with a word processing document and a spreadsheet simultaneously. Programs such as Microsoft Works for the Apple Macintosh microcomputer, Framework for the IBM PS/2 microcomputer, and AppleWorks for the Apple II microcomputer are examples.

intensity (1) Amount of light in a graphics display device. Level of brightness emitted by a cathode ray tube. On most visual display devices, intensity can be controlled by manipulating a switch. (2) The relative purity or brilliance of a hue.

Intensity Red Green Blue A type of color encoding used in IBM's color graphics adapters: CGA, EGA and VGA.

interactive graphics Any graphics system in which the user and the computer are in active communication.

interactive graphics system Computer graphics system in which workstations are used interactively for computer-aided design, all under full operator control, and possibly also for text-processing, generation of charts and graphs, computer-aided engineering, and generation of 35 mm slides or animation pictures.

interface A hardware and/or software link which enables two systems, or a computer and its peripherals, to operate as a single, integrated system. A shared boundary.

International Standards Organization (ISO) An international agency that reviews and approves independently designed products for use within specific industries. ISO is also responsible for developing standards for information exchange.

interpolation A method of determining intermediate values between those provided, such as shades of pink between the colors white and red.

intersection A method of combing two objects into one. The area where the objects' overlap remains, creating a new object.

intrinsic font A font for which a bit image (an exact pattern) exists that can be used without modification.

inverse video Process that shows dark text on a light background display screen. Normally, light text is shown on a dark background. Same as reverse video.

inversions Words that can be read right side up, upside down, and every which way. In some cases the inversion is the same word whether you look at it right side up or upside down.

inversion

invert (1) To turn over; reverse. To highlight text or objects by reversing the on-screen display or printout. For example, to invert the colors on a monochrome display means to change light to dark and dark to light. (2) To convert a logic value to its opposite, i.e., zero to one and one to zero.

invert

ion deposition A printing technology that is used in high speed page printers

ionographic printer A printer that uses ion deposition. The image is formed on a dielectric surface and then transferred to plain paper.

IRGB See Intensity Red Green Blue.

ISO See International Standards Organization.

isometric A two-dimensional representation of a three-dimensional object.

isometric view In computer graphics, a display method that shows three-dimensional objects with height and width but without the change in perspective that would be added by depth. In other words, a picture of a three-dimensional object that shows all three dimensions in equal proportions. A drawing in which the horizontal lines of an object are drawn at an angle to the horizontal and all verticals are projected at an angle form the base. Isometrics can be generated automatically by CAD. In computer-aided mapping, isometric drawings are frequently used to display digital terrain models, three-dimensional subsurface models, or other landform representation.

ISOMETRIC VIEW   PERSPCTIVE VIEW

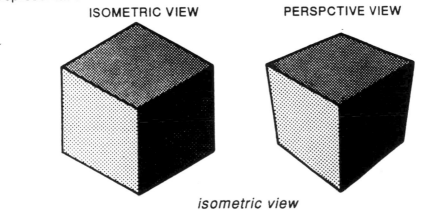

isometric view

147

italic A typeface that slants to the right and commonly is used for emphasis.

ITC Avant Garde A modern sans serif typeface designed by the International Typeface Corporation (ITC) and included as a built-in font with many PostScript laser printers.

ITC Bookman A serif typeface design owned by the International Typeface Corporation (ITC) and included as a built-in font with many PostScript laser printers.

ITC Zapf Chancery An italic typeface owned by the International Typeface Corporation (ITC) and included as a built-in font with many PostScript laser printers. The typeface was developed by Herman Zapf, a German typeface designer.

Iterated Function Systems (IFS) A system, developed by Michael Barnsley, consisting of several sets of equations, each of which represents a rotation, a translation, and a scaling. By starting with a point and randomly applying one set of equations, according to specified probability rules, the system will generate classic fractals. IFS can be used to generate ferns and other shapes from nature.

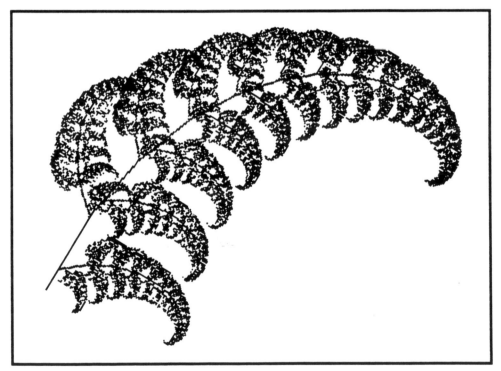

iterated function systems

iterative (1) A technique for solving a problem by repeatedly applying the same operations. (2) In fractal geometry, the repeated evaluation of successive output points.

jacket The plastic cover for a disk. It has holes and slots cut into it to expose the hub and afford the head-of-disk drive access to the disk. 5.25-inch disks use a stiff plastic jacket, with glued or crimped seams. 3.5-inch disks use rigid plastic envelopes, with spring-loaded sliding metal shutters to protect the disk surface from being touched accidentally.

jaggies In a computer graphics display, the stairstepped or saw-toothed effect of diagonals, circles, and curves.

LOW RESOLUTION   HIGH RESOLUTION

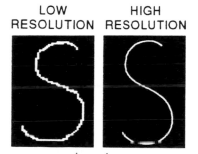

jaggies

jargon The vocabulary peculiar to a group or profession.

jargon

jitter Brief instability of a signal, applied particularly to signals on a video display.

joystick A lever, pivoted to move in any direction, that controls the movement of a cursor on a display screen. Similar to a mouse, but used mostly when playing video games.

joystick

JPEG Acronym for Joint Photographic Experts Group, the International Standards Organization's proposed standard for image compression on the Apple Macintosh microcomputer.

Julia set Set of all points which do not converge to a fixed point or finite attracting orbit under repeated applications of the map. Most Julia sets are fractals, displaying an endless cascade of repeated detail. Julia sets were named after French mathematician Gaston Julia, who studied this field of mathematics during the 1910-1925 period.

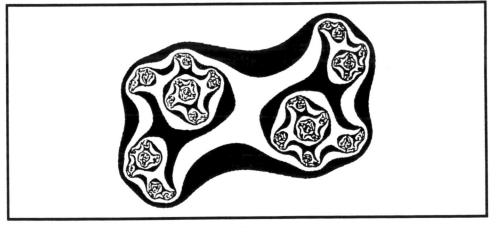

Julia set

justification (1) Act of adjusting, arranging, or shifting digits to the left or right to make them fit a prescribed pattern. (2) Alignment of text margins on both right and left sides. Justified text is both flush left and flush right. Contrast with ragged left and ragged right.

justify To align the characters in a field. For example, to right justify, the last character (the least significant digit) is written in the last, or rightmost, character position in the field. Alphabetical lists are commonly left justified.

kaleidoscope picture A kaleidoscope is a tubelike device with mirrors that generates random patterns with high radial symmetry. Computers can be used to produce kaleidoscope-like pictures.

kerning Adjusting the space between characters to create wider or tighter spacing. Reduction of excess white space between specific letter pairs. For example, the pair To can be placed more closely together than the pair Tk because the arm of the T fits over the top of the o. Kerning is especially important with large type sizes.

keyboard Input device used to key programs and data into the computer's storage. Since the keyboard is the most frequently used part of the computer, a good keyboard is an essential part of any computer system intended for business purposes.

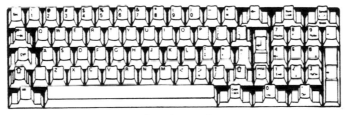

keyboard

kill (1) To terminate a process before it reaches its natural conclusion. (2) Method of erasing information. (3) To stop, frequently to abort.

kinematic programs In CAD/CAM, visual simulation programs used for solving those design problems which involve moving parts.

kinetic Art that incorporates movement into a composition.

knots Scalar values that influence a curve shape.

Koala Pad An inexpensive digitizing tablet for microcomputers. Similar to a graphics tablet, but with a much smaller surface area. Also referred to as a touch tablet. Manufactured by Koala Technologies Corporation.

Kurta Corporation A manufacturer of graphics workstations, data tablets and digitizers.

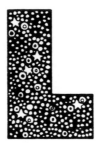

lacunarity The property of a fractal having large intervals, such as empty circular or spherical regions, so that it appears not to fill space. The term was coined by Benoit Mandelbrot.

LAN See local area network.

landscape An orientation in which the data is printed across the wider side of the form.

landscape mode A video display screen whose width is greater than its height, like a pastoral landscape painting. Contrast with portrait mode.

landscape monitor

landscape monitor A monitor with a screen shape wider than it is high.

152

laptop computer A personal computer, small and portable enough to be used comfortably in the lap of a person seated in an automobile or an airplane. Laptop computers are battery powered in their normal operation. Laptop computers today feature full-sized keyboards, flat-screen monitors that fold up and down, hard disks, floppy disks, and powerful microprocessors. Also called a lap computer.

laptop computer

LaserJet A series of desktop laser printers from Hewlett-Packard Company. Introduced in 1984, it set the standard for the desktop laser printer market.

laser printer A printer that uses a light beam to transfer images to paper. Laser printers print a full page at a time. A laser is used to "paint" the dots of light onto a photographic drum or belt. The toner is applied to the drum or belt and then transferred onto the paper. In 1975, the IBM Corporation introduced the first laser printer, called the IBM 3800, which was designed for high-speed printing. In 1978, the Xerox Corporation introduced the Xerox 9700 high-speed printer. In 1984, the Hewlett-Packard Company introduced the first desktop laser printer, which has revolutionized personal computer printing and has spawned desktop publishing. Desktop laser printers is technically more like an office copier than a conventional printer. They are very fast in operation and relatively silent.

laser printer

LaserWriter A series of desktop laser printers from Apple Computer, Inc.

lasso On many graphics programs, a tool that selects irregularly shaped regions from the image for further processing.

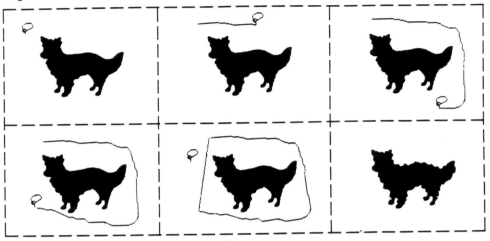

lasso

layer (1) In computer graphics drawing programs, an overlay on which text or images can be stored. In SuperPaint, for example, you can create illustrations on two layers: a paint layer for bit mapped graphics and a draw layer for object-oriented graphics. In some graphics programs you can draw and paint on many different layers. (2) Third dimension in a three-dimensional array.

layer discrimination The process of selectively assigning colors to a layer, or highlighting entities via gray levels, to graphically distinguish among data on different layers displayed on a CRT.

layering (1) Logical concept that associates subgroups of graphic data within a single drawing. Allows a user to view only those parts of a drawing being worked on and reduces the confusion that might result from viewing all parts of a very complex file. (2) Organizing data in layers.

layers User-defined logical subdivisions of data in a graphics database which may be viewed on the CRT individually or overlaid and viewed in groups.

layout (1) In desktop publishing, the design for process of arranging text and graphics on a page. (2) The arrangement of data items on a data record. (3) Overall design or plan, such as system flowcharts, schematics, diagrams, format for printer output, and makeup of a document (book).

layout sheet Grid paper designed to map the display screen for purposes of program planning. Text and graphics can be sketched in terms of rows and columns or the graphics X-Y coordinates.

LCD printer Short for Liquid Crystal Display printer, an electrophotographic printer that uses an electrostatically charged drum to transfer toner to a piece of paper. Similar to laser printers and LED printers.

154

LCS Short of liquid crystal shutter, a type of optical technology based on using LCD (liquid crystal display) panels to block or pass light through for display or reaction. LCS technology competes with laser beam methods in the design of high quality page printers.

leader (1) In page layout and word processing programs, a row of dots and dashes that provide a path for the eye to follow across the page. Leaders are sometimes used in table of contents to lead the readers' eye from the entry to the page number. (2) Blank section of tape at the beginning of a reel of magnetic tape.

leading The vertical spacing between lines of type, measured from baseline to baseline. Font styles which have long ascenders and descenders need more leading than fonts that don't. In publishing, the font size and leading is described as a fraction. For example, 10/12 (which is read "10 on 12") indicates 10 point type with 2 point leading.

leading edge (1) In optical scanning, the edge of the document or page that enters the read position first. (2) Buzz word implying technological leadership: "on the leading edge of technology."

LED printer Short for Light Emitting Diode printer, an electrophotographic printer that uses an electrostatically charged drum to transfer toner to a piece of paper. Similar to laser printers and LCS printers.

legend (1) Text beneath a graph; it explains the colors, shading, or symbols used to label the data points. (2) Text that describes or explains a graphic.

LetraStudio A graphics program from Letraset USA that has the ability to condense, stretch, slant, scale, rotate, flip-flop, or distort a design in real time.

letter quality printing High-quality output produced by some printers. Laser printers, daisy-wheel printers and ink-jet printers are letter quality printers. High-end, 24-pin dot matrix printers provide near letter quality printing.

library (1) Published collection of programs, routines, and subroutines available to every user of the computer. (2) A storage area, usually on hard disk or a diskette, used to store programs. (3) A collection of items, such as clip-art, intended for inclusion in other programs.

ligature In typography, two or more characters designed and cast as a distinct unit for aesthetic reasons. Letter combinations such as ae, fi, ff, fl, ffi, ffl, and oe commonly are printed as ligatures. Some outline fonts available for PostScript laser printers and imagesetters include ligatures for desktop publishing applications.

light Being closer to white than black. Having a high color value.

lightface In desktop publishing, an extra light version of a typeface.

lighting model A mathematical formula for approximating the physical effect of light from various sources striking objects.

lightness Amount of light or dark present in a particular color.

light pen Electronic input device that resembles a pen and can be used to write or sketch on the screen of a graphics display. The user points the light pen at a location on the graphics display. When the electron gun illuminates the phosphor, the light pen detects the light and sends a signal to the graphics system, which records the pixel event at that moment.

light pen

light source One of several types of light used by a lighting model. Light source types include ambient, directional, positional, and spot.

linear perspective A picture or drawing which gives the illusion of depth. Linear perspective is often shown by parallel lines which recede from the spectator and meet in a point (the vanishing point) on the horizon or eye-level.

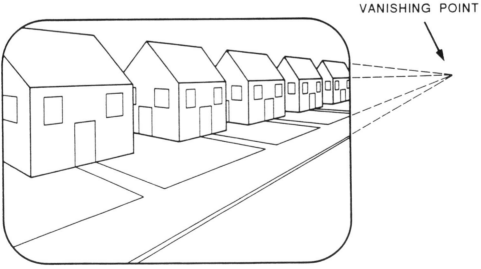

VANISHING POINT

linear perspective

line art Artwork containing only blacks and whites with no shading. Line art can be reproduced accurately by low to medium resolution printers.

line art

line art mode A scanner setting for digitizing an image by characterizing each point either as black or white with no shades of gray.

line chart Method of charting business data.

linecut The reverse of a black on white line drawing.

line cut

line drawing Drawing where an object's image is represented by a solid-line outline of the surface.

line feed (LF) Operation that advances printer paper by one line. See form feed.

line filter Device used to correct electromagnetic interference that comes in over the power line.

line graph Graph made by connecting data points with a line. Shows the variations of data over time or the relationships between two numeric variables.

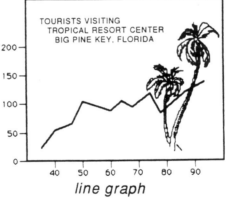

line graph

line join The way in which two line segments meet.

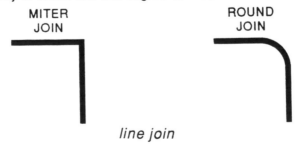

line join

line plot Graph with displayed data points, and straight lines connecting the points.

line printer A printer that assembles all characters on a line at one time and prints them out practically simultaneously. Line printers are high-speed printing devices that are usually connected to mainframes and minicomputers.

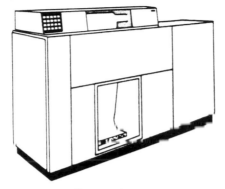

line printer

line screen frequency When a continuous tone image is screened, this is the number of halftone dots per inch making up the screen. Typical line screens are 53, 65, 85, 100, 120, 133, and 150 lines per inch: 200-500 lines per inch for high-quality products.

line segment Portion of a longer line defined by its two end points.

lines per inch Abbreviated lpi, lines per inch is the yardstick used to measure halftone resolution.

line style In computer graphics, the method of representing a line in a graphics system, such as with dashes, solid lines, or dots.

line styling In computer graphics, the type of line used when a line is drawn on the screen. For instance, line styling may call for the use of a bold, solid, or dashed line.

line width Actual, physical thickness of a line in a graphics system.

line work Any non-continuous tone image, i.e. without shades of gray or other colors. Usually black-and-white line art or diagram, but can also include EPS art created on a computer that incorporates flat color tints (comic-book coloring).

line work

Linotronic A series of high-quality typesetting machines known as Linotronic laser imagesetters, which can print at resolutions over 1200 dots per inch (dpi). Imagesetters are commonly used with PostScript desktop publishing systems.

liquid crystal display (LCD) A flat display used in many portable computers because it is small, and requires little power. The display is made of two sheets of polarizing material sandwiched together with a nematic liquid crystal solution between them. Images are produced when electric currents cause the liquid crystals to align so light cannot shine through.

Lisa A microcomputer introduced in the early 1980s by Apple Computer, Inc. It featured a graphical user interface and a mouse. The Lisa had its own Apple-generated operating system, called the Lisa Operating System. This was designed to perform file management, memory management, event handling and exception handling. The Lisa was built around a Motorola, Inc. microprocessor. The Lisa was the forerunner of the Apple Macintosh microcomputer.

list price The manufacturer's suggested retail price of a product. See street price.

local area network (LAN) Communications network connecting various hardware devices together within a building by means of a continuous cable or an in-house voice-data telephone system.

locator device A graphics input device used to specify coordinate data.

lofting An interactive graphics technique in which the third dimension is obtained from a two-dimensional representation – as in elevating the contours of a topographic map.

logarithmic graph In presentation graphics, a graph displayed with a y-axis incremented exponentially in powers of 10. On an ordinary y-axis, the 10 is followed by 20, 30, 40, 50, and so on. On a logarithmic scale, however, 10 is followed by 100, 1000, 10,000, 100,000, and so on.

logical graphic function/logical operations A computer-aided design capability which applies Boolean operations (AND, OR, NOT) to areas of graphic entities. This provides the user with interactive tools to create new figures from existing ones or to expand a design – rules checking program – for example, in integrated circuit design.

LOGO High-level programming language that assumes the user has access to some type of graphics terminal. Designed for students and easily employed by those in the younger age groups, it has wide-ranging application in graphic reports of business and industry. Highly interactive, permitting users to learn quickly how to draw geometric patterns and pictures on the screen. One important feature of LOGO is turtle graphics. Turtle graphics enable the programmer to make simple drawings by telling the "turtle" on the screen to move forward, right, left, and so on. Once he or she masters the simple drawing environment, the programmer starts to discover the more sophisticated features of the language. Developed in 1968 at the Massachusetts Institute of Technology by Seymour Papert.

lower case Noncapitalized alphabetic letters. Contrast with upper case.

low-res graphics Abbreviation of low-resolution graphics, a blocky and jagged picture on a display screen produced by a small number of pixels. Contrast with hi-res graphics.

low-res graphics

low-resolution Pertaining to the quality and accuracy of detail that can be represented by a graphics display. Resolution quality depends upon the number of basic image-forming units (pixels) within a picture image – the greater the number, the higher the resolution. Low-resolution pictures, produced by a small number of pixels, are not as sharp and clear as high-resolution pictures.

Lumena A professional draw/paint graphics program designed for use by visual communications professionals who design sophisticated images for output to print, film, and video. It runs on IBM-compatible microcomputer systems. Features include 250 draw/paint tools, color mixing, color separations, and several bit mapped and vector fonts.

luminance (1) A measure of the amount of light radiated by a given source, such as a computer display screen. (2) Portions of composite video signal controlling brightness.

luminance decay Reduction in screen brightness on a visual display terminal that inevitably occurs over time.

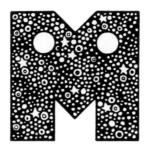

Mac A nickname for the Apple Macintosh computer.

MacDraw A fast, flexible and precise drawing program for the Apple Macintosh computer. Nine drawing tools are provided which have become drawing program standards: line, text, selection, rectangle, rounded rectangle, oval, arc, polygon, and freehand drawing. Up to 16,000 black-and-white or color patterns and 255 customizable pen widths can be used in a document. Font sizes and line spacings can vary from 1 to 127 points; and objects and text can be rotated from 0 to 360 degrees. Multiple, overlapping, transparent layers can be hidden, shown and rearranged in any order. Drawing features include an enhanced polygon, a bezigon tool, a freehand tool and zoom while drawing, duplicate while dragging and edit points while drawing polygon and bezigon objects. Users can interchange with standard file formats such as MacDraw, PICT, CGM, and EPSF.

MacDraw file format The object file format used by the MacDraw drawing program and other programs.

MacDraw Pro An advanced version of the MacDraw drawing program with features to aid specific needs, such as desktop publishing.

machine-aided graphics for illustration and composition (MAGIC) An interactive program for preparation, editing and storage or graphic designs and technical documentation for computers using the UNIX operating system.

machine vision The gathering and interpreting of visual data, particularly for industrial applications such as robot guidance or parts inspection.

Macintosh A series of popular microcomputers from Apple Computer, Inc., introduced in 1984. It used the Motorola 68000 family of microprocessors and a proprietary operating system that simulates a user's desktop on screen. This standard user interface, combined with its built-in QuickDraw graphics language, has provided a visual, easy-to-use microcomputer. The Macintosh uses a mouse as a primary input device, in addition to a keyboard. Since the introduction of the Macintosh, Apple Computer, Inc. continues to offer progressively faster and more powerful models of the Macintosh.

Macintosh 128K The original Macintosh introduced in 1984. It had a 68000 microprocessor running at 8 MHz, and it had 128K of memory and a built-in 400K disk drive. It was a revolutionary system due to its ease of use.

162

Macintosh 512K An upgrade to the Macintosh 128; a system with 512K of main memory.

Macintosh 512Ke A 1986 upgrade to the Macintosh 128K and 512K systems. The upgrade included new ROMs and a 800K double-sided disk drive.

Macintosh Classic The Macintosh Classic, introduced in 1990, replaces the Macintosh Plus and the SE. The Classic runs up to 25 percent faster than the Macintosh Plus. The Classic uses a Motorola 68000 processor, a 1.4 MB floppy disk unit and has an optional 40 MB internal hard disk unit. It is the lowest-priced Macintosh system offered to date.

Macintosh Classic

Macintosh Classic II A 1991 upgrade to the Macintosh Classic. The Classic II uses a Motorola 68030 microprocessor running at 16 MHz which doubles the performance of the Classic.

Macintosh draw programs See Canvas, ColorStudio, DeskPaint/DeskDraw, Freehand, Illustrator, MacDraw, and Photoshop.

Macintosh LC A low priced color-capable modular Macintosh system. The LC is powered by the Motorola 68020 microprocessor running at 16 MHz. It is up to 100 percent faster than the SE and Classic systems. The LC includes a 2 megabyte ROM memory, a 1.4 MB floppy disk unit, and an internal 40 megabyte hard disk unit. The Macintosh LC was introduced in 1990.

Macintosh paint programs See DeskPaint/DeskDraw, Easy Color Paint, MacPaint, Oasis, PixelPaint, Studio 1, Studio 8, Studio 32, SuperPaint, UltraPaint, and VideoPaint.

Macintosh Plus This computer had 128K ROMs, an internal 800K disk drive, and 1 megabyte of memory. This machine quickly became the standard for a minimum configuration. Many programs for the Macintosh require a minimum 1 megabyte memory. This computer also introduced the now standard SCSI (Small Computer System Interface) port, which allows the easy addition of one or more hard disks and other peripherals. Apple Computer, Inc. introduced the Macintosh Plus in 1986.

Macintosh Portable When the original Macintosh was introduced, many people liked it because it was "portable". In reality, it was luggable if you did not have to carry it very far. Since then, the Macintosh has been evolving into larger, heavier, harder-to-move systems. In 1989, Apple Computer, Inc. released a portable Macintosh. The portable is powered by a Motorola 68000 microprocessor running at 16 MHz. This battery operated computer used a liquid crystal display of 640 by 400 pixels and a standard 4 MB RAM memory.

Macintosh PowerBooks Three notebook Macintoshes, called the Macintosh PowerBook 100,140 and 170, were introduced in 1991. These notebook computers have a built-in hard disk, built-in floppy drives (140 and 170), and an optional internal fax/data modem.

Macintosh Quadra 700/900/950 High performance Macintoshes, introduced in 1991 and 1992, that use Motorola 68040 microprocessors.

Macintosh SE SE stands for System Expansion. It indicates that this system offers a single expansion slot for adding a card to attach a peripheral. The SE was very similar to the Macintosh Plus in performance. The SE was introduced in 1987.

Macintosh SE/30 This is a high performance Macintosh that uses the more powerful Motorola 68030 microprocessor, has a disk drive that is capable of storing 1.4 megabytes, and a math coprocessor. The SE/30 was introduced in 1989.

Macintosh SE/30

Macintosh II First serious Macintosh for professional production; introduced in 1987. The Macintosh II was the first of the "modular" Macintoshes. The system unit does not contain a monitor, allowing each user to choose a monitor that will perform best in the user's environment. The Macintosh II was the first Macintosh to support color and multiple video screens. It has stereo sound and six expansion slots. It was powered by the Motorola 68020 microprocessor running at 16 MHz and had a math coprocessor. The Macintosh II had a 1 megabyte RAM and a built-in hard disk drive.

Macintosh IIci The IIci is a faster version of the Macintosh IIcx, with a processor that operates about 1.5 times faster (a Motorola 68030 running at 25 MHz). The Macintosh IIci has a standard 5 MB RAM memory. The IIci was introduced in 1989. The IIci contains fewer parts than earlier Macintoshes due to its use of 13 special Apple-designed VLSI chips.

Macintosh IIci

Macintosh IIcx Introduced in 1989, this Macintosh II upgrade used a Motorola 68030 microprocessor running at 16 MHz. The IIcx is a compact version of the Macintosh IIx.

Macintosh IIfx A Macintosh computer designed for intensive graphics, CAD, and numeric calculations. The IIfx uses a Motorola 68030 microprocessor running at 40 MHz, or 1.6 times faster than the IIci's 25 MHz speed. The IIfx has two additional processor (each with the power of an Apple II microcomputer) to handle the flow of information inside the computer. The IIfx uses a standard 4 MB RAM memory and available as an option is a 160 MB internal hard disk unit. The Macintosh IIfx was introduced in 1990.

Macintosh IIsi The Macintosh IIsi, introduced in 1990, uses a Motorola 68030 microprocessor running at 20 MHz and runs about five times faster than the Macintosh Classic. The IIsi uses a standard 3 MB RAM memory, a 1.4 MB floppy disk unit and a 40 MB internal hard disk unit.

Macintosh IIx This Macintosh II update used a Motorola 68030 microprocessor, a 68882 math coprocessor and a standard 4 MB RAM memory. The Macintosh IIx was introduced in 1988.

165

Macintosh user interface The method of operating an Apple Macintosh microcomputer, originally developed by Xerox Star workstation. It uses a graphics screen that places objects on a two-dimensional desktop. Programs, files, folders and disks are represented by small pictures (icons) that look like the objects they represent. A mouse is used to select, activate or delete an object represented on the desktop. The Macintosh user interface style has been adapted to many non-Macintosh products, including Windows, GEM and Presentation Manager.

MacPaint A full-featured paint program for the Apple Macintosh microcomputer from Claris Corporation. Originally developed by Bill Atkinson at Apple Computer, Inc. and bundled with every Macintosh microcomputer until Claris Corporation was formed in 1987. Claris produces a more advanced version of the program. MacPaint provides a versatile set of tools for graphic expression. It is an excellent program that uses a mouse to draw lines and shapes on the screen, select patterns, edit drawings, erase lines, shade drawings, manipulate images, stretch shapes and a variety of other graphics functions. MacPaint displays a portion of a page within a drawing window. It provides a variety of tools from a drawing tool palette. Images may easily be copied to other parts of the screen or to other documents via the clipboard. The MacPaint paint program style has been imitated in a variety of other popular paint programs.

MacPaint file format Bit map graphics format used by MacPaint and some other Apple Macintosh paint programs. MacPaint files are limited to a resolution of 72 dpi, the same as the screen on the original Macintosh computers.

MacWrite A full-featured word processing program for the Apple Macintosh microcomputer from Claris Corporation. Originally developed by Apple Computer, Inc. and bundled with every Apple Macintosh microcomputer until Claris Corporation was formed in 1987. Claris enhanced MacWrite by adding many new word processing features.

magazines See computer graphics magazines.

MAGIC See machine-aided graphics for illustration and composition.

magazette A magazine recorded on a diskette.

magenta A purplish red color, containing no green hue. One of the three subtractive primary colors. In 1850 King Emmanuel of Sardinia made a pact with Napoleon III to declare war on Austria, which at that time controlled part of what is now northern Italy. They succeeded in destroying the Austrian army in two small towns west of Milan and very soon afterward a purplish red dye was discovered there. The new dye was named for one of the towns: Magenta.

magnetic bubble memory Memory that uses magnetic "bubbles" that move. The bubbles are locally magnetized areas that can move about in a magnetic material, such as a plate of orthoferrite. It is possible to control the reading in and out of this bubble within the magnetic material. Andrew Bobeck, Richard Sherwood, Unberto Gianola, and William Shockley, of Bell Laboratories, invented magnetic bubble memory. At present, bubble memories are more expensive than disks; they are used in very lightweight, portable computers when a disk drive is too bulky or too fragile.

magnetic disk Disk made of rigid material (hard disk) or heavy Mylar (floppy disk). The disk surface is used to hold magnetized data, which is written on the disk and retrieved from the disk by a disk drive.

magnetic media Generic name for floppy disks, tapes, and any other devices that store data in the form of magnetic impulses.

magnetic printing A process where a magnetic write head is used to create a latent image on a drum or a belt, which is then toned, usually with a dry toner. The toned image is transferred to the paper and fixed with either heat or pressure.

magnetic resonance imaging (MRI) A medical imaging technique that is used for image capture.

magneto-optic disc An erasable storage disc, similar to a CD-ROM disc. Uses a recording method that combines laser and magnetic technologies to create high-density erasable storage discs. Magneto-optic (MO) drives are immune from disc head crash damage since nothing physically touches the media, provide greater storage capacity than magnetic media, and provide more flexibility of use since the media is removable from the drive.

mainframe Large, expensive computer generally used for information processing in large businesses, colleges, and organizations. Originally, the phrase referred to the extensive array of large rack and panel cabinets that held thousands of vacuum tubes in early computers. Mainframes can occupy an entire room and have very large data-handling capacities. Far more costly than microcomputers or minicomputers, mainframes are the largest, fastest, and most expensive class of computers. Supercomputers are the largest, fastest, and most expensive of the mainframes. Before minicomputers became popular in 1965, all computers were mainframes.

mainframe

management graphics Charts, graphs, and other visual representations of the operational or strategic aspects of a business, intended to aid management in assimilating and presenting business data.

Mandelbrot, Benoit B. A mathematician who invented the terms fractal and fractal geometry. A fractal is a complex geometric shape that has an infinite number and variety of corners, twists, and curves. These shapes are used to study and simulate natural phenomena, such as atmospheric turbulence, geographical landscapes, cloud formations, and the distribution of stellar systems throughout the universe. In the simplest of terms, fractals imitate nature. Mandelbrot is an IBM Fellow at the Thomas J. Watson Research Center and a visiting professor at Harvard University.

Mandelbrot set The Mandelbrot set is probably the most well-known fractal. In many magazines, you will come across an article of the Mandelbrot set and some examples of the pictures of its displays. Originally, the Mandelbrot set was discovered by Benoit Mandelbrot when he was investigating the behavior of the iterate function

$$Z_n = Z_{n-1}^2 + C$$

where both Z and C are complex numbers. Mandelbrot developed a new way of mapping this equation: the Mandelbrot set. This set also turned out to be a kind of catalog of all possible Julia sets, from which particular interesting Julia set parameters may be selected for mapping.

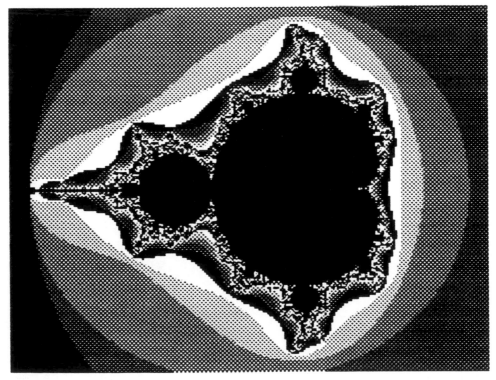

Mandelbrot set

manufacturer's software Operating system or set of programming aids that the computer manufacturer supplies or makes available with a computer. See systems programs.

map A detailed representation in which the positions of points have a known correspondence to the positions of real or allocated points on the object being represented.

map generalization An automatic mapping process for reducing the amount of graphic and nongraphic information displayed on a map. Often used in the creation of composite maps from a series of large-scale maps. The process may employ line filtering, symbol revision, reclassification, and other generalizing techniques.

mapping (1) The transformation of one coordinate system into another. (2) An application for computer graphics systems. (3) A computer graphics technique for taking a two-dimensional image and applying (mapping) it as a surface onto a three-dimensional object.

marquee A rectangular area surrounded by dotted lines, used to select objects or selected portions of an image in a drawing/painting program.

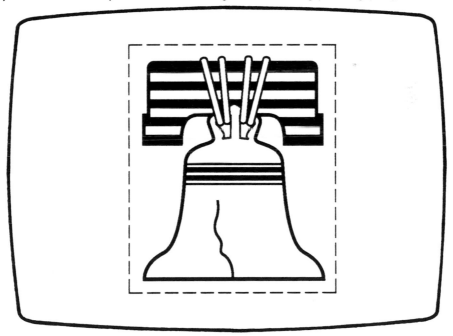

marquee

mass properties The physically related properties of an object, such as volume, weight, inertia, and center of gravity.

math coprocessor A special chip added to a computer to handle advanced mathematic functions, thereby freeing up the processing power of the main CPU.

169

mathematics Study of the relationships among objects of quantities, organized so that certain facts can be proved or derived from others by using logic. Because computers can calculate and display in visual form the roots of equations and other mathematical objects, computer generated pictures are also starting to prove useful in areas of mathematics far from geometry. For the first time, mathematicians are getting to "see" the content of the abstract theorems they prove and to use their eyes, not just their minds, to probe new mathematical territory and to bag new game.

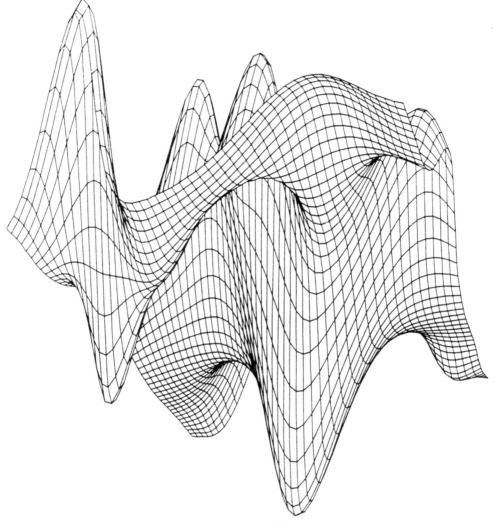

mathematics

matrix printer Character printer that uses a matrix of dots to form an image of the character being printed. See dot matrix printer.

MCAD Acronym for Mechanical Computer Aided Design. CAD for mechanical design.

MCGA Acronym for Multi-Color Graphics Array; a type of display adapter for IBM PS/2 compatible computers.

MDA Acronym for Monochrome Display Adapter. A video adapter that provided text on IBM Personal Computers. MDA cards were often replaced with adapter cards which provided both text and graphics. MDA was superseded by VGA.

mechanical computer-aided design (MCAD) A specialized computer graphics market for the design of mechanical structures, such as airplanes, automobiles, and their parts.

mechanical mouse A mouse that uses a rubber ball that makes contact with several wheels inside the unit. Contrast with optical mouse.

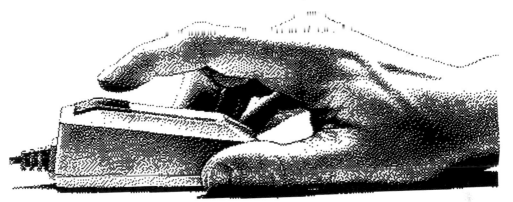

mechanical mouse

mechanicals Camera-ready pages with text and art in position.

media compatibility The ability of two or more different style units to use the same type of disks as blank disks, whether or not each can read data recorded by the other.

media interchangeability The extent to which disks recorded on one machine can play back on another with the same type of drive. Media interchangeability is excellent for floppy disks, but some removable cartridge hard disks have problems with it.

medical imaging A field that employs various image-generation techniques, such as computed axial tomography (CAT), magnetic resonance imaging (MRZ), and x-ray to collect image samples from a patients' internal tissue for analysis. Computers have revolutionized medicine. They have led to completely new insights into the anatomy and physiology of the living body, through computerized imaging techniques. Computer-generated imagery offers an effective means for presenting three-dimensional medical data to the clinician.

medium Any physical substance upon which data are recorded, such as floppy disk, magnetic disk, magnetic tape, and paper.

MEGA A personal computer series from Atari Corporation that is compatible with the Atari ST series of microcomputers.

megabyte (MB) Specifically, 2^{20}, or 1,048,576 bytes; 1024 kilobytes. Roughly, 1 million bytes of 1 thousand kilobytes.

megapel display In computer graphics, a display system that handles a million or more pixels. A resolution of 1000 lines by 1000 dots per line requires a million pixels for a full screen image.

memory Storage facilities of the computer, capable of storing vast amounts of data.

memory chips A semiconductor device used to store information in the form of electrical charges. There are two types of memory chips: ROM holds information permanently while RAM holds it temporarily.

memory map A diagram that show how memory is used. For example, in a display unit there is a memory map of the screen display, with one memory location corresponding to each pixel display.

Menger sponge A three-dimensional analog of the Sierpinski carpet. Starting with a cube, dividing it into 27 smaller cubes, and removing the central cube as well as the cubes lying at the center of each face of the original cube (7 in all) leads to a form called the Menger sponge. Its fractal dimension is log 20/log 3=2.727.

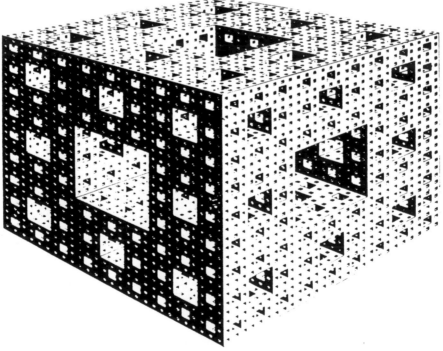

Menger sponge

menu A list of command options available to the user of a computer software program. An on-screen list of command choices.

menu-driven software Computer programs that made extensive use of menus. Software of this type is designed so it may be used easily by people with minimal computer experience. Menus are used to select tasks to be performed.

mesh A graphical object with a mesh surface constructed from polygons. The polygons in a mesh are described by the graphics system as solid faces, rather than as hollow polygons, as is the case with wireframe models.

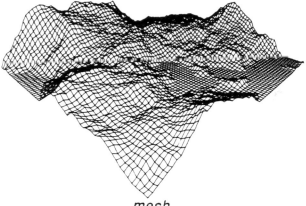

mesh

metamerism The condition of a color changing hue under different lighting conditions, e.g. yellow appears green under certain fluorescent lighting.

metamorphosis The change, over a varying period of time, from an object of one shape to an object of another shape.

metamorphosis

metaphor In software development, the use of words or pictures to suggest a resemblance. For example, the Apple Macintosh computer uses a desk-top metaphor with its icons for paper, folders, wastebaskets, and so on.

mezzotint An engraving that is produced by scraping a roughened surface to produce the effect of gray tones. Image editing and processing software can produce this effect with a process called error diffusion.

MFLOP One million floating-point operations per second. Used as a rough measure of a computer's processing speed.

173

microcomputer The smallest and least expensive class of computer. Any small computer based on a microprocessor. Also called a personal computer.

microcomputer

microcomputer system System that includes a microcomputer, peripherals, operating system, and applications programs.

microdisk A 3.5-inch diskette.

microfloppy disk A 3.5-inch floppy disk, which in recent years has become the disk of choice. A 3.5-inch disk holds more data and are much easier to store, transport and handle than their 5.25-inch counterparts. The microfloppy disk was developed by Sony.

microfloppy disk

Micrografx Designer A graphic arts and technical illustration program for the IBM PC. Designer mixes, edits, and manipulates different font types. Using advanced spline technology, Designer provides curves, parabolas, and a variety of freehand drawing capabilities.

micrographics The use of photographically digitized information for convenient storage, retrieval, and examination of documents, files and records.

microjustification In some word processing programs, the ability to add small slivers of blank space between words and between letters within words. The result is easier to read than ordinary justified copy, in which the computer merely adjusts space between words.

microprocessor The complex chip that is the central processing unit (CPU) of the computer. The job of the microprocessor is to control what goes on inside the computer. All processing that a computer does takes place in the microprocessor.

Microsoft Corporation A leading software company founded in 1975 by Williams H. Gates and Paul G. Allen. The company's first product was Microsoft BASIC for the Altair 8800 microcomputer. Following products include MS-DOS, Microsoft Windows, Microsoft Word, Microsoft Works, GW-BASIC, as well as many other software systems. Microsoft's position as the supplier of the major software to the world's largest computer base (IBM-compatible microcomputers) gives it considerable influence over the future of the computer industry.

Microsoft Windows A graphics-based operating environment for IBM-compatible microcomputers from Microsoft Corporation. It runs in conjunction with DOS. Some of the graphical user interface features include pull-down menus, multiple typefaces, desk accessories, and the capability of moving text and graphics from one program to another via a clipboard.

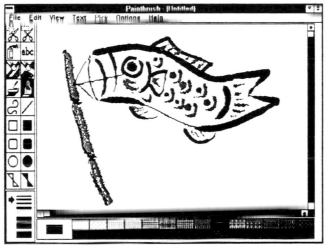

Microsoft Windows

Microsoft Word A full-featured word processing program for IBM-compatible microcomputers and Apple Macintosh computers from Microsoft Corporation. It has a spelling checker, hyphenation, style sheets, a glossary, mail merge, automatic text wrap, and a column design feature.

Microsoft Works An integrated application program that includes a spreadsheet, a database, and a word processor. It provides desktop publishing with drawing and word processing documents. The drawing tools and linked columns of the desktop publishing section let you create professional style layouts.

microspacing Feature of some printers that allows them to move extremely small distances. Used to do microjustification and shadow printing.

minicomputer A class of computers with capabilities and a price between microcomputers and mainframes. In 1959, Digital Equipment Corporation (DEC) launched the minicomputer industry with its PDP-1. In 1965, DEC introduced the PDP-8, the first popular, low cost minicomputer. In 1970,

DEC introduced the PDP-11, which became the most widely used minicomputer in the world. Data General Corporation, Hewlett-Packard Company, Prime Computer, Inc., IBM Corporation, Wang Laboratories, Inc., and other companies have produced a variety of minicomputers.

minicomputer

minifloppy A 5.25-inch diskette, introduced by Shugart in 1978.

MIPS One million instructions per second. A measure of the processing speed of a computer. Used to describe the average number of machine-language instructions a large computer performs in one second. A computer capable of 2.0 MIPS can execute 2,000,000 instructions per second. A mainframe can typically perform 10 to 50 MIPS; a microcomputer might be in the 0.05 MIPS range.

mirroring Display or creation of graphic data that portrays an image in exactly the reverse orientation it originally had. Many computer graphics systems will automatically create a mirror image of a graphic entity on the display screen by flipping the entity or drawing on its X or Y axis.

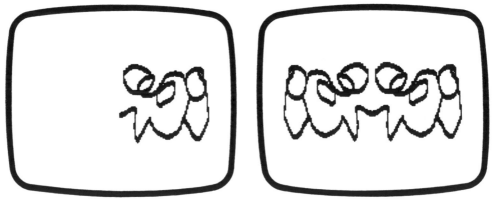

mirroring

miter The treatment of thick lines at a corner intersection so that each line is beveled to make the join.

MITERED

ROUNDED

NOT MITERED

miter

model coordinates The coordinate system used for describing a single object.

model, geometric Complete, geometrically accurate two-dimensional or three-dimensional representation of a shape, a part, or a geographic area, designed on a computer graphics system and stored in the database.

model, geometric

modeling The method of creating an object in computer graphics through computational descriptions of the object's polygonal makeup, surface shape, and attributes.

modeling, geometric See geometric modeling.

modeling, molecular See molecular modeling.

modeling, solid See solid modeling.

177

modern art Generally indicative of the art of the twentieth century that is nonobjective or abstract in nature.

modern art

modular constraint In computer graphics, a limitation on the placement of images such that some or all points of an image are forced to lie on the intersections of an invisible grid.

modulation depth The difference in brightness between black-and-white in a CRT display.

modulation transfer function (MTF) The curve that expresses the luminance contrast between black-and-white lines on a display screen as the number of lines increases.

moire pattern (1) An interference pattern created when two patterns are asymmetrically superimposed. (2) An undesirable grid pattern that may occur when a bit mapped graphic with gray fill patterns is reduced or enlarged. (3) In scanning, an objectionable pattern caused by the interference of halftone screens. Often produced when you rescan a halftone and a second screen is applied on top of the first.

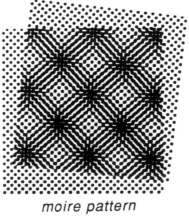

moire pattern

molecular modeling A sophisticated chemical engineering application using computer graphics to simulate chemical reactions in molecules.

monitor (1) A device on which images generated by the computer's video adapter are displayed. (2) Control program or supervisor.

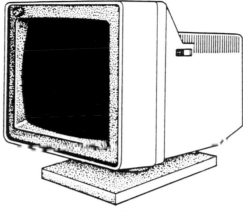

monitor

monochrome (1) A term applied to a monitor that displays a single color (white, amber or green) image on a contrasting (black) background, producing a sharp, clear display that is easy to read. (2) A single color.

monochrome adapter A video adapter capable of producing one foreground color.

monochrome display A video display capable of displaying only one color. It generally has a higher resolution than a color monitor and is often more suitable for word processing and information processing use, which require long periods of user viewing.

monochrome display

monospace A typeface in which the width of all characters is the same, producing output that looks like typed characters. Courier is an example of a monospace typeface.

montage

montage A series of images that generate a powerful effect.

mosaic (1) A form of pictorial representation in which an image is created out of small, colored pieces of stone, tile, or some other material. This effect can also be created by computers with the right imaging software. (2) Synonym for tessellation or tiling.

mosaic

motion graphics See animation.

Motorola, Inc. A leading manufacturer of semiconductor devices that was founded in 1928 by Paul V. Galvin in Chicago. Although the company produces many consumer electronics, they are best known in the computer business as the manufacturer of the 68000 family of microprocessors.

Motorola 68000 family A family of microprocessors developed by Motorola, Inc.: MC 68000 (a 16-bit processor) developed in 1979, MC 68010 (a 16-bit processor) developed in 1983, MC 68020 (a 32-bit processor) developed in 1984, MC 68030 (a 32-bit processor) developed in 1987, MC 68040 (a 32-bit processor) announced in 1987. The MC 68000 family of microprocessors is used in several popular microcomputers including the Apple Macintosh, Commodore Amiga, and Atari ST.

mouse A hand-operated pointing device that senses movements as it is moved across a flat surface and conveys this information to the computer. The mouse also has one or more buttons that can be pressed to signal the computer. The mouse's main advantage is that is can move a cursor around on the display screen, including diagonally, with great precision.

mouse

181

mouse button Switch on top of the mouse that transmits commands to the computer. See click and double-click.

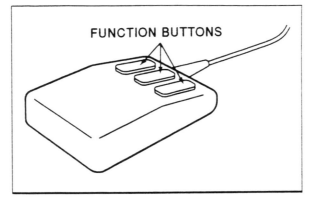

mouse button

mouse pad A surface to be used with a mouse. As you move the mouse across the mouse pad, the cursor moves across the screen in the same direction.

mouse pad

mouse pointer The on-screen icon or cursor, the movement of which is controlled by the mouse.

movement A sense of activity or change in position. It is created in drawings by use of character shapes, lines, color and lighting.

movement

182

MPEG Acronym for Motion Picture Experts Group, the ISO's proposed standard for moving images.

MRI See magnetic resonance imaging.

MS-DOS Acronym for Microsoft-Disk Operating System, the standard operating system for IBM-compatible microcomputers. MS-DOS was created by Microsoft Corporation and released in 1981. MS-DOS oversees such operations as disk input and output, video support, keyboard control, and many internal functions related to program execution and file maintenance.

MS-DOS

MS-Windows See Windows.

multi-bit Any scan that uses more than one bit to store information about a pixel.

multifunction optical drive An optical drive that has both WORM and erasable capabilities and can read or write. A multifunction drive in conjunction with a CD-ROM drive, will provide enormous capabilities and storage facilities.

multimedia Multiple types of media, such as film, videotape, computer disks, sound recordings, photographs, paper, slides, etc.

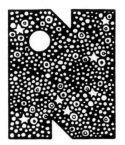

National Computer Graphics Association (NCGA) Nonprofit professional and trade organization dedicated to developing, promoting, and improving computer graphics applications in business, government, science, and the arts. NCGA brings together users and producers of computer graphics technology in a common, independent forum to share experience and knowledge. This exchange of ideas and viewpoints between the computer graphics industry and the creative people it serves identifies potential applications and spurs development of new technology. Holds an annual meeting that includes presentations, equipment exhibits, and art show. More application oriented than SIGGRAPH. NCGA was founded in 1979.

National Computer Graphics Association

NDC See normalized device coordinates.

near letter quality Printing produced by dot matrix printers with 24-pin printheads.

neighborhood operator A procedure applied to a pixel that incorporates information about the pixels that surround and touch it.

NEO Neochrome bitmap graphics format used by many programs for the Atari ST computer.

NEOchrome A color paint program for the Atari ST microcomputer. Developed by Dave Staugas, an engineer at Atari Corporation.

network (1) When two or more computers are connected to allow them to share the same software and information. Used primarily in businesses and schools. (2) System of interconnected computer systems and terminals. (3) Structure of relationships among a project's activities, tasks, and events. (4) A means of organizing data in artificial intelligence systems. A type of knowledge representation in artificial intelligence.

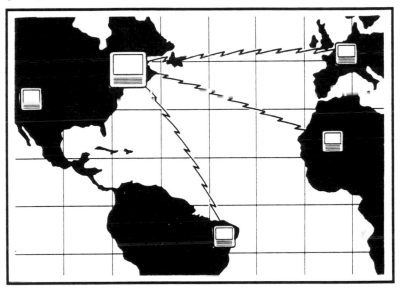

network

New Century Schoolbook An easily read typeface developed for textbooks and magazines. new Century Schoolbook often is offered as a built-in font in PostScript laser printers.

newspaper columns A page format in which two or more columns of text are printed vertically on the page so that the text flows down one column and continues at the top of the next column.

Newton A pocket-size, pen-based computer introduced by Apple Computer Inc. in 1992. Newton combines electronic calendar, card index, notetaking and telecommunications functions.

Newton-Raphson Interactive procedure used for solving equations. See iterate.

NeXT Computer A UNIX-based computer system introduced in 1988 by NeXT, Inc. It includes a 68030 microprocessor, high-resolution (1120 x 832) graphics and a 256 MB erasable optical disc. NeXT, Inc. was founded in 1985 by Steven Jobs, co-founder and former chairman of Apple Computer, Inc.

nodal point Central point on the axis movement.

noise Irrelevant data that hamper the recognition and interpretation of the data of interest.

nonimpact printer Printer that uses electricity, heat, laser technology, or photographic techniques to print output. A printer that prints without striking the paper.

nonimpact printer

normal (1) At right angles to another line segment, object, or plane. (2) The vector that is perpendicular to a surface at a specific point.

normalized device coordinates (NDC) The coordinate system between the user's world coordinates and the graphics system's physical device coordinates in the viewing pipeline.

notation Any defined, symbolic system for representing data.

nude (1) A picture of a person without clothing. (2) A Caucasian skin color.

number crunching The rapid processing of large quantities of numbers. Number crunching can be repetitive, mathematically complex, or both, and involves considerable internal processing. Parallel processing and the use of math coprocessors greatly enhance the ability of computers to perform these tasks. Complex mathematical calculations are required in many computer graphics applications.

numerical art A graphic work in which printed numbers are positioned in various ways to convey a "meaning" though not exclusively in terms of numbers.

numerical art

numeric coprocessor A microprocessor support chip that performs mathematical computations in conjunction with the main microprocessor of a system. It works in tandem with another central processing unit to increase the computing power of a system.

NURB An acronym for Non-Uniform Rational B-Spline, a complex curve that can be represented by a series of piecewise curve segments. This process is done with a sequence of "knots", which are values that join the separate splines in a curve, each knot interval representing one curve segment. NURBs have a high precision and flexibility due to the use of the knot sequence. Their relative spacing has an impact on the curve shape, and because the knots can be non-uniformly spaced, the user can exert extra control over the shape of the curve. A relatively small amount of memory is required to represent NURBs, making them an efficient curve defining method.

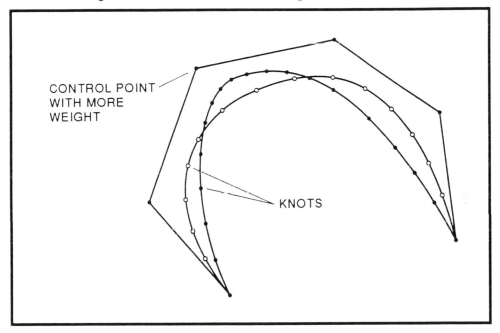

NURB

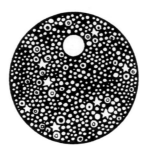

Oasis An Apple Macintosh graphics program designed specifically to take advantage of input from a pressure sensitive digitizing tablet. It offers 18 brushes with pressure control, including its ArtistBrush that allows virtually any traditional or fine art medium to be replicated, including oil paint, water color, gouache, chalks, ink, pastels, magic marker, finger paint and charcoal. The brush uses pressure input to produce strokes and to control attributes such as wetness, dry-out speed and gradient. Used with a pressure-sensitive tablet, computer artists can create the look of traditional media.

object (1) In computer graphics, a distinct entity. For example, a polygon might be an object in a graphics program. (2) A shorthand term for object code. (3) In object-oriented programming, a variable comprising both routines and data that is treated as a discrete entity. The primitive element in object-oriented programming. Something you can do things to. An object has state, behavior, and identity; the structure and behavior of similar objects are defined in their common class.

object file graphic formats See CDR, CGM, DFX, EPS, GEM, HPC, HPGL, MacDraw, PIC, PICT, SLD, WMF, and WPG. Contrast with bitmap file formats.

object-oriented graphics Computer graphics that are based on the use of "construction elements" such as curves, lines, and squares. Object-oriented graphics describe an image mathematically as a set of instructions for creating the objects in the image. Object-oriented graphics enable the user to manipulate objects as entire units. Because objects are described mathematically, object oriented graphics can also be rotated, magnified and layered relatively easily. Object-oriented graphics can usually be displayed or printed at the full resolution of the monitor or output device, offering more precision than bit mapped images.

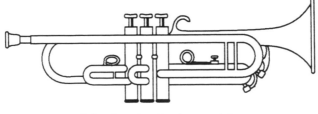

object-oriented graphics

188

object-oriented interface A graphical interface that uses icons and a mouse, such as the Apple Macintosh Finder, Microsoft Windows on IBM-compatible microcomputers, or GEM environment on Atari ST microcomputers.

object-oriented programming (OOP) A programming technology that is generally more flexible and adaptable than standard programming. Object-oriented programming lets you create procedures about objects whose exact type is not known until run time. Xerox's Smalltalk was the first object-oriented language and was used to create the graphical user interface whose derivations and imitations are so popular today. C++ is an object-oriented programming language that combines traditional C programming with object-oriented features.

object space The coordinate system in which a graphics object is defined.

oblique A style of text created by slanting a Roman font to simulate italics when a true italic font doesn't exist on the computer or printer.

oblique axis An axis that is placed at an angle to the margins of a page.

occlusion The result of an object or a portion of an object surface being drawn behind another solid object or opaque surface. An occluded object is one that is hidden from view.

offset printing A widely used printing process in which a page is reproduced photographically on a metal or paper plate attached to a revolving cylinder. Ink is transferred from the plate to a rubber blanket from which it is transferred to paper.

one-point perspective Perspective in a drawing having a single vanishing point.

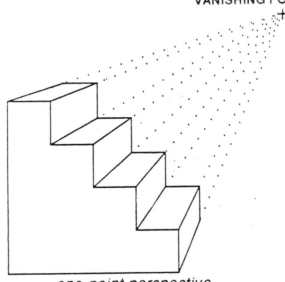

one-point perspective

189

on-screen help Operating assistance for applications that appear directly on the monitor, saving you the bother of looking them up in a manual.

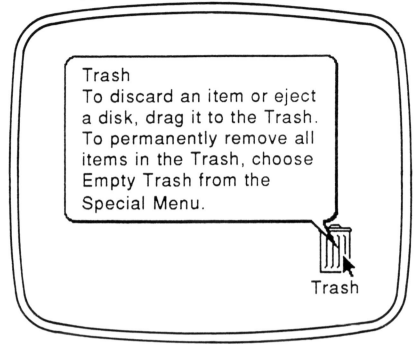

on-screen help

on-screen pasteup A layout on a computer monitor.

opacity As applied to a graphic element, the degree to which an element will hide anything in layers below it.

Op Art An art style of the mid-20th century concerned with optical stimulation and manipulation, including the creation of optical illusions.

open prepress interface Developed by the Aldus Corporation, a system for automating the placement of color photographs, usually when sending desktop files to a high-end system.

open system A vendor-independent system that is designed to interconnect with a variety of products that are commonly available.

operating system (OS) The master set of programs that manage the computer. Among other things, an operating system controls input and output to and from the keyboard, screen, disks, and other peripheral devices; loads and begins the execution of other programs; manages the storage of data on disks; and provides scheduling and accounting services.

optical computer A type of computer, still largely experimental, that uses laser beams instead of wires to process information and works far faster than traditionally wired computers.

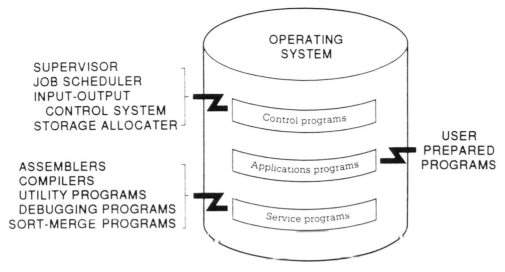

SUPERVISOR
JOB SCHEDULER
INPUT-OUTPUT
 CONTROL SYSTEM
STORAGE ALLOCATER

OPERATING
SYSTEM

Control programs

Applications programs

Service programs

USER
PREPARED
PROGRAMS

ASSEMBLERS
COMPILERS
UTILITY PROGRAMS
DEBUGGING PROGRAMS
SORT-MERGE PROGRAMS

operating system

optical art A form of visual fine art in which an object (usually consisting of clearly defined geometrical figures) is designed so as to produce a strong visual effect. Also called op art.

optical art

191

optical disc A large capacity storage device. Several types of optical discs are available: CD-ROM (compact disc, read-only memory), WORM (write once, read many) and erasable optical disc drives that let you write data as well as read it. Erasable optical discs are impervious to magnetic fields and can hold data for many years. This storage technology uses a laser beam to store large amounts of data at relatively low cost.

optical disc

optical illusion A visual image that confuses the viewer and is deceptive.

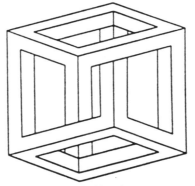

optical illusion

optical mouse A mouse that uses reflected light to determine position and movement. Contrast with mechanical mouse.

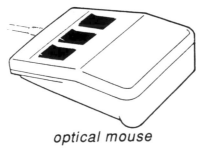

optical mouse

optical scanning Any input method by which information is converted for machine processing by evaluating the relative reflectance of that information to the background on which it appears.

optomechanical mouse A type of mouse in which motion is translated into directional signals through a combination of optical and mechanical means.

ordinate The perpendicular distance of a point form the x-axis. Contrast with abscissa.

origin (1) The location in Cartesian coordinates from which the axis originate. This is the location (0,0) in two-dimensional graphics and (0,0,0) in three-dimensional graphics.

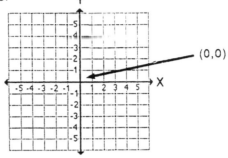

origin

origin point The lower left corner where the two axes of a graph or chart intersect.

orphan (1) First line of a paragraph sitting alone at the bottom of a page of text. Considered undesirable in all forms of printing. (2) Personal computer that has been discontinued and is no longer supported by its manufacturer.

orthogonal view A "straight-on" view of an object (front, side, or top) that is perpendicular to both the viewing angle and the lines of projection.

orthographic Type of layout, drawing, or map in which the projecting lines are perpendicular to the plane of the drawing or map.

OS Acronym for Operating System. A group of programs that control a computer and make it possible for users to enter and run their own programs. Some examples of OS are: MS-DOS, OS/2, System 7 and UNIX.

OS/2 A microcomputer operating system from Microsoft Corporation and IBM Corporation that allows multitasking by a single user. OS/2 was introduced in 1987. Several important OS/2 subsystems include Presentation Manager, which provides a graphical user interface, and LAN Manager, which provides networking facilities. OS/2 is designed for use on microcomputers based on Intel 80x86 processors: 80286, 80386 and 80486.

outdent In word processing, a line of text that extends farther to the left than other lines in the same paragraph. Opposite of indentation.

outline drawing A drawing consisting of an outline shape or a repeated sequence of outline shapes.

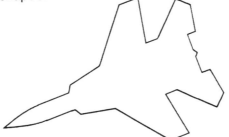

outline drawing

outline font A font that is made up of basic outlines for each character. A printer or screen font in which a mathematical formula generates each character, producing a graceful and undistorted outline of the character, which the printer then fills in at its maximum resolution. You can scale outline distortions. Outline fonts are available as built-in fonts in many PostScript printers and as downloadable fonts provided on disk.

outline font

output device Unit used for taking out data values from a computer and presenting them in the desired form to the user, such as a printer or display screen.

output device

output media Physical substance upon which output information is recorded, such as paper, magnetic disk, or magnetic tape.

output primitive Simple graphical objects provided by a graphics library for use in the construction of more complex objects.

overhead scanner A digital scanner that resembles a photographic enlarger. The original is placed on a table or bed beneath the sensor head, which is suspended about a foot over the copy. No internal light source is required. Ambient illumination in the room provides the sensor with enough light. A pivoting mechanism inside the sensor head directs the scanner's "eye" at each line of the original in turn.

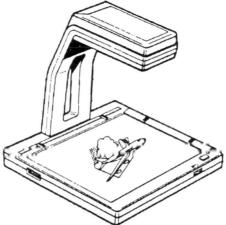

overhead scanner

overlay (1) In computer graphics, a graphics image superimposed over a portion of another image. (2) In desktop publishing, a sheet laid on top of another to specify spot colors for printing. (3) In programming, a portion of a program that is called into memory as needed, overlaying the previous redundant section of the program. Overlays allow writing programs that are much bigger than those which could fit into memory all at once.

overprint Process of printing more than once at the same position in order to emphasize or improve the type. For example, to print an element of one color over one of another color.

overstriking Ability of a hard-copy printer to strike a character more than once to produce special effects: boldface characters, character with a line through it, etc.

packaged software Software that is packaged and sold in stores and by mail order. The prepared package consists of the program on diskette(s), operating manual and possibly other documentation.

packaged system A fully integrated computer system that includes both hardware and software.

pad Any keyboard input device associated with a computer graphics system.

paddle A hand-held input device used to move the cursor on the display screen through the use of a dial. Paddles are commonly used in computer games.

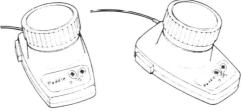

paddle

page (1) That area of a computer memory large enough to store a complete image. (2) A leaf in a book.

page break (1) In word processing, the location where one page ends and another begins. (2) A special code placed in a documentation to mark the end of a page.

page composition Adding type to a layout.

page composition program A program for designing and producing professional looking documents. Also called a desktop publishing program.

page description language (PDL) A programming language with specialized instructions for describing how to print a whole page. If an application generates output in a page description language, the output can be printed on any printer that supports it.

page design The process of specifying the boundaries of text or graphics on a page. Includes choosing margins, page length, headings and footings.

page layout In publishing, the process of arranging text and graphics on a page.

page layout program In desktop publishing, an application program that assembles text and graphics from a variety of files, with which you can determine the precise placement, scaling, sizing, and cropping of material in accordance with the page design represented on-screen. Popular page layout programs are PageMaker, Quark XPress, and Ventura Publisher.

pagination The integration of text, illustrations and pictures into a whole page.

PageMaker A desktop publishing program for IBM-compatible and Apple Macintosh microcomputers. It was introduced in 1985 by Aldus Corporation. This program set the standard for desktop publishing. Paul Brainerd, president of Aldus, coined the term of desktop publishing.

page makeup program A program for designing and producing professional looking documents. Also called desktop publishing program.

page-out Process of swapping programs or data from the computer's main storage to disk storage.

page preview A mode found on many page layout and word processing programs that shows a full-page view of how a page will look when printed out, including added elements such as headers, footers, and margins.

page printer Printer in which an entire page of characters is composed and determined within the device prior to printing. The most common example is a laser printer.

page printer

page reader Piece of optical scanning equipment that scans many lines of information, with the scanning pattern being determined by program control and/or control symbols intermixed with input data.

page recognition A program that recognizes the content of a printed page which has been scanned into the computer.

page Amount of text or graphic material displayed on a screen at one time.

pagination (1) Electronic manipulation of graphics and blocks of type for the purpose of setting up an entire page. (2) Breakup of a printed report into units that correspond to pages. (3) Process of numbering or ordering pages.

paint In computer graphics, the process of creating a graphic image (painting) on the display screen using a paint program and a mouse or graphics tablet.

paint

paintbrush In computer paint programs, a tool used to sketch or paint brushstrokes of varying width and, in some cases, calligraphic or shadowing effects.

paintbrush software A program that generates drawings or illustrations.

paint file format A bit mapped graphics file format found in paint programs such as Deluxe Paint, MacPaint, PC Paintbrush and SuperPaint.

painting (1) The process of displaying graphic data on a visual display screen. (2) In a paint program, filling a selected area with a solid color or pattern. (3) Displaying the trial of movements of a graphical input device.

Painting Effects An image editing/paint program for IBM-compatible microcomputer systems operating in MS-DOS. The program imports video or scanned images and can create different variations of the scanned or captured image.

paint program A program for creating and manipulating pixel images, as opposed to creating and manipulating object-oriented graphics. A paint program, because it treats a drawing as a group of dots (pixels), is particularly appropriate for freehand drawing. Paint programs create raster graphics images.

Palatino A serif typeface included as a built-in font with many PostScript laser printers.

palette (1) Set of available colors or patterns in a computer graphics system. (2) In a paint program, a collection of drawing tools, such as patterns, colors, different line widths, brush shapes, from which the user can choose.

palette

pan (1) In computer graphics, to move (while viewing) to a different part of an image. (2) To move the cursor across a spreadsheet. (3) A function allowing the user to view an off-screen section of a drawing.

pane Term for each of the windows that result from splitting a single window.

panning Movement of displayed graphic data across a visual display screen. Moving a graphic image inside a frame to see its various sections.

Pantone Matching System (PMS) Specific ink color specifications widely used in printing and color graphics. Catalog of Pantone colors are available which describe about 1000 colors; each assigned a unique PMS number. The Pantone color-selection system is supported by a variety of high-end illustration programs. A color system standardized by the Pantone Corporation.

paper feed Method by which paper is pulled through a printer.

paperless engineering The use of Computer-Aided Design and Drafting (CADD) systems to design products and buildings without the use of paper materials.

parabola A graphics curve that can be obtained by cutting a right circular cone by a plane parallel to one of the elements. It may also be described as the path of a point which moves so that it remains equidistant from a fixed point and a fixed line. See conic sections.

parallax Refers to the apparent displacement in space of the position of an object viewed from two or more different places not in a straight line. Used to permit the calculation of the image of three-dimensional objects displayed on graphic output devices.

parallel Describes lines or planes in a graphics file that are an equal distance apart at every corresponding point.

parallel printer Printer that receives information from the computer one character (letter, number, etc.) at a time through eight wires. Additional wires are used to exchange control signals. A parallel printer is designed to be connected to the computer's parallel port.

parallel projection The process of projecting an image from the three-dimensional view volume onto the two-dimensional graphics display with parallel projectors. Objects at any distance from the eye point maintain their apparent size under parallel projection.

PARC Acronym for Palo Alto Research Center. An advanced research and development arm of the Xerox Corporation which developed many of the underlying techniques for Smalltalk and graphical user interface.

part The graphic and nongraphic representation of a physical part designed on a graphics system.

particle systems A method of graphically producing the appearance of amorphous substances, such as smoke, fire, and clouds.

Pascal High-level structural programming language that has gained wide acceptance as a tool for both applications programming and system development. Pascal was developed in the early 1970s by Niklaus Wirth. Pascal was named after the French mathematician Blaise Pascal. The language provides a flexible set of control structures and data types to permit orderly, top-down program design and development. Pascal is used extensively in the educational field for teaching programming principles and practices.

passive graphics Non-interactive graphics, as, for example, in the applications of instrumentation and process control − where the operator is simply receiving visual information.

paste To place information previously cut from a document into a new position. With some computer systems, areas of text or graphics may be cut from a document, saved, and later pasted into another document. See cut-and-paste.

pasteboard In desktop publishing, the work area displayed on a screen upon which art and text will be placed.

patch A portion of an object surface defined by some number of points.

path (1) A route from one point to another. (2) In computer graphics, an accumulation of line segments or curves, to be filled or overwritten with text. (3) Hierarchy of files through which control passes to find a particular file.

pattern A set of objects in space, distinguishable from or comparable to another set.

pattern fill A graphics technique which involves creating a pattern by drawing a pattern element, then placing it into temporary storage. This pattern element can then be accessed and used for filing a bounded area.

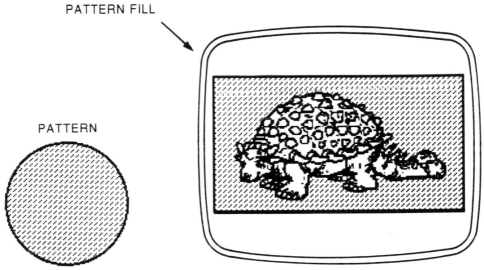

PATTERN FILL

PATTERN

pattern fill

pattern generation Transforming CAD integrated circuit design information into a simpler format (rectangles only, or trapezoids only) suitable for use by a photo or electron-beam machine in producing a reticle.

pattern matching The search for similarities between symbolic expressions; i.e., matching a pattern with images or templates in a database.

pattern recognition (1) Recognition of forms, shapes, or configurations by automatic means. A subfield of artificial intelligence. (2) Using a computer to identify patterns. (3) The use of statistical techniques and templates to process and classify patterns of data. (4) In image processing, the analysis, description, identification, and classification of objects.

PC Acronym for Personal Computer, Pocket Computer, Portable Computer, Printed Circuit, and Program Counter. The most common use of PC is to refer to IBM Corporation's Personal Computer line. Thus, for example, PC-compatible refers to a computer that can run the same programs as IBM PC or IBM PS/2 microcomputers.

PC compatibility Refers to a microcomputer that is compatible in some way with the popular IBM Personal Computer and IBM PS/2. Many levels of compatibility are possible.

PC-DOS Acronym for Personal Computer-Disk Operating System. IBM Corporation's trade name for its version of MS-DOS, an operating system developed and licensed by Microsoft Corporation for computers that use Intel Corporation microprocessors. There is effectively no difference between PC-DOS and MS-DOS.

PC Paint A popular painting program for microcomputers, developed by Mouse Systems Corporation.

PC Paintbrush A popular paint program for IBM-compatible microcomputers. Virtually every paint program for the IBM-compatible microcomputers is in some way a subset of Paintbrush. The industry standard PCX graphic format is a product of Paintbrush. Paintbrush creates, refines and retouches images. It includes image editing, automatic text effects, and 256 on-screen colors. The program also offers the capability to blend, smudge, and add gradient flood fills. The program can control many black-and-white, gray-scale, or color scanned images. Aside from normal draw/paint tools, other features include image capture software, outline bit mapped fonts, and built-in scanner and pre-scan controls.

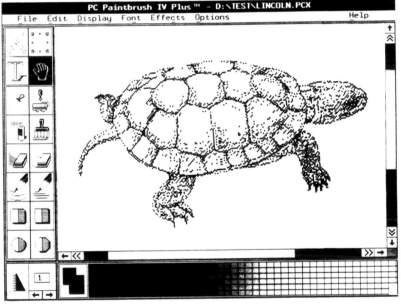

PC Paintbrush

PCX A bit mapped graphics file format, originally developed for the PC Paintbrush paint program and now used by many other programs.

PDL Acronym for Page Description Language. A standardized coding system that presents all the elements on a page — type, images and graphics, using the same descriptive metaphors. Common PDLs are PostScript, Apple Computer's QuickDraw and Hewlett-Packard's HPGL. PostScript has become the default standard for most desktop systems and PostScript interpreters are designed to convert the others to PostScript.

pel Picture element. See pixel.

pencil tool A freehand drawing tool found in all popular paint programs.

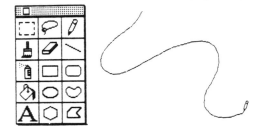

pencil tool

pen plotter An output device that generates hard copy of displayed graphic data by means of a ballpoint pen or liquid ink. Provides exceptional uniformity and density of lines, precise positional accuracy, as well as various user-selectable colors.

performance, graphic The degree to which visual graphics achieves its specified result(s). Useful measurement criteria include: display screen resolution, picture element resolution, display writing speed, internal intelligence, working area, accuracy and precision.

perfory Detachable perforated strips on the two sides of fanfold computer paper.

perfs Perforations in paper to facilitate removing pin-feed edges and tearing continuous paper into separate pages.

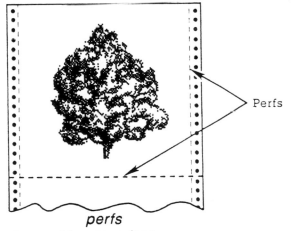

Perfs

perfs

periodicals See computer graphics magazines.

peripheral equipment Input/output units and auxiliary storage units of a computer system, attached by cables to the central processing unit. Used to get data in and data out, and to act as a reservoir for large amounts of data that cannot be held in the central processing unit at one time. The laser printer, hard disk and graphics tablet are examples of peripherals.

persistence (1) In computer graphics, the rate of decay of luminance of a CRT display after the stimulus is removed. In essence, the "staying power" of a lighted phosphor. Since a phosphor begins to dim after its excited by the electron gun(s), a long-persistence screen allows the phosphor to dim more slowly. (2) In object-oriented programming, the permanence of an object, particularly relevant in the context of object-oriented databases, which maintain a distinction between objects created only for the duration of execution and those intended for permanent storage. Persistence is one of the fundamental elements of the object model. (3) In artificial intelligence, the length of time data are kept during a program run.

personal computer The smallest and least expensive class of computer. A computer designed for use by one person at a time. Abbreviated PC. Also called a microcomputer.

personal computer

perspective rendering Computer graphics generated from a three-dimensional database, but displayed two-dimensionally.

perspective view In computer graphics, a display method by which an illusion of depth is achieved on a two-dimensional surface and by which the space depicted is organized from one point of view.

perspective view

PFS: First Publisher An entry-level desktop publishing program for people who want to create newsletters, memos, flyers, and reports. PFS: First Publisher directly reads files from most popular word processing programs and supports a wide variety of printers.

PGA Acronym for Professional Graphics Adapter, a type of display adapter for IBM-compatible microcomputers.

PHIGS Acronym for Programmer's Hierarchical Interactive Graphics System. An international standard thru-dimensional graphics library consisting of a graphical tool for application programmers. PHIGS is designed for easy portability to many graphics systems.

Phong shading A sophisticated smooth shading algorithm that was originated by Phong Bui-tuong. The algorithm is best known for its ability to render precise, realistic specular highlights. Phong shading achieves excellent realism by calculating the amount of light on the object at tiny points across the entire surface. Each pixel representing the image is given its own color based on the lighting model applied at that point.

phosphor Rare earth material used to coat the inside face of cathode ray tubes. Holds the light generated by a monitor's electron guns. Each dot on the screen is actually a phosphor that glows for a given length of time. The dots are used to create an image.

phosphor burn-in What occurs when the same image is left on the screen for extended periods of time, burning itself in so the image can be seen even when the monitor is turned off.

photocomposition Application of electronic processing to the preparation of print. Involves the specification and setting of type, and its production by a photographic process. In desktop publishing, the use of laser printers and imagesetters to accomplish the same ends.

PhotoMac A Macintosh graphics program from Avalon Development that is designed for manipulating and color separating scanned images. The program features many powerful separation controls. Like all color separation programs, PhotoMac produces four separate versions of a page.

Photon Paint A paint program intended for Macintosh II computer systems equipped with a color card.

photo plotter A CAD output device that generates high-precision artwork masters photographically for printed circuit board design and IC masks.

photorealism The process of creating images that are as close to photographic quality as possible. In computer graphics, photorealism requires powerful computers and highly sophisticated software and is heavily mathematical.

photorealism

Photoshop This powerful and versatile 24-bit image processing program, for the Apple Macintosh computer, can be used as a paint, pre-press, color correction and darkroom system. Designers can work with scanned photos, slides, electronic artwork or create original graphics using a full range of filters, painting, drawing and selection tools. It includes sophisticated image manipulation tools, antialiased text in any size and resolution and EPS graphics support.

phototypesetter Computer-controlled device that converts text into professional-quality type. A printer similar to a laser printer, but capable of resolutions over 2000 dpi. See imagesetter.

PIC Acronym for PICture File Format, a graphics file format used by some spreadsheet and graphing programs for IBM-compatible microcomputers.

pica (1) A unit of measure used in typography. A pica is one sixth of an inch, or equivalent to 12 points. (2) A character font that has a print density of 10 characters per inch.

picking A feature of a graphics library that enables an application user to select primitives and objects with a pointing device.

picking device Input device, such as a light pen, mouse, or joystick, used to enter data on a display screen.

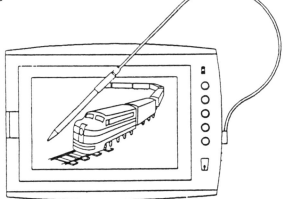

picking device

PICT Acronym for PICTure file format, a black-and-white object/bit mapped formatted used by many programs for the Apple Macintosh line of microcomputers and by some programs for the IBM-compatible microcomputers.

pictorial That having to do with the art of painting and drawing.

PICT2 Acronym for PICTure file format 2, a graphics file format used in many programs for the Apple Macintosh line of microcomputers that can support both black-and-white and color images.

picture element See pixel.

206

picture graph Bar graph that uses symbols instead of bars.

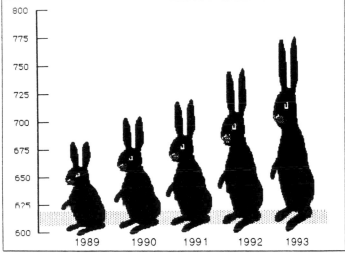

picture graph

picture processing (1) In computer graphics, method for processing pictorial information by a computer system. Involves inputting graphic information into a computer system, storing it, working with it, and outputting it to an output device. (2) In artificial intelligence, the transformation of an input image into a second image, which has important properties that will help in better understanding the scene.

Picture Publisher A graphics program that allows you to work with scanned images. You can adjust contrast, brightness, gray map, and other parameters, and edit the image on a pixel-by-pixel basis. Image processing choices let you sharpen, blur, or posterize the image.

P & ID An acronym for Piping and Instrumentation Diagram. A schematic, two-dimensional drawing which shows the major equipment, pipelines, and components to be used in a particular process plant design. Can be constructed on a CAD system.

pie chart Graphical representation of information; charting technique used to represent portions of a whole.

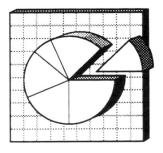

pie chart

207

PIL Acronym for Publishing Interchange Language. An Apple Macintosh file format which let applications exchange page-description information.

pin-feed Paper-feed system that relies on a pin-studded roller to draw paper, punched with matching sprocket holes, into a printer.

pitch Density of characters on a printed line, usually expressed in terms of characters per inch; for example, 10 pitch means that 10 characters are printed in every inch.

pixel Short for "picture element," a picture cell; a single dot on the computer display screen. The visual display screen is divided into rows and columns of tiny dots, squares, or cells, each of which is a pixel. Smallest unit on the display screen grid that can be stored, displayed, or addressed.

EACH PIXEL IS A DOT OF LIGHT ON THE SCREEN

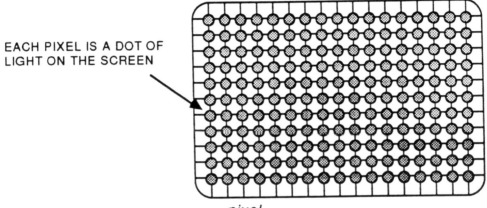

pixel

pixel graphics A technique for representing a picture image as a matrix of dots.

pixel image The representation of a graphic in a computer's memory.

pixel operations Pixel data is stored as numbers which are converted into color, or other information. Arithmetic and logical operations can be performed on this data for image modification.

PixelPaint Professional A popular Apple Macintosh paint program. Features capabilities include the ability to create a masking tool from any brush, tool, or image. A WetPaint feature allows repositioning and editing of any shape or text before merging it with the rest of the bit map. A gradient editor creates precise color ramps with multiple anchor points. A unique feature of PixelPaint that creates surface textures such as charcoal paper, linen, concrete, canvas and slate; other textures can be scanned in. File formats supported include MacPaint, PICT, TIFF and EPSF. Artwork can be printed to PostScript or QuickDraw printers or produced as 4-color or spot color separations.

pixmap The array of values in the frame buffer for a given picture.

planar (1) In computer graphics, a term applied to objects lying on a plane. (2) In the fabrication of chips, planar refers to a processing method used to create silicon-based transistors.

plane Any flat or level surface.

plane figures Any set of points in a plane. Some common plane figures are angles, triangles rectangles, and circles.

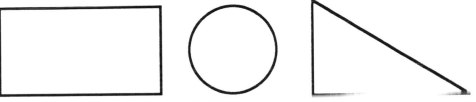

plane figures

plasma display panel Type of VDT utilizing trapped neon/argon gas. The image is created by turning on points in a matrix (energized grid of wires) comprising the display surface. The high-resolution image is steady, long-lasting, bright, and flicker-free; selective erasing is possible.

plate A thin, flexible sheet of metal, paper, or plastic used in offset printing. It contains a photographic reproduction of the page being printed.

platen A backing, commonly cylindrical, against which printing mechanisms strike to produce an impression, such as the roller in a printer against which the keys strike.

platform (1) The compute hardware in a graphics system (or other computer system). (2) A software library.

platonic objects Figures constructed from regular polygons: tetrahedron, cube, octahedron, icosahedron, and dodecahedron.

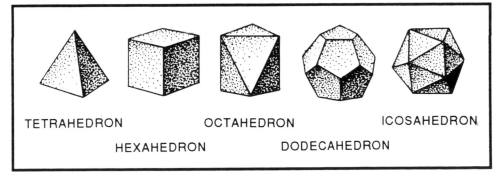

TETRAHEDRON   OCTAHEDRON   ICOSAHEDRON

HEXAHEDRON   DODECAHEDRON

platonic objects

PLB An acronym for Picture Level Benchmark, a graphics system performance indicator that measures frames per second, or the length of time it takes to draw a picture on the display screen. The PLB is intended to provide a consistent method of measuring graphics performance.

plot To diagram, draw, or map with a plotter. To create an image by drawing a series of lines.

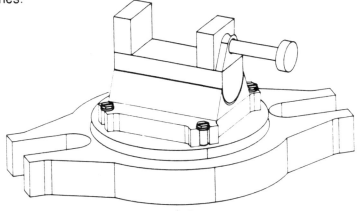

plot

plotter An output device that draws images with ink pens. A plotter draws images as a series of point-to-point lines. Plotter types includes: pen, drum, electrostatic, and flatbed.

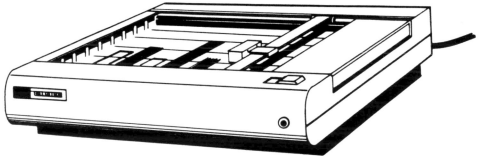

plotter

plotting a curve Locating points from coordinates and connecting these points with a curve that approximates or resembles the actual curve that pictures the relationship existing between variables.

PLT Abbreviation for plotter, a peripheral device for providing output of graphs and technical drawings.

PMS See Pantone Matching System.

point (1) Typographic measurement equaling approximately 1/72 inch, abbreviated pt. (2) Smallest unit of graphic information, representing a single location on a coordinate system.

point and click To position the cursor over an object displayed on the screen (point) and press the mouse or pointing device to select it (click).

pointer (1) A indicator on a screen that shows where the next user computer interaction will be. Also called a cursor. (2) Address or other indication of one storage location as held in another storage location. Used in a network database to point to related records in the same or different files. (3) A device such as a mouse or tablet stylus that moves the cursor on the screen. (4) The additional connections in a network database between parent nodes and child nodes. (5) A variable that holds the address of another memory object.

pointer tool A tool used in layout and drawing programs to select objects or an entire block of text. It is usually represented by an on-screen arrow.

pointillism A painting procedure in which dots or spots of color are used to create colors and values by optical mixing. In a computer graphics system, the paintbrush tool, found in most paint programs, can be used to procedure the pointillism type of art form.

pointillism

pointing device A input device, such as a mouse or graphics tablet, that is used to move the cursor on the display screen.

pointing device

point set curve Curve defined by a series of short lines drawn between points.

point size The vertical measurement of type, roughly equivalent to the distance between the highest ascender and lowest descender, plus a small bit of breathing room on top and bottom.

polar coordinates Graphic system for specifying the location of a point by reference to an angle and a distance from a fixed point. Contrast with Cartesian coordinate system.

polarizing filter Accessory for terminal screens to reduce glare.

polygon A shape formed by three or more connected lines enclosing an area. Rectangles, triangles, squares, and any irregular-shaped lines that close on themselves are examples of polygons. An n-gon is a polygon with an undetermined number of sides. A polygon is one of the standard graphics primitives.

polygon

polygon mesh A portion of a mesh model surface constructed from polygons.

polyhedron A solid formed by portions of plane surfaces which are called the faces (usually more than six faces). A cube is a polyhedron.

  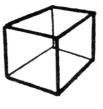

FACE

polyhedron

polyline In computer graphics, a line consisting of multiple connected segments.

polyline

polymorphic tweening An animation technique that, based on information about its starting and ending shapes, creates the necessary "in-between" steps to change one object into another.

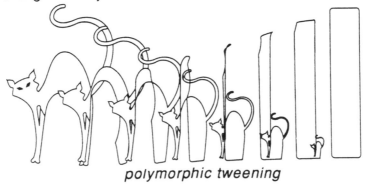

polymorphic tweening

212

Pop Art A style of drawing that used popular and commercial symbols and images as subject matter.

Pop Art

pop erase A method for erasing graphic entities that clears parts of the screen in a single action, so that all dots appear to turn off simultaneously.

pop-up menu A menu that appears on-screen anywhere other than in the standard menu bar location.

port That portion of a computer through which a peripheral device may communicate. Plug-in/socket on the back of the computer for connecting cables for peripherals.

portability Ease with which a program can be moved from one computer environment to another. Many programs written in high-level languages may be used on different machines. These programs are, therefore portable.

portable computer A self-contained computer that can be easily carried and moved. Compared to desktop models, it has limited expansion slots and disk capacity.

portable computer

Portfolio A professional illustrative graphics program for IBM-compatible microcomputers. Aside from an enhanced list of usual drawing tools, there's a raster and vector based system, a full featured text editor with scalable fonts and spelling checker, a feature to import files directly from word processors, an autotrace feature and templates of two-dimensional and three-dimensional charts and graphs.

portrait An orientation in which the data is printed across the narrow side of the form.

portrait mode A video monitor display screen whose height is greater than its width, like a portrait painting. Contrast with landscape mode.

portrait monitor A monitor with a screen shape higher than it is wide. A popular type monitor in desktop publishing systems.

portrait monitor

position stat A copy of a halftone which can be placed on a mechanical to illustrate positioning and cropping of the image.

posterization A photographic effect in which the number tones and colors in an image is reduced to achieve a poster-like effect. The same effect can be achieved in computer graphics by reassigning the color values, substituting one color scale for another.

posterize To transform an image to a more stark version by rounding tonal values or color values to a smaller number of possible values.

posterize

PostScript A proprietary language developed by Adobe Corporation to tell a printer what to print on a particular page. PostScript's chief benefit is its device independence, that is to say that the same file can be printed to printers of varying resolutions.

PostScript font A font defined in terms of the PostScript page-description language rules and intended to be printed on a PostScript-compatible printer.

PostScript laser printer A laser printer that includes the processing circuitry needed to decode and interpret printing instructions phrased in PostScript – a page description language widely used in desktop publishing. The printer converts the PostScript instructions (sent by the computer) into the dots that make up the printed image.

PostScript Level 2 An updated version of the PostScript language that adds support for color, forms handling, data compression and many other features.

posture The slant of the characters in a font.

PPM Acronym for Pages Per Minute, a measure of output for printing devices, i.e., the number of printed pages output per minute.

preprocessing The steps that may be used on an image between the capturing of the image and any analysis. Typically, preprocessing might include contrast enhancement, averaging and so on.

presentation graphics High quality professional looking business graphics. Used in proposals, business presentations, manuals and other business related documents. An easy-to-understand display of numerical information. Presentation graphics are visually appealing and easily understood by an audience.

presentation graphics

presentation graphics program An application program designed to create and enhance charts and graphs so that they are visually appealing and easily understood by an audience.

Presentation Manager The graphical user interface provided in OS/2, jointly developed by Microsoft Corporation and IBM Corporation. Presentation Manager brings to IBM-compatible microcomputers, running the OS/2 operating system, many of the graphical user interface features associated with the Apple Macintosh computer – pull-down menus, multiple on-screen windows, desktop accessories, and multiple on-screen typefaces.

press Act of pushing down and holding the button on a mouse. See click.

pressure-sensitive pen Stylus used with a digitizer. Contains a pressure transducer that detects and transmits writing pressure as Z-axis data.

primary colors Set of colors from which all others can be derived , but which cannot be produced from each other. The additive primaries (light) are blue, green, and red. The subtractive primaries (colorant) are cyan, magenta, and yellow. The psychological primaries are the pairs red/green, yellow/blue, and black/white.

primitive (1) In computer graphics the most basic graphic entities available. Primitives are the elements which large graphic designs are created. Graphics primitives include point, line segment, circle, ellipse, polyline, triangle, rectangle, square, and characters. (3) The basic building blocks of a language. In the English language individual words are primitives. In this vein, keywords in BASIC or Pascal may be considered as primitives.

print A impression produced on a graphics printer or plotter.

print

print buffer Extra RAM in the printer or an add-on board which allows you to send a print job to the printer all at once thereby freeing up the computer for other work.

print chart Form used to describe the format of an output report from a printer. Also called printer spacing chart, printer design form, and print layout sheet.

print control character Control character for operations on a line printer, such as carriage return, page ejection, or line spacing.

print density Number of printed characters per unit of measurement, such as the number of characters on a page.

print element That part of a printer that actually puts the image on paper.

print engine Part of a laser printer. The mechanism that uses a laser to create an electrostatic image of a page and fuse that image to a sheet of paper.

printer Output device that produces hard copy output.

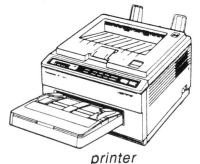

printer

printer engine The part of a page printer, such as a laser printer, that actually performs the printing.

printer font A font available for printing. There are three types of printer fonts: built-in fonts, cartridge fonts, and downloadable fonts.

printer format Pertaining to printing paper divided into print zones. Only one value can be printed in each zone.

printer resolution The number of dots a laser printer can print on a linear inch. For example, most laser printers image at 300 dpi, while high-end imagesetters print at resolutions of 1270, 2540, and higher.

printing orientation See landscape or portrait.

printing orientation

print layout sheet Chart used for establishing margin and spacing requirements for a printed report. See print chart.

printout Form of computer system output, printed on a page by a printer. See hard copy.

print quality Quality of a printout produced on a printer.

Print Shop A simple graphics package that performs several useful printing services easily and well. It prints standard and customized signs, greeting cards, posters, and letterheads, as well as multipage banners on fan-fold paper with a wide selection of fonts, icons, borders, and graphics. Developed by Broderbund Software.

procedural modelling Time-saving methods for constructing computer models whereby the object geometry is not defined directly but is represented as a procedure, e.g. a staircase is created with three input variables: height, width and stair type.

process camera A camera used in graphic arts to photograph mechanicals and create printing plates.

process color Printing that used only four standard colored inks to create the illusion of thousands of colors. The inks are (in order of typical printing); Yellow (Y), Magenta (M) (sort of a hot pink color), Cyan (C) (sort of a turquoise color), and Black (K). The actual hues are strictly controlled within the ink industry.

processing Computer manipulation of data in solving a problem.

processor (1) The central processing unit of a computer. (2) A computer is sometimes referred to as a language processor. (3) In addition to the central processing unit, many sophisticated graphics systems contain a dedicated processor for graphics acceleration.

processor bound Pertaining to system performance that is slowed by the time it takes the central processing unit to perform the actual processing or computations. Same as compute-bound.

Professional Graphics Adapter (PGA) A video adapter introduced by the IBM Corporation and used primarily for computer-aided design applications.

Professional Write A full-featured word processing program designed for executive users.

profile An outline; especially refers to the face seen from the side.

profile

program Series of instructions that will cause a computer to process data. It may be in a high-level source form, which requires intermediate processing before the computer can execute it, or it may be in an object form directly executable by the computer.

programmer Person whose job is to design, write, and test software.

programming The process of setting up a procedure for problem solving which can be understood by a specific computer.

projection Producing a two-dimensional graphics display of a three-dimensional scene.

projective geometry The study of those properties of geometric configurations that are invariant under projection.

219

prompt Any message output by a computer graphics system that requires some response from the operator.

CHOOSE SCREEN EFFECT
❑ MEZZOTINT
❑ HORIZONTAL LINE
❑ TILE
❑ CROSSHATCH

prompt

proof (1) A trial copy of a page or publication used to check accuracy. (2) Short for proofread, meaning to check for mistakes.

proofreaders' marks In desktop publishing, a standard set of notations for indicating errors or corrections on a proof.

proportion The relation, or ratio, of one part to another and of each part to the whole with regard to size, height, width, length, or depth.

proportional font A set of characters in a particular style and size in which a variable amount of horizontal space is allotted to each letter, number or special character. In a proportional font, the letter l, for example, is allowed less space than the letter w.

proportional spacing If the horizontal space allotted to a printed character is proportional to the width of that character, the spacing is said to be proportional. Since this book is typeset in proportional spacing, the "w" in the word "write" consumes more space than the "i." Standard typewriter style, in contrast, allots equal space to all characters.

PS/1 A home computer from IBM Corporation introduced in 1990.

PS/2 A series of personal computers from IBM Corporation introduced in 1987. This second generation of IBM personal computers superseded its original personal computer series. The PS/2 introduced three major changes: VGA graphics, Micro Channel bus, and 3.5-inch floppy disks.

PS/2

publication window In desktop publishing, a display screen consisting of a pasteboard, icons, scroll bar, ruler, and toolbox.

public domain software Software not protected by copyright laws and therefore free for all to reproduce and trade without fear of legal prosecution. Any computer program donated to the public by its creator. Public domain software may be duplicated by others at will.

Publish It! A full-featured desktop publishing program that allows the designing, layout, production, and printing of professional looking documents. Publish It! runs on IBM-compatible microcomputers.

puck Hand-held, manually controlled, graphics input device used to pinpoint coordinates on a digitizing tablet. Has a transparent window containing cross hairs and allows coordinate data to be digitized into the system from a drawing placed on the digitizing tablet surface.

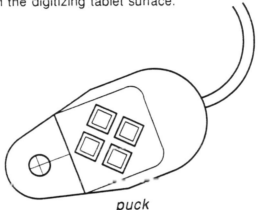

puck

pull-down menu A second-level menu, or list of commands, that appears from the top of the screen when a command needs to be given and then disappears when the selection has been made. A pull-down menu is usually used as an extension to a menu bar. To select an option on a pull-down menu, one presses and holds down the mouse button while dragging the mouse pointer down the menu until the wanted option is highlighted.

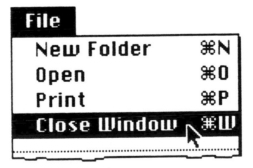

pull-down menu

pull-down quote In desktop publishing, a quotation extracted from the copy of text and printed in larger type in the column.

221

quad An abbreviation for quadrilateral.

quadrilateral A closed polygon with four vertices, and thus four sides.

quadrilateral mesh A surface defined by four-sided polygons, each attached to other quadrilaterals.

quantization In image processing, a process in which each pixel in an image is assigned one of a finite set of gray levels.

Quark Xpress A page layout program for the Apple Macintosh computer from Quark, Inc. It is noted for its precise typographic control and sophisticated graphics capabilities. Quark XPress allows unlimited document length and includes many word processing features.

QuickDraw A graphics language system built into the ROM of the Apple Macintosh computer. Application programs call on QuickDraw for on-screen displays. QuickDraw consists of a series of primitive shapes, lines, and fill patterns which can be mathematically modified. When printing to PostScript printers, QuickDraw must be translated during the printing process by a program called a PostScript interpreter.

QWERTY keyboard Keyboard arrangement that is standard on most keyboards found on typewriters, word processors, and computers. Developed more than a century ago to slow down swift typists and prevent jamming of the old mechanical typewriters. The design is called QWERTY after the first six letters on the top alphabetic line of the keyboard. Now that electronics can accommodate high-speed typing, QWERTY is no longer efficient. Many businesses are replacing QWERTY keyboards with the more efficient Dvorak keyboard. Some computer companies now offer keyboards with a switch that will change from one keyboard to the other.

QWERTY keyboard

radial fill A varying color or tint that changes smoothly from one color or brightness to another, usually moving from the center of an object out toward the edges.

radial symmetry A radially symmetrical object is generated around a central axis, much like an object is shaped on a lathe. Many three-dimensional programs allow you to set the number of segments the object should have.

radio button In a graphical user interface, the round option buttons that appear in dialog boxes. Only one radio button can be selected within a group of radio buttons.

Radio Shack A manufacturer and distributor of electronic equipment, including microcomputer systems sold under the name of TRS-80 or Tandy. A division of the Tandy Corporation.

radiosity A technique that calculates the lighting in a complex diffuse lighting environment, based on the geometry of the scene.

rag The irregularity along the left or right ends of the lines on a printed page. See ragged left margin and ragged right margin.

RAGGED
RIGHT

Of Australia's
roughly 200 species of
marsupials (mammals
whose young develop
further in their mothers'
abdominal pouches af-
ter birth), the 40-odd
species of kangaroos
are the best known.
The red kangaroo
(Macropus rufus) is the
largest of all marsupi-
als, with a head-and-
body length of about 65
inches and a weight of

JUSTIFIED

Of Australia's roughly
200 species of marsupi-
als (mammals whose
young develop further in
their mothers' abdominal
pouches after birth), the
40-odd species of kanga-
roos are the best known.
The red kangaroo
(Macropus rufus) is the
largest of all marsupials,
with a head-and-body
length of about 65 inches
and a weight of about 180
pounds. It can jump up to

RAGGED
LEFT

Of Australia's roughly
200 species of marsupi-
als (mammals whose
young develop further in
their mothers' abdomi-
nal pouches after birth),
the 40-odd species of
kangaroos are the best
known. The red kanga-
roo (Macropus rufus) is
the largest of all marsu-
pials, with a head-and-
body length of about 65
inches and a weight of
about 180 pounds. It

rag

ragged left margin Refers to text printed with a straight right margin and an uneven left margin. Also called flush right. Contrast with left justify.

ragged right margin Text printed with a straight left margin and an uneven right margin. Also called flush left. Contrast with right justify.

RAM Acronym for Random Access Memory, a memory into which the user can enter information and instructions (write) and from which the user can call up data (read). Working memory of the computer, into which applications programs can be loaded from outside and then executed.

random scan A term used for describing display devices which allow the drawing of vectors between specified endpoints.

raster display Video display that sweeps a beam through a fixed pattern, building up an image with a matrix of points. See raster graphics. Contrast with vector display.

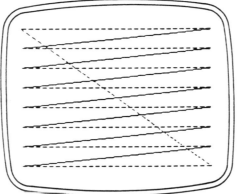

raster display

raster fill Process used by a graphics camera to fill in the spaces between the raster lines of a video screen to give a screen picture a more finished appearance.

raster graphics Manner of storing and displaying data as horizontal rows of uniform grid or picture cells (pixels). Raster scan devices recreate or refresh a display screen thirty to sixty times a second to provide clear images for viewing. Raster display devices are generally faster and less expensive than vector tubes.

raster image A display image formed by a pattern of pixels in a rectangular array.

raster image file format (RIFF) A file format for paint-style graphics developed by Letraset USA. It is an expanded version of the TIFF format used by many scanner markers.

raster image processor A devise that converts a vector image into a raster image prior to printing on an output device that requires raster technology.

rasterization The conversion of vector graphics to equivalent images composed of pixel patterns (bit mapped images).

raster scan Generation of an image on a display screen made by refreshing the display area line by line.

ray tracing In computer graphics, a method of adding a degree of realism to an image through the use of reflections, refractions, and shadows. A sophisticated and complex approach to producing high-quality computer graphics. Ray tracing is a very process-intensive operation.

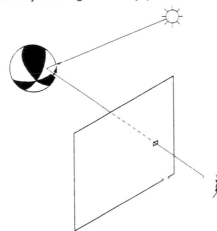

A RAY BEING TRACED
FROM THE EYE POINT
TO THE OBJECT, AND
BACK TO THE LIGHT SOURCE

ray tracing

readout Manner in which a computer represents the processed information, such as by visual display, printer, and digital plotter.

read/write head Small electromagnet used to read, write, or erase data on a magnetic storage device, such as a disk or tape.

real time The accelerated graphics processing that makes objects appear to move naturally and at a speed that appears realistic.

real-time image generation Performance of the computations necessary to update an image being completed within the refresh rate, so the sequence appears correctly to the viewer. An example is flight simulation, in which thousands of computations must be performed to present an animated image, all within the rate of 30-60 cycles per second at which the frames change.

rectangular coordinate system System in which every point in a plane is given an address in the form of a pair of numbers, called the coordinates of the point. Same as Cartesian coordinate system.

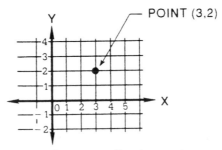

rectangular coordinate system

recto The right-handed (odd-numbered) page in a two-sided printing of a book or document.

recursive The use of something to define itself. An object is said to be recursive if it partially consists of or is defined in terms of itself. A recursive operation invokes itself as an intermediate operation.

reduced instruction set computer (RISC) A microprocessor that has only a relatively small set of instructions. RISC design is based on the premise that most of the instructions a computer decodes and executes are simple, thus RISC architecture limits the number of instructions that are built into the microprocessor but optimizes each so it can be carried out very rapidly.

reduction The changing of a larger format picture into a smaller format picture.

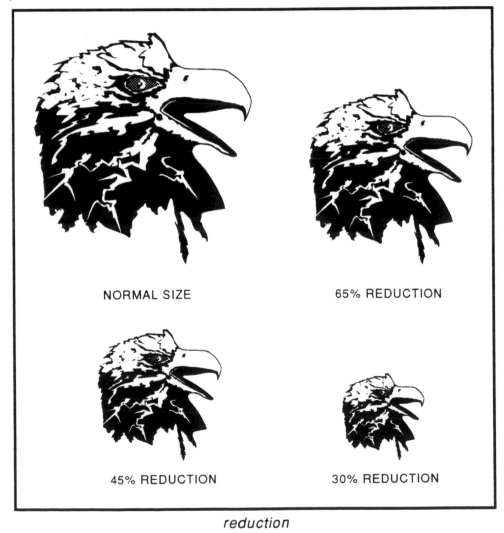

NORMAL SIZE   65% REDUCTION

45% REDUCTION   30% REDUCTION

reduction

reflect To make a mirror image of an object around a specified point or line.

reflect

reflectance In optical scanning, a relative value assigned to a character or color of ink when compared with the background.

reflectance ink In optical scanning, ink that has a reflectance level that very nearly approximates the acceptable paper reflectance level for a particular optical character reader.

reflective art Any image that is viewed by reflected light such as a drawing or photograph on paper, as opposed to transparencies which are illuminated by light shining through. Reflective art includes black-and-white photos, color prints, line art, had-drawn color art, etc.

refresh circuitry Electronic circuitry necessary to restore (1) the information displayed on a visual display screen, and (2) the data stored in dynamic RAM, which steadily lose their charge.

refresh display cycle Time between successive raster scans or passes through the vectors to be displayed on a vector device. The phosphors on the face of a CRT are excited and glow as the result of each pass of the electron beam in each refresh cycle. The refresh rate usually occurs at a level fast enough to eliminate the flicker from the brightening and fading of the phosphors each time they are struck. Typically, the image must be regenerated at a rate of 1/30th or 1/60th of a second.

refreshing Process of constantly reactivating or restoring information that decays or fades away when left idle. Phosphor on a CRT screen needs to be constantly reactivated by an electron beam to remain illuminated. Typically, the image must be regenerated at a rate of 30 to 60 hertz to avoid flicker. Likewise, cells in dynamic memory elements must be repeatedly accessed to avoid losing their contents. See dynamic RAM and raster scan.

refresh memory Area of computer memory that holds values indicating whether a particular dot of a graphics raster is on or off. May also contain information on brightness and color.

refresh rate Rate at which the graphic image on a CRT is redrawn in a refresh display; time needed for one refresh of the displayed image.

regeneration The production of a new screen image after a change in scale, position or elements.

region fill In computer graphics, the technique of filling a defined region on the screen with a selected pattern, color, or other attribute.

registration The degree of accuracy in the positioning of one larger or overlay in a graphic image or artwork, relative to another layer, as reflected by the clarity and sharpness of the resulting image.

relative coordinates Coordinates relative to a coordinate system whose origin is set at the initial position of a point selected on an object.

relative vector In computer graphics, a vector with end points designated in relative coordinates.

release number The number that identifies a specific version of a program. A program labeled 3.5, for example, is the sixth release of Version 3 of the program (the first was Version 3.0).

release version Version of a program currently available for purchase.

reliability Measure of the ability of a program, system, or individual hardware device to function without failure.

religious art Art pertaining to religion, as the Buddha, Christ, the Virgin Mary, etc.

religious art

228

remote Physically distant from a local computer, such as a terminal or printer.

COMPUTER

COMMUNICATIONS
LINK

REMOTE TERMINAL

remote

remote sensing A method of gathering image data remotely, such as by satellite or aerial photography.

renderer A program or function that takes a geometric model or description of a scene and produces the corresponding images.

rendering In computer graphics, a three-dimensional image that incorporates the simulation of effects, such as reflections, shadows, smoothness, texture and color. Usually, this means filling in a graphic object or image with color and brightness. Realistic rendering takes a lot of computing power and advanced techniques.

rendering

229

repagination Process in which a page layout or word processing program adjusts a multipage document as it is revised to ensure uniform page length and appearance.

repaint Redrawing of an image on a visual display device to reflect updated graphic or textual data. Feature on many graphics systems that automatically redraws a design displayed on the visual display screen.

repeat key Keyboard key that can be held down so it repeatedly makes contact without need for additional pressing.

replace In word processing, command that enables users to search for a word and replace it with another one.

repligraphics In computer-aided design and drafting (CADD), a concept for obtaining multiple copies of plots.

representational art Art that reproduces reality with little or no change or distortion.

representational art

reprographics Technology that includes reproduction and duplication processes for documents, written materials, pictures, drawings, and films, as well as methods of their mass reproduction, such as photocopy, offset printing, microfilming, and offset duplicating.

reset key Key on a keyboard that normally is used to restart the computer.

resident font Built-in font in a printer.

resident program Program that occupies a dedicated area of a computer's main memory (ROM or RAM) during the operating session.

resizing Process of scaling a graphics file or entity according to predetermined parameters.

resolution A term used to describe the amount of information that a video display can reproduce. A pixel is the smallest unit on the display screen grid that can be stored, displayed, or addressed. The resolution of a picture is expressed by the number of pixels in the display. A high-resolution picture looks smooth and realistic. It is produced by a large number of pixels. A low-resolution picture is blocky and jagged. It is produced by a small number of pixels. Low-resolution pictures represent surfaces with ragged edges, while high-resolution produces a finely defined image. A picture with 640 x 480 pixels is much sharper than a picture with 512 x 342 pixels. Also, 1200 dots per inch is considered to be excellent print resolution.

LOW-RESOLUTION   HIGH-RESOLUTION

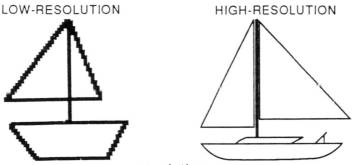

resolution

resolution, plotter Measure of the quality of a plotted image. The number of addressable points on a digital plotter determines the resolution: the more points, the higher the resolution.

resource Any component of a computer configuration. Memory, printers, visual displays, disk storage units, software, materials, and operating personnel are all considered resources.

RETURN key Key on a computer keyboard used to make the display cursor or a printer carriage move to the beginning of the next line. Used like an ENTER key on other keyboards to execute a command.

reverse print Having white type or graphics on a black background (or some variation on that theme) instead of the usual black type or graphics on a white background.

reverse print

231

reverse video A term used to indicate, in some video terminals, the ability to display dark characters on a light background. The inverse of the normal foreground and background colors on a video screen. For example, the reverse video of light characters on a dark background would be dark characters on a light screen background. Commonly used to highlight text or special items on the screen

reverse video

RF modulator A device which converts computer signals to signals which can be displayed on a TV screen.

RGB (Red, Green, Blue) The most common color model. It's the way color is created on computer monitors. Red, green and blue are called the additive primaries, because they create white light when combined, and any two produce the subtractive primaries: cyan, magenta and yellow.

RGB monitor A display screen that requires separate red, green, and blue video signals from the video source. RGB monitor is synonymous in IBM-compatible microcomputer computing with the Color Graphics Adapter (CGA) standard.

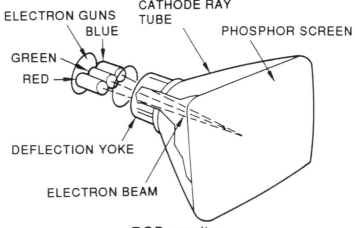

RGB monitor

RIB Acronym for RenderMan Interface Bytestream, an Apple Macintosh file format for three-dimensional images rendered in Pixar's RenderMan.

232

RIFF Acronym for Raster Image File Format. A graphics file format used to store gray-scale images. Used most often in Letraset's ImageStudio and Ready, Set Go software packages.

Rio-Sable A true color object oriented draw and image processing program. It allows users to compose scenes that combine video capture, TV-quality electronic color images or high resolution scanned images with vector-based text and geometric shapes. The program includes flexible draw and edit features for high resolution and video captured files operating in MS-DOS.

RIP Short of Raster-Image Processor, the part of a printing system that translates from the input data in the form provided by the computer to the actual dots or lines sent to the marking device.

ripple sort See bubble sort.

RISC Short for Reduced Instruction Set Computer, a computer system designed to minimize the number of different underlying operations that the microprocessor does in hardware in order to optimize the execution speed. Such systems depend on the software for functions that formerly were handled by the microprocessor.

river In desktop publishing, the presence of irregular white space between words that accidently line up vertically or diagonally.

roam To move a display window around on a visual display screen.

robo stick An input device used to manipulate the cursor and to create graphics.

rolling ball Another name for a track ball.

roll paper Printer paper in continuous form on a spool. Contrast with fanfold paper.

ROM Acronym for Read-Only Memory. Generally, a solid state storage chip programmed at the time of its manufacture and that cannot be reprogrammed by the computer user. Also called firmware, since this implies software that is permanent or firmly in place on a chip.

Roman In typography, a medium-weight typeface in which all letters are upright.

ROM cartridge Plug-in module that contains software permanently stored in ROM. A method of entering data and/or programs into a computer. The module can contain one or more printer fonts, programs, games or other information.

roping An aliasing effect in a graphics image in which a line or thin polygon appears to vary in width, color, or brightness according to a repeating pattern that suggests the braiding of a rope.

rotation In computer graphics, the turning of a computer-modeled object relative to an origin point on a coordinate system. In three-dimensional graphics, an object can be rotated in space, usually around the axis, to provide different views. In two-dimensional graphics, an object can revolve around a point.

rotation

rough draft In desktop publishing, the preliminary page layouts done by the designer using pencil sketches to represent page design ideas. A roughly drawn sketch of a finished document.

RTF Acronym for Rich-Text Format, a de facto document-formatting standard, developed by Microsoft Corporation, for exchanging information between program applications running within its Windows environment.

rubberbanding In computer graphics, changing the shape of an object made up of connected lines by "grabbing" a point on a anchored line and "pulling" it to the new location.

rubber stamp The ability to duplicate an electronically drawn object on other parts of the display screen, as many times as desired, through a single, simple command.

rule (1) A statement about the relationships of various facts or data. (2) A line, available in several sizes, and used as a box or border, or in the form of a fancy design.

ruler An on-screen ruler, marked off in inches or other units of measure, is used to show line widths, paragraph indents, center of page, tab settings, etc.

runaround Type with measures adjusted to fit around an illustration or another design element on the page.

running head A line of text at the top margin of a page; usually the title of the book, the name of the chapter, the page number, and so on. Also called header.

SAGE Acronym for Semi-Automatic Ground Environment. A U.S. Air Force command and control system developed in the mid-1950s. One of the first computer systems to use computer graphics.

SAGE

sample rate The frequency of the points used to determine an object's placement on the display device.

sampling A procedure that samples many points across an object's lines or surfaces to determine its placement in pixels.

sampling ratio When electronically scanning art or photographs, the number of pixels recorded from the original image verses the final line screen during printing. The scanner may record at 300 dpi but the finished price is printed at 150 dpi, a ratio of 2:1. The desired ratio of desktop scans is 1.5:1 to 2:1, that is 1.5 or 2 pixels are scanned for every halftone dot printed.

sans serif Letters of typefaces without serifs – the ornate, widened bases and tops seen on some characters of some type fonts. As a matter of fact, sans means "without" in French. Sans serif fonts have very clean lines and are typically considered friendly, casual and familiar.

SANS SERIF   SERIF

ABC   ABC

sans serif

satellite imaging Using computer-enhanced images taken from orbiting satellites, scientists are able to gather data and better study the Earth. Satellite imaging systems are capable of acquiring imagery that has a wider dynamic range than that of the human eye or photographic film. This imagery can be processed and manipulated into data that can be analyzed and studied by scientists for a wide variety of uses and applications.

saturation In the HSB color model, one of the three characteristics used to describe a color. Saturation refers to the degree that a color is pure or the degree of white it contains. A highly-saturated color is one that contains little white; a less-saturated color looks washed out.

save To store information somewhere other than in the computer's internal memory, such as on a tape or disk, so it can be used again.

scalable font Characters which can be scaled to any size via a page description language. By contrast, bit map fonts must be loaded for every size, using up storage space. Scalable fonts provide more flexibility than bit mapped fonts by eliminating the need to store a variety of different font sizes in the computer's memory.

scale (1) To change the size of a graphics file by a specified quantity to make it fit a specified boundary. (2) Quantity by which graphic data are multiplied or divided to fit size limitations. (3) A relationship of size between objects or elements in a visual field.

scaling (1) Process of changing one bit map density into a bit map of another density. Scaling usually involves enlarging or contracting an image. (2) Process of changing the size of an image. Scaling by a factor of three multiplies all dimensions of an image by 3.

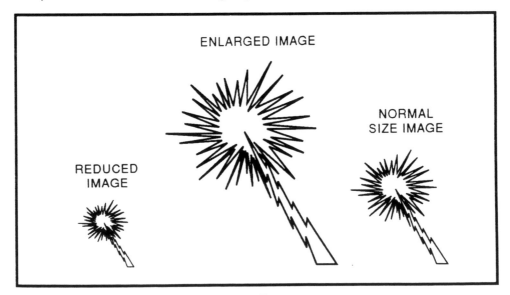

scaling

scan (1) Operation required to produce an image on a visual display screen. Involves moving a electron beam across the inner surface of the screen, one line at a time, to light the phosphor that creates a displayed image. (2) In optical technologies, to view a printed form a line at a time in order to convert images into bit mapped representations.

scan conversion The process of converting picture data in digital form to pixel data in analog form.

scan head An optical sensing device in an optical scanner or facsimile machine that is moved across the image to be scanned.

scan line (1) The parallel horizontal lines that are defined by the scan of the electron beam inside the cathode ray tube. (2) One line of pixels in the frame buffer.

scanned image A bit mapped, or TIFF, image generated by an optical scanner. Many layout programs can scale or crop scanned images before placing them into a page.

scanned image

scanner An optical reading device that can recognize text, drawings and photographs and convert them into electronic representation of the images. Scanners can be differentiated by whether they process color or are limited to shades of gray. Scanner resolution is determined by the amount of information available from the scanning sensor for a given area. Common resolutions in desktop scanners are 200-600 dots per inch. More powerful systems can scan up to 8000 lines per inch or more.

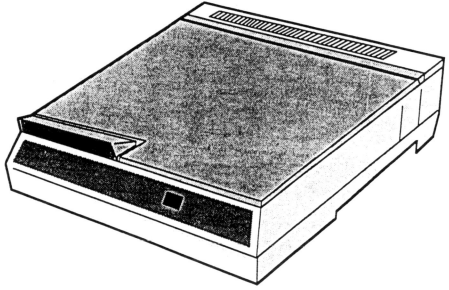

scanner

scanning area The dimensions of the largest original image that can be captured by a particular scanner.

scan rate The number of times a CRT screen is refreshed in a given time period.

scatter diagram An analytical graphic in which data items are plotted as points on x-y coordinate axes.

scene matching A pattern recognition technique that involves recognizing a portion of a scene when other images of the same scene have been taken at different times and under different viewing conditions.

scientific visualization Technology that enables scientists to store vast amounts of mathematical data, generate graphical models that represent the data, and visually analyze the results, usually through interactive software programs. Scientific visualization is a multidisciplinary methodology which employs the largely independent, but converging fields, of computer graphics, image processing, computer vision, signal processing, and computer-aided design. Its specific goal is to act as a catalyst between scientific computation and scientific insight. Scientific visualization came into being to meet the ever increasing need to deal with highly active, very dense data sources, which, for example, include satellite data and data from supercomputer computations.

scissoring Automatic erasing of all portions of a design on the visual display device that lie outside user-specified boundaries.

scrapbook A storage location for frequently used text and pictures. The stored images can be inserted into new documents as required.

scraperboard drawing A drawing that resembles a white line engraving. Obtained by scratching or scraping on a black surface. Can also be produced with a computer graphics system by using the tools found in all paint programs. Also called scratchboard drawing.

scraperboard drawing

screen (1) A television-like output device that can display information. (2) A pattern of tiny dots used as shading in a graphic.

screen angle The angle at which a halftone screen is printed.

screen capture (1) The transfer of the image on the current display screen into a graphics file. (2) A printout of the current screen display.

screen coordinates Alternate name for device coordinates.

screen cursor An indicating symbol generated by the display hardware and moved by the user around the screen area. Its position on the screen can be made to correspond to the position of a hand-held input device, such as a mouse moved across a mouse pad.

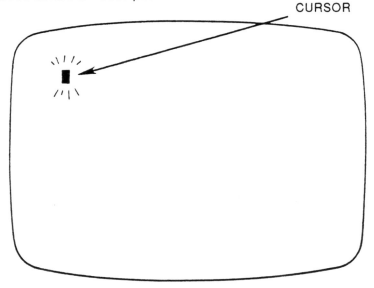

screen cursor

screen dump Process of transferring the information currently appearing on a display screen to a printer or saved as a file on disk; a "snapshot" of the screen.

screen fonts The bit mapped representations of a printer font that is used to display the font on the screen. A screen font is designed to mimic the appearance of printer fonts when displayed on medium-resolution monitors.

screen generator Special utility program used to create customized screen displays.

screen overlay (1) A clear, fine-mesh screen that reduces the glare on a video screen. (2) A window of data that in part overlays another window of data.

screen position Physical location of graphic data on a visual display screen.

screen resolution A measure of the crispness of images and characters on a screen, usually specified in terms of the number of pixels in a row or column.

HIGH-RESOLUTION   LOW-RESOLUTION

screen resolution

screen saver A program that produces moving patterns on the screen after a specified number of minutes without keyboard or mouse activity. Pressing a key on the keyboard or moving the mouse restores the screen. Screen savers are used to prolong the life of a monitor; they prevent one image from being burned into the screen phosphors. See also phosphor burn-in.

screen size Measure of the amount of information that a video display screen can display. Screens can be measured diagonally, as TV sets (usually a diagonal measure in inches), or by the number of vertical and horizontal dot or character positions. See resolution.

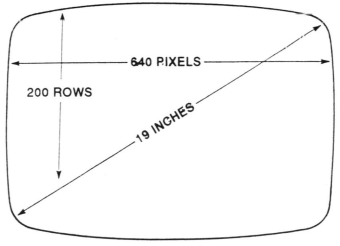

screen size

screen space The space defined by pixel coordinates.

screen update Process of changing screen contents to reflect new information.

scribble A quick-gesture drawing in which the drawing tool does not leave the drawing surface.

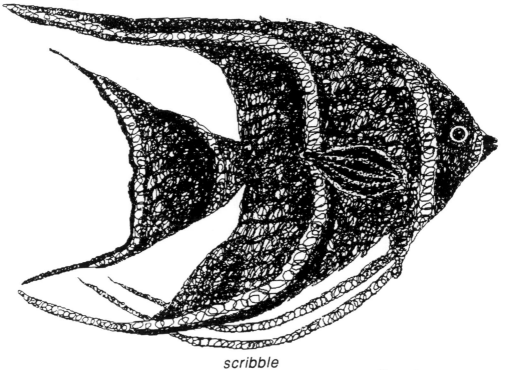

scribble

script font A typeface that looks like fine handwriting or calligraphy.

scroll To move information (graphics or text) up/down or right/left on a computer screen.

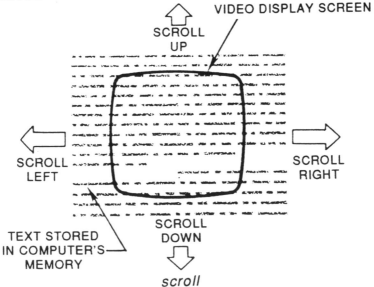

scroll

scroll arrow An arrow displayed at the ends of each scroll bar. Clicking or holding the mouse pointer on the scroll arrow causes the document in the window to move.

scroll bar In some types of graphical user interface, a vertical or horizontal bar at the side or bottom of a window that can be used with a mouse for moving around in a document.

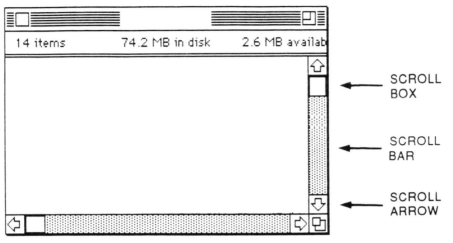

scroll bar

scroll box A box that slides in a scroll bar to indicate the relative position of a displayed document.

scrolling The vertical or horizontal movement of information (text or graphics) on a display screen in order to display additional information.

scrolling area An area on the screen in which scrolling takes place.

SCSI Stands for Small Computer Systems Interface. The SCSI is a general purpose parallel interface designed for connecting one or more computers and one or more peripherals – a total of 8 devices may be connected to one bus. It is an industry standard interface for high-speed access to peripheral devices. Used extensively on the Apple Macintosh computer. SCSI's great advantage is its ability to chain together multiple devices on a single I/O card, each of which has a unique address.

search and replace Software feature that finds a designated character sequence and replaces it with a new one. Important in word processing applications. See global search and replace.

second generation computers Computers belonging to the second era of technological development of computers, when the transistor replaced the vacuum tube. Prominent form 1959 to 1964, when they were displaced by computers using integrated circuitry.

section A cross-section, or cut-through view, of an object.

243

sectioning & paneling Computer-aided mapping functions that allow the cartographer to create new maps joining a number of smaller-scale maps. The two functions trim extraneous data, allow maps with common boundaries to be merged, and correct small inconsistencies.

sector chart A pie chart.

seed filling Filling a bounded area with color by switching just one pixel (or very few pixels) to the chosen shade.

segment A portion of a picture, such as a line segment.

selective erase A graphics feature for deleting portions of a display without affecting the remainder or having to repaint the entire CRT display.

self-similarity Central to the theory of fractals is the old idea of self-similarity, a theory that dates back to Aristotle. Self-similarity is where small sections of the objects contain, in some sense, scaled down versions of the whole object. The self-similarity characteristic has been used to model apparently complex forms recursively, e.g. ferns, grasses, trees, and other similar plant forms.

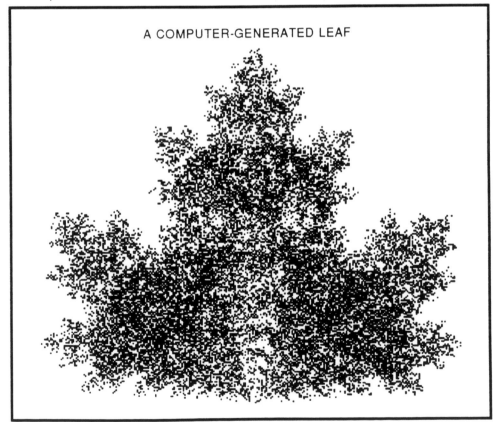

A COMPUTER-GENERATED LEAF

self-similarity

separated graphics Graphics characters with spaces between them. When a set of characters, with a space at one side and at the top or bottom, is printed in adjacent positions, the spaces will separate the graphics characters.

separations Transparencies or pages used for color reproduction. Each separation is used to reproduce a particular color.

serial mouse A mouse that connects to a computer's serial port.

serial port Input/output port in a computer through which data are transmitted and received one bit at a time.

serial printer Printer that receives information from the computer one bit at a time through a single wire. (One character equals eight bits.) One or more additional wires may be necessary to exchange control signals. Prints one character at a time. Serial printers are designed to be connected to the computer's serial port.

serif An ending stroke on the arms, tails and stems of characters in certain typeface designs. Serif type styles are typically considered businesslike, formal, and authoritative.

A SERIF TYPEFACE   A SANS SERIF TYPEFACE
TIMES ROMAN AVANT GARDE

serif

serif face A typeface that contains serifs, or finishing strokes.

server In the client/server model for a network system, the server is a machine with compute resources (and is sometimes called the compute server), and large memory capacity.

shade (1) In computer graphics, the quantity of black mixed with a pure color. (2) To give added dimension to an image by including changes in appearance caused by lightness and darkness. A particular shade occurs as a direct result of the shape of the object and the way it's lit. For clarity's sake, "shade" is confined to the surface of the illuminated object; "shadow" is the gray or black image cast by the object onto another surface.

shade

shading (1) Changing the brightness and color of parts of an image to simulate depth or otherwise enhance definition. (2) As applied to graphic objects, the way light reflects off a surface.

shading symbols Block graphics characters that are part of some computer graphics built-in character sets. Provide different dot densities, giving the appearance of different levels of shading.

shadow mask A metal plate with tiny holes positioned inside the CRT hardware. The electron beam passes from the electron gun, through a hole in the shadow mask, which guides the beam and ensures its precise placement on the inside of the display surface.

shadow printing A style applied to text in which a duplicate of each character is shifted, often down and to the right, to create a shadow effect.

ABCDEFGHIJKLM

shadow printing

shape Any area defined by line, color, tones, or the edges of forms. The visible configuration or outward form of something.

shape fill The automatic painting-in of an area of a drawing, defined by user-specified boundaries.

shape fill

shapes in nature Fractals have become the natural way of representing many of the shapes in nature. Thus, just as Euclidean geometry is the natural way of describing man-made shapes such as squares, triangles or cubes, so fractals are the natural language for describing clouds, trees, leaves, and other natural objects.

shapes in nature

shareware Software that is passed around. The authors let you copy and share their programs freely, but retain the copyrights. Shareware provides income to its author in the form of "contributions," much like public TV. Payment is strictly voluntary. Even though shareware is given away free, the maker hopes that satisfied users will voluntarily pay for it.

sharpen Any image enhancement technique that enhances edges and details in an image.

sharpness Charity and quality of an image produced on a visual display device, digital plotter, printer, film recorder, and other devices. See resolution.

Shatter The first computer-generated comic book, which was published in 1984. The original work was drawn on a a Apple Macintosh microcomputer with a monochrome paint program. The black-and-white output was hand painted with an airbrush and traditional tools.

Shatter

shattered image An image, broken into pieces to achieve a desired aesthetic effect, through the use of computers and imaging software programs.

shattered image

shear In painting and drawing programs, to slant an object along a specified axis.

shear

sheetfed scanner A digital scanner in which the original artwork is fed through the device, passing over the scanning sensor one line at a time.

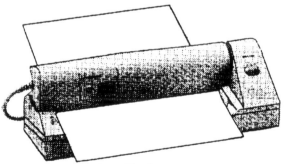

sheetfed scanner

sheet feeder Device that attaches to the printer, designed to automatically insert and line up single sheets of paper or envelopes in much the same way as an operator would perform the task. Usually sits above the printer platen and is operated either mechanically or electrically by the printer. See friction-feed.

shell An operating environment layer that separates the operating system from the user. The shell provides a graphical icon-oriented or menu-driven interface to the system in order to make it easier to use.

sidebar A block of text or a graphic image placed to the side of the main body of text in a document.

Sierpinski gasket A fractal that starts as a triangle and all the drawing and cutting takes place within the figure. Marking the midpoints of the three sides and joining those points creates a new triangle embedded within the original triangle into four smaller triangular pieces: one central and three corner triangles. Cutting out the central triangle leaves the three corner triangles. Then the process of finding midpoints and drawing in a triangle is repeated within each of the remaining triangles. The central triangle that sits within each of these corner pieces is cut out, leaving nine small triangles. The pattern seen in the first step is thus duplicated in each of the corner triangles within the figure. The process continues indefinitely to generate an arrangement of triangles nested within triangles nested within triangles, and so on, resulting in a two-dimensional sieve punctured by an infinite number of holes. The Sierpinski gasket has an area of zero and a fractal dimension of log 3/log 2 = 1.584.

Sierpinski gasket

Sierpinski square A fractal that starts as a square using a procedure similar to that used in producing a Sierpinski gasket. Dividing each side of a square into three parts to create a 3 by 3 grid and removing the central square is the first stage in generating an infinitely moth-eaten Sierpinski carpet. Its fractal dimension is log 8/log 3 = 1.8928.

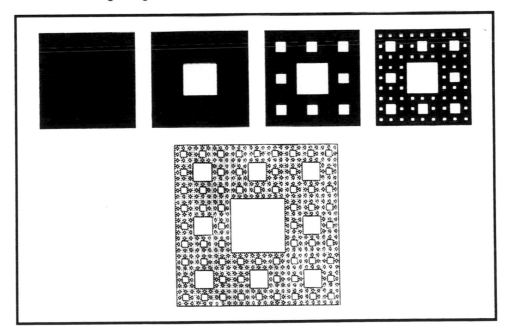

Sierpinski square

SIG Acronym for Special Interest Group. Often a sub-unit of a professional organization. Made up of members with common interests, e.g., a "Computers in Education" SIG, a "Computer Graphics" SIG, or a "Computers in Medicine" SIG.

SIGGRAPH A special interest group on computer graphics that is part of the Association for Computing Machinery (ACM). Each year SIGGRAPH holds an annual conference. The conference has become a focus for the exchange of information regarding fundamental discoveries and the latest innovations in the field of computer graphics. The conference includes lectures, exhibits, films and a computer art show. Approximate attendance records since 1980 are as follows:

YEAR	LOCATION	TOTAL ATTENDANCE
1980	Seattle	6,000
1981	Dallas	9.474
1982	Boston	16,557
1983	Detroit	14,169
1984	Minneapolis	20,390
1985	San Francisco	27,400
1986	Dallas	22,000
1987	Anaheim	30,541
1988	Atlanta	25,000
1989	Boston	26,000
1990	Dallas	25,000
1991	Las Vegas	28,000
1992	Chicago	30,000

SIGGRAPH

silhouette A form as defined by its outline.

silhouette

silk screen A type of artwork which can be generated by a CAD/CAM system for printing component placement and/or identification information on a PC board.

simulation See graphics simulation.

size The physical magnitude of objects, forms, elements, and quantities.

sizing The process of changing the size or shape of a window.

sketching Freehand drawing of lines and colors with an interactive display.

sketching

sketch pad Working storage area displayed on a visual display screen that permits the operator to add and delete graphic or textual information easily before it is entered into permanent storage.

skew In computer graphics and optical scanning, a condition in which a character, line, or reprinted symbol is neither parallel with nor at right angles to the leading edge. See stair stepping.

skip factor In a computer graphics program, an increment that specifies how many data points the program should skip as it constructs a chart or graph.

slave tube Cathode ray tube connected to another in such a way that both tubes perform identically.

SLD A slide file format for AutoCAD.

sleeve Protective envelope for storing a diskette.

slew To move paper through a printer.

slide A photographic representation of a visual display screen.

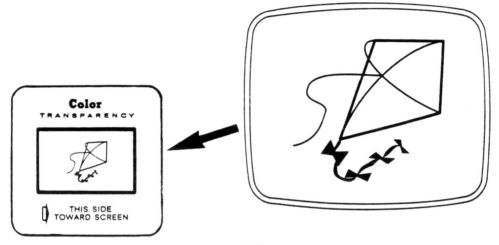

slide

slide show Computer graphics software that displays graphics images in a timed sequence on the video display screen, similar to a slide show. Some programs can produce interesting effects, such as fading out one screen before displaying another and enabling you to choose a path through the images available for display.

slug (1) In desktop publishing, a code inserted in headers or footers that generates page numbers when the document is printed. (2) In line printers, a metal casting that carries the image of a printable character. The character is printed when the casting strikes the paper.

small caps A font of capital letters that are smaller than the standard capital letters in that typeface.

smoothing (1) Any image enhancement technique in which the effect of noise in the original image is reduced. (2) Fitting together curves and surfaces so that a smooth, continuous geometry results.

smooth shading A shading method that blends colors smoothly across the object.

252

smudge A feature on some graphics programs that blends colors or softens edges that are already in place in an image. The effect is supposed to resemble what would happen if the image was made of wet paint and you ran a finger over the area.

snap, snap to (1) The automatic movement of a selected object or point to the nearest designated grid line, grid intersection, or connection point. (2) A CAD command that moves the screen cross hairs by predetermined increments, such as every .25-inch, .50-inch, 1-inch, 1-foot, etc.

soft clip area Limits of the area where data can be presented on a plotting device.

soft copy Data presented as a display screen image, in audio format, or in any other form that is not hard copy.

soften A filtering effect that decreases contrast in an image.

soft font A font that is downloaded from a computer to a printer from files stored on a disk.

soft hyphen Conditional (nonrequired) hyphen printed only to break a word between syllables at the end of a line. Contrast with hard hyphen.

soft keys Keys on a keyboard that can have a user-defined meaning. Called soft keys because their meaning can change from user to user or program to program.

soft return Combination line feed/carriage return command, entered by a program containing the word wrap feature to begin a new line within a paragraph. Unlike a hard return, it is conditional – the computer executes the command only when the current word doesn't fit in the line in progress.

software The generic term for any computer program or programs; instructions that cause the hardware to do work. Contrast with the "iron" or hardware of a computer system.

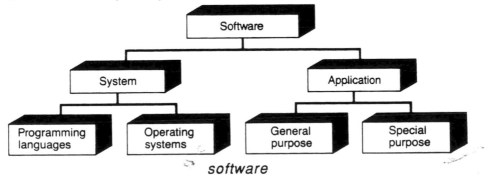

software

software package A prewritten program that can be purchased for use with a specific computer to perform a specific task. Usually includes the programs, stored on a storage media (floppy disk, CD-ROM, and so on), and an operating manual. Examples of software packages for microcomputers include word processing packages such as WordPerfect and Microsoft Word, paint packages such as SuperPaint and Deluxe Paint, educational packages, desktop publishing packages such as PageMaker, Ventura Publisher, and Quark Xpress, game packages, and so on.

software piracy Copying of commercial or proprietary software without permission of the originator.

software portability Ease with which a program can be moved from one computer environment to another. As third-party software becomes more prevalent in the computer industry, portability becomes a more valuable attribute of that software.

solarization An effect achieved by changing the intensity levels in an image in a way that particularly brightens or transforms the middle levels.

solarization

solid A black or one-color area on a printed page that contains no artwork, text or patterns.

solid modeling A type of three-dimensional modeling in which the solid characteristics of an object under design are built into the database so that complex internal structures and external shapes can be realistically represented. This makes computer-aided design and analysis of solid objects easier, clearer, and more accurate than with wire-frame graphics.

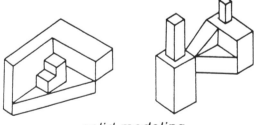

solid modeling

254

sonic pen A pencil-shaped device using sound to select a screen location.

space figures A set of points which may have one, two or three dimensions. Cubes, spheres and pyramids are space figures. Sometimes they are called solids, solid geometrical figures or solid shapes.

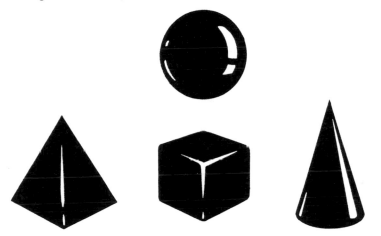

space figures

spatial Having the attributes of two- or three-dimensional space.

spatial digitizer Device often used in computer graphics to simulate three-dimensional objects; a three-dimensional scanner.

spatial resolution The number of pixels used to represent an image from side-to-side and top-to-bottom.

SpectraColor A color paint program for the Commodore Amiga computer.

spectral color The color of a single wavelength of light, starting with violet at the low end and proceeding through indigo, blue, green, yellow and orange and ending with red.

specular highlight Light reflected from a shiny surface.

spherization Turning an image into a sphere.

Splash! A paint program for IBM-compatible microcomputers. With a palette of over 256,000 colors, 60 patterns and brush sizes, color fills, stamps, and spray cans, the Splash! user is equipped to prepare drawings for publications.

spline In computer graphics, a piecewise polynomial with at least first-order continuity between the pieces. Mathematically simple and elegant way to connect disjoint data points smoothly, hence used not only for generating smooth curves and surfaces between sparse data points, but also for smooth motions between parameters sparsely located in time, such as those used to describe the keyframes in an animation.

spline curve See B-spline curve.

split screen Display screen that can be partitioned into two or more areas (windows) so different screen formats can be shown on the screen at the same time. It implies that one set of data can be manipulated independently of the other.

split screen

splitting a window Act of dividing a window into two or more panes.

spot In referring to the output of an imagesetter or film recorder, the smallest element that can be written. Also called a pixel or dot.

spot color A color that is added as a second or third (or more) color to a print job. Often used in dressing up a formatted section such as a rule or a headline.

COLOR 1   COLOR 2

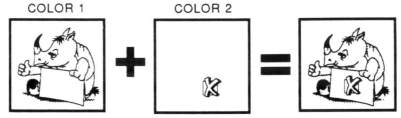

spot color

spot size In vector displays, the diameter of the focused electron beam of the display surface.

spraying A feature of a paint program mimicking the action of a spray gun by painting a fine pattern of pixels.

spraying

spray can One of the capabilities found in several computer graphics systems. A spray can provides the computer graphics artist with a method of shading or "spraying" an area with a specific pattern or color.

spread Enlarging the width of lines in an image to overlay gaps between the line and an adjoining fill area.

sprites Small, high-resolution objects that can be moved independently of other text or graphics on the monitor. The shape might be a flying airplane or a smiling face. Sprites allow programmers to generate particular shapes and to move them about quickly. They can change color and size and move in front of or behind other objects on the monitor. Used to create animated sequences.

sprocket holes Equally spaced holes on both edges of continuous forms for use by a tractor-feed mechanism to feed paper through a printer.

squash and stretch The technique of exaggeration of a drawing. The distortion given to a normal reaction to make it more forceful.

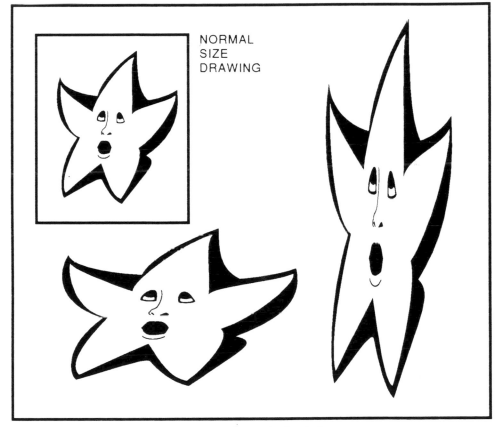

NORMAL
SIZE
DRAWING

squash and stretch

ST A personal computer series from Atari Corporation. The Atari ST family of personal computers are high-performance personal computers with capabilities for computer graphics in color.

stacks A term given to a "stack" of cards (information displayed on screen) created through HyperCard.

staircasing A characteristic of lines drawn on dot matrix screens that makes them appear jagged rather than smooth. The degree of staircasing depends on the angle at which the line is drawn (horizontal and vertical lines do not exhibit staircasing) and the resolution of the screen. Finer screens exhibit far less staircasing than coarse ones. Synonym of aliasing.

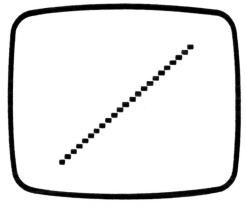

staircasing

stair-steps See aliasing and antialiasing.

standalone program A program, such as a word processing or drawing program.

standalone system (1) Self-contained computer system that can work independently, not connected to or under the control of another computer system. A standalone system contains all the hardware and software a user requires. (2) Not connected to a network, or operating as if not connected to a network.

standalone system

258

Star A workstation from Xerox Corporation that introduced the desktop user interface in 1981. Although the Star was not successful, it was the inspiration for Xerox's subsequent machines and for Apple's Macintosh computer.

startup screen A graphics file that, when placed in the System Folder on a Apple Macintosh computer, is displayed when the computer is turned on. Any bit mapped graphic image can be used as a startup screen. For example, you can display a fish, a tree, or even a picture of a favorite movie star.

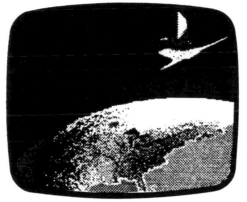

startup screen

state-of-the-art Phrase that implies being up-to-date in technology, pertaining to the very latest technology; at the forefront of current hardware or software technology.

stem In typography, the main vertical stroke of a character.

stereopsis The dimensional perception resulting from two different views of the same image.

stick model A model made of lines, or vectors. For example, in dancing applications, the limbs of a person are converted into lines so that the dance steps can be visually observed and studied.

stickup initial In desktop publishing, an enlarged initial letter at the beginning of a paragraph that rises above the top of the first line.

stickup initial

259

still life An arrangement of inanimate objects – fruit, flowers, pottery, etc. – taken as the subject or motif of a work of art.

still life

stippling (1) The technique of applying color or tone as a mass of small dots, made with the point of a fine brush, a drawing instrument, or the paintbrush facility of a computer paint program. (2) To fill a region with a stipple, a pattern of dots.

stippling

stitch To combine several images, especially combining side-by-side strips made by hand scanners, into a single image.

stochastic painting A term used for paintings in which the designs, the distribution of color and, possibly, the color selections are made by chance, following a predetermined methodology or a set of rules for making use of the chance factor.

260

storyboard Preliminary sketches or diagrams made in panels to suggest the sequence of action and dialogue for movies, TV ads, etc.

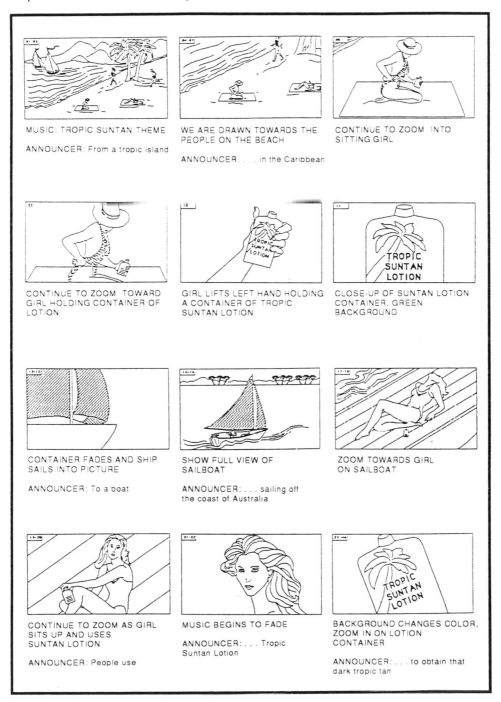

storyboard

straight line drawing A graphics image composed of only straight lines.

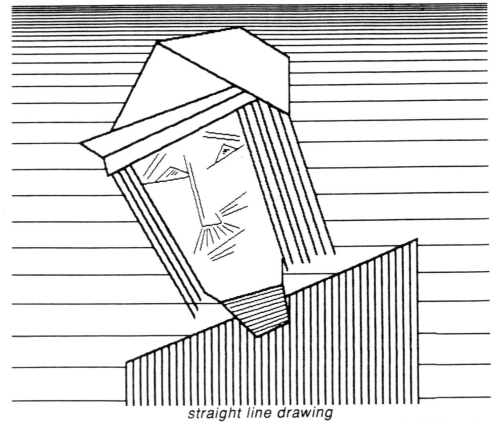

straight line drawing

streaming cartridge A type of cartridge tape drive that records whole tracks of a cartridge at one time, rather than stopping and starting for individual blocks. Because the mechanism is simpler, it is less expensive than incremental recorders and can hold more data per cartridge. Used primarily for backup of hard disk drives.

street price The current price of a computer product at a computer store, mail order business, or other retail business. The street price of a product is often considerably lower than the retail price of a product. It is an average price charged by dealers around the country. See list price.

stretch A graphics aid that enables the user to automatically expand a displayed entity beyond its original dimensions.

strikethrough A line drawn through a selected range of text. Marking text in this manner indicates that the text is to be deleted at some future time.

strip To paste an item, often a drawing or halftone onto a page.

strobing A peculiar jitter effect that results in computer animation when an object is moved too fast, and leaves a representative trail behind it.

stroke (1) In computer graphics, a line created as a vector. (2) In data entry, a keystroke. (3) In paint programs, a "swipe" of the paintbrush made when creating a graphic image. (4) In printing, the weight, or thickness, of a character.

stroke beam A technique for displaying information on a CRT that directs the beam from point to point on the display screen of the CRT. The beam traces only the points required to display the desired information.

stroke display An alternative name for a CRT vector display.

stroke writing A graphics picture-generating technique. A beam is moved simultaneously in X and Y directions along a curve or straight path in much the same way as an Etch-A-Sketch children's toy.

structure The compositional relationships in a work of art

structure

Studio/1 An Apple Macintosh graphics program that combines black-and-white painting, scanning and animation with a computer slide-show capability. Very advanced black-and-white graphics can be created; all basic painting tools are included, and some not-so-basic capabilities such as polygon selection, rotating ellipse, Bezier curves and sophisticated distortion, shearing, and bending options. A built-in scanner interface allows images to be input directly from a scanner while in the program. Most unique is the ability to also create full animation incorporating graphics, art, motion and sound. Designers can define complex paths for objects and have the program create the animation, or use a feature which allows automatic painting on consecutive frames. With a built-in HyperCard driver, Studio/1 can also import/export in PICT, MacPaint, PICS, TIFF, EPSF and compressed animation formats.

Studio/8 An Apple Macintosh paint program that supports color. Studio 8 can select any part of an image and turn it into a custom paintbrush. The program remembers up to eight brushes. Images can be tinted, smoothed, smeared, and blended.

Studio/32 A powerful Apple Macintosh paint program that supports 32-bit full color, giving computer artists virtually unlimited colors and tools to work with. Even better than its power is its unintimidating, intuitive interface which lets users easily handle advanced features such as masking, transformation effects and color control. Special features include selection techniques, tear-off menus, three-dimensional perspectives, custom gradients, variable dithering and slide-show presentation utilities. It has the ability to keep text as a separate layer for editing. Strong Pantone color matching support is provided with an interface allowing users to locate colors by number or color qualities. Other color editing modes supported include CMYK, HSV and RGB. Files can be imported and exported in PICT, MacPaint, TIFF and EPSF formats.

style Variation in the appearance of a typeface (e.g., italic, bold, shadow, outlined, normal).

style sheet In word processing and desktop publishing, a file that contains formatting instructions but not text. Style sheets contain such information as margin sizes, column widths, paragraph indention, spacing, fonts, size, and style. Applying a stylesheet to text automatically formats the text according to the stylesheet's specifications.

stylus In computer graphics, a pointer that you operate by placing it in a display space or a graphics tablet. To draw a point, the user touches the stylus (also called a pen) tip to the surface of the graphics tablet. The stylus and graphics tablet are preferred drawing devices for artists.

stylus

subtraction A method of combining two objects into one. The subtracted object "carves away" the overlapping portion of the second object.

subtractive color Cyan, magenta, and yellow, produced from reflected light. These colors cannot be made by mixing other inks together. Inks do not add to light, but subtract from it. Pure Cyan, magenta and yellow together yield black.

Summagraphics Corporation A major manufacturer of data tablets and digitizers, founded in 1972.

supercomputer Largest, fastest, and most expensive mainframe computer available. Used by businesses and organizations that require extraordinary amounts of computing power. Sometimes called number crunchers because they perform between hundreds of millions to several billions of operations per second. They are very expensive and are typically used for the most complex computational tasks. Some applications of supercomputers include nuclear energy research, petroleum exploration, electronic design, realtime animated graphics, and structural analysis. Supercomputers are typically 50,000 times faster than microcomputers.

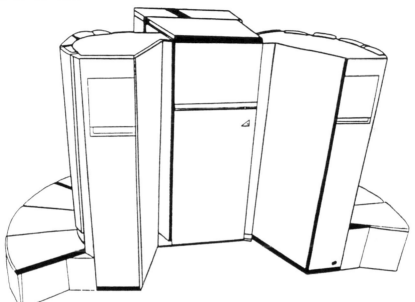

supercomputer

superimposition (1) The combination of two separate drawings into a single drawing. (2) To lay one image, or portion of an image, over another.

SuperPaint An Apple Macintosh graphics program that combines drawing and paint capabilities. Drawing features include a freehand drawing tool capable of creating editable Bezier paths, hairline widths and varying vertical and horizontal widths for lines, PostScript halftone gray values available as fill patterns and a capability to align selected objects in relationship to each other. Editing capabilities include mixing of fonts, styles and sizes within a single block of text; the ability to edit text in the Draw layer after performing any transformation command; group/ungroup and lock/unlock commands; the ability to simultaneously open and edit multiple points along a Bezier curve; and snap-to-grid options. SuperPaint was introduced in 1986. The latest version, SuperPaint 3.0 was released in late 1990. This version of SuperPaint supports color.

Super 3D An Apple Macintosh graphic program. It includes built-in animation and its enhanced version uses color blending techniques. Super 3D can set up any number of key frames and automatically creates the in between frames with multiple light sources and a choice of rendering algorithms.

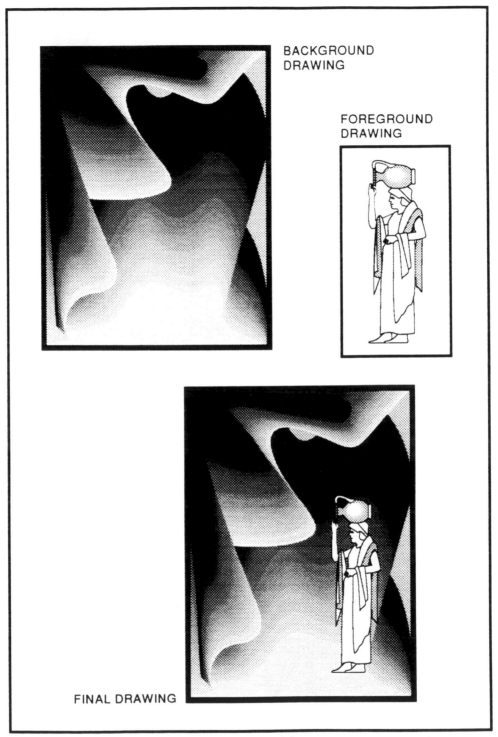

BACKGROUND
DRAWING

FOREGROUND
DRAWING

FINAL DRAWING

superimposition

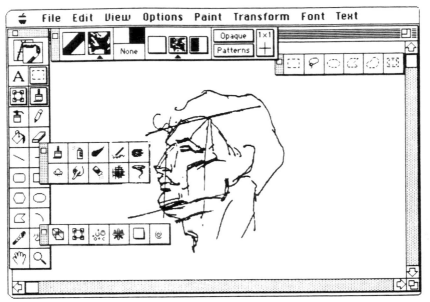

SuperPaint

surface A surface consists of sets of points. Usually, surface is undefined in geometry. There are plane surfaces such that a straight line joining any two of its points lies completely in the plane. There are curved surfaces of which no part is a plane. A surface may consist of plane and curved surfaces.

surface modeling A display method used by some computer-aided design (CAD) programs that gives on screen constructions the appearance of solidity. Surface modeling creates the appearance of a firm surface either by filling the shape or by removing hidden lines from within it. Surface modeling is a more complex method for representing object than wireframe modeling, but not as sophisticated as solid modeling.

surface modeling

267

surface of revolution Figure resulting from the rotation of a curve around a fixed axis set at a specified angle.

sweeping Generating a surface implicitly by moving a curve over a trajectory.

Survival 3D An Apple Macintosh three-dimensional program that can be used to create, manipulate and render complex objects. The program also includes image mapping, independent light sources and environment mapping.

System 7 Operating system for the Apple Macintosh computer. System 7 expands the Macintosh capabilities including an upgraded finder, file sharing capability, truetype fonts, interapplication communications and virtual memory.

system disk The disk that contains the operating system and other systems programs that are necessary to start the computer.

system error A malfunction of the hardware or systems software within a computer system.

system error

system folder In a Apple Macintosh environment, the folder that contains the System File and the Finder, the two components of the Macintosh's operating system.

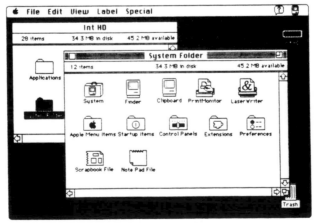

system folder

table plotter See flatbed plotter.

tablet In computer graphics, a locator device with a flat surface and a mechanism that converts indicated positions on the surface into coordinated data.

tagged image file format (TIFF) A common file format used to store bit mapped graphic images. TIFF simulates gray-scale shading.

Tandy Corporation A leading manufacturer of personal computers and electronic equipment. In 1977, Tandy introduced one of the first personal computers, the Radio Shack TRS-80 Model I. Several other TRS-80 models were developed, and in 1984, Tandy started selling IBM-compatible microcomputer systems through their company-owned Radio Shack stores.

tangram A puzzle made by Chinese mathematicians about 4000 years ago that showed how shapes are related. It was basically a square made of 7 pieces. Hundreds of pictures can be made with these 7 pieces.

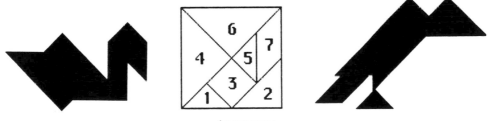

tangram

TARGA Acronym for Truevision Advanced Raster Graphics Adapter. A file format created by Truevision image capture boards, compatible with NTSC standards.

Targa board A video graphics board from Truevision that is used in high-resolution graphics applications.

target printer A specific printer selected for printing a job.

tear-off menu A screen menu that can be moved off its primary position, relocated to any part of the display screen and kept active.

template (1) In computer graphics, the pattern of a standard, commonly used component or part that serves as a design aid. Once created, it can be subsequently traced instead of redrawn whenever needed. (2) In a spreadsheet program, a worksheet that has already been designed for the solution of a specific type of problem. (3) Plastic sheet placed over keyboard keys to help the user remember tasks performed by each key. (4) In page layout and word processing programs, templates are predesigned page formats. You use the template by loading the file, adding the text and/or graphic images, and printing. (5) Plastic guide used in drawing geometric flowcharting symbols.

Tempra An image editing program for IBM-compatible microcomputers operating in MS-DOS. Features include color mapping, video capture, show and print utilities. Virtual paint canvas allows importing, creating, and/or retouching images up to 8192 x 8192 pixels for precision editing and printing.

terrain modeling Generating realistic-looking natural surfaces, most often through the use of fractals.

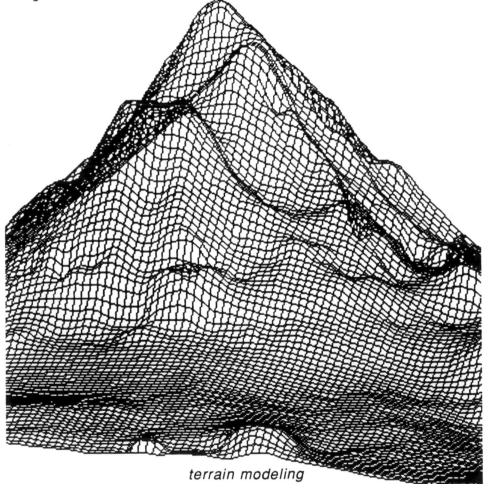

terrain modeling

tessellate To subdivide a surface into a collection of smaller geometric forms.

tessellation The division of smooth surfaces into polygons that fit together like a mosaic.

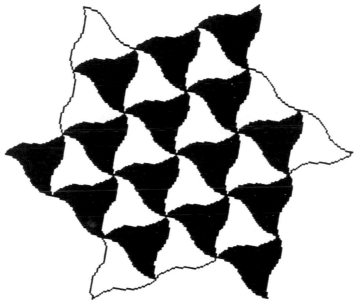

tessellation

text composition In desktop publishing, evenly spaced lines, usually set in the same type size and style.

text editing General term that covers any additions, changes, or deletions made to electronically stored material.

text editor Computer program used to manipulate text; for example, to erase, insert, change, and move words or groups of words. The manipulated text may be another computer program.

text formatting (1) The process of controlling the appearance of a document so that it will look good on paper. (2) Output generated by computer software that closely resembles galleys set on conventional composing machines.

text generation The process of constructing meaningful text using a computer.

text letter A typeface that looks like early brush stroke lettering.

text graphics Graphic images created by combining ASCII characters.

text processing Manipulation of alphabetic data under program control.

textual Composed entirely of text, without graphic images or other data.

texture In computer graphics, a two-dimensional pattern used to add the appearance of complexity to a three-dimensional surface without actually modeling the complexity. For example, a surface could be made to appear reflective to simulate glass or metal, or a brick texture pattern could be used on an architectural drawing of a brick house.

texture

texture mapping In computer graphics, the application of graphic representations of surface textures to objects.

text window Area on some computer graphics systems display screens within which text is displayed and scrolled.

TGA Bitmap format for images created on high-resolution video boards. Because of their resolution, these files can be very large. Because they can have up to 16 million colors, the palette often has to be compressed before the files can be used. See TARGA.

thematic map A map specifically designed to communicate geographic concepts such as the distribution of densities, relative magnitudes, gradients, spatial relationships, movements and all the required interrelationships and aspects among the distributional characteristics of the earth's phenomena. CAD systems allow the quick assignment and identification of both graphic and nongraphic properties, thus facilitating the use of thematic maps.

thermal wax-transfer printer A nonimpact printer that uses heat to melt colored wax onto paper to create an image. It uses pins to apply the heat.

thesaurus program With a word processing program, this program provides a list of synonyms and antonyms for a word in a document.

thick and thin The weight of a line, its graphic quality.

third generation computers Computers that use integrated circuitry and miniaturization of components to replace transistors, reduce costs, work faster, and increase reliability. Introduced in 1964 and still the primary technology for digital computers. Compare first generation computers, second generation computers, fourth generation computers, and fifth generation computers.

three-dimensional digitizer A piece of digitizing equipment for taking coordinate data directly from a physical three-dimensional object.

three-dimensional graphics (3-D) A graphic image in three dimensions – height, width and depth. A three-dimensional image is rendered on a two-dimensional medium; the third dimension, depth, is usually indicated by shading or by means of perspective.

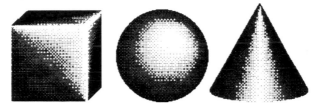

three-dimensional graphics (3-D)

three-point perspective Representations drawn in perspective so as to show height, width and depth.

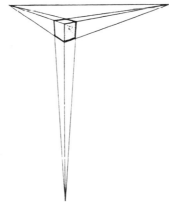

three-point perspective

threshold A predefined level used by a black-and-white scanner to determine whether a pixel will be represented as black or white. The result is a high-contrast black-and-white image that highlights certain features.

thumbnail layout In desktop publishing, a quickly drawn sketch that shows major elements in a document.

Thunderscan An inexpensive high-resolution scanner that replaces the ribbon cartridge in an Apple ImageWriter printer, and converts photographs and printed images into data that can be stored on a disk. Developed by Thunderware, Inc.

TIFF Acronym for Tagged Image File Format; which is basically a standardized header (tag) defining the exact data structure of the images to be processed. A common bit mapped file format. The TIFF format will handle gray-scale shading and images with a resolution up to 300 dpi. TIFF was developed by the Aldus Corporation. TIFF files are very large.

TIFF-24 A version of the Tagged Image File Format (TIFF) that encodes 24 bits of information for each point in the image.

tile (1) A single sheet or portion that can be combined with others to form an oversize page, or to split a page into such sections. (2) To cover a surface with non-overlapping polygons or other contiguous geometric objects.

tiled The display of objects side by side.

tiled windows A screen display divided into nonoverlapping windows.

tiling (1) In computer graphics, the filling of an object with a design or pattern instead of a solid cover. Tiling is used to cover defined areas of the screen with particular images. (2) Synonyms for tessellation or mosaic.

tile

tilting screen Video display screen that can be angled back and forth from top to bottom for easier viewing – one result of ergonomics.

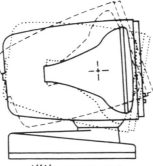

tilting screen

274

Time Arts, Inc. A leading developer of computer graphics software for art and illustration; founded in 1982.

Times Roman An attractive and easy-to-read serif font that is included as a built-in font with many laser printers.

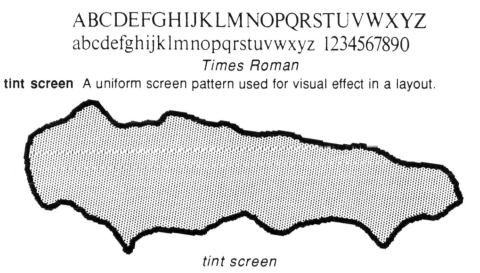

ABCDEFGHIJKLMNOPQRSTUVWXYZ
abcdefghijklmnopqrstuvwxyz 1234567890

Times Roman

tint screen A uniform screen pattern used for visual effect in a layout.

tint screen

TIPS An imaging program for IBM-compatible microcomputers.

title bar In a graphics environment, the line of text at the top of a window that indicates the name of the application or file in that window.

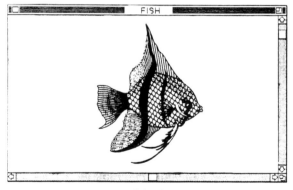

FISH

title bar

toggle (1) A keystroke that turns a function of a program on or off. (2) A device having two stable states. (3) The ability to go back and forth between two distinctly separate functions on a CRT.

tonal range The spread between the lightest and darkest parts of an image.

tone A term describing the effect of shadow used to suggest the three-dimensional quality of form; adding "tone" to a drawing means creating the effect of light and shade.

toner Very fine black powder which is fused to paper in laser printing. The equivalent of black ink.

toner cartridge In a laser printer, the disposable container that holds the electrically charged dry ink and drum used in creating an image on the paper.

tone value All colors have a tone value, according to whether they are light or dark. Tone value is that quality which distinguishes a light color from a dark color.

tool (1) An object or icon used to perform operations in a computer program. Tools are often named either by what they do or by the type of object on which they work. (2) In some computer systems, an applications program.

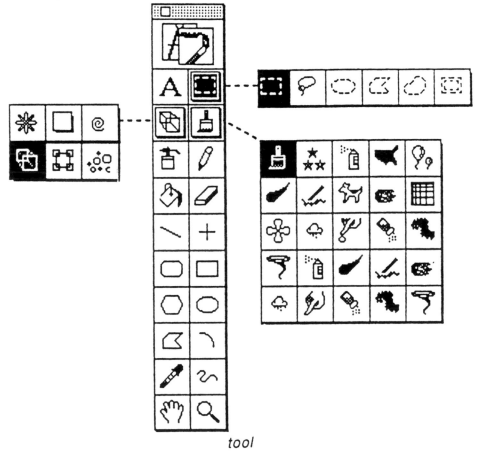

tool

toolbox (1) A set of standard routines (pointing, cropping, drawing, etc.) provided by a program or operating system that can be called on by other programs or by the user. (2) An on-screen group of icons representing these routines.

tool palette A collection of on-screen functions that are grouped in a menu structure for interactive selection.

topographic landscape A landscape in which the actual features are depicted as accurately as possible.

topology A branch of geometry concerned with the general properties of shapes and space.

torus A surface or solid generated by the revolution of a circle or other conic section about an axis; for example, a solid ring of circular or elliptic section, a doughnut-shaped surface.

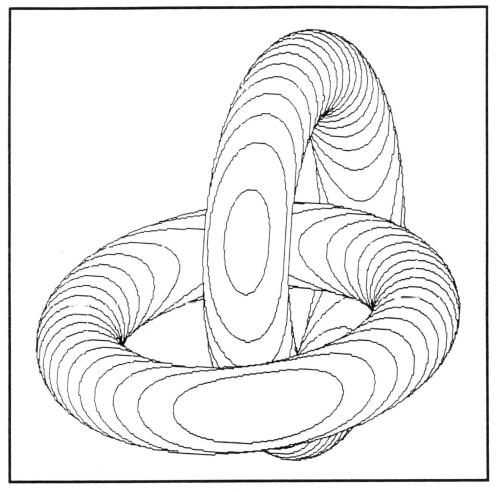

torus

touch-sensitive screen Display screen on which the user can enter commands by pressing designated areas with a finger or other object. This method takes advantage of an individual's natural instinct to point.

touch-sensitive tablet Input device that converts graphics and pictorial data into numerical form for use by a computer. Graphic data can be generated by pressing the tablet with a stylus.

track ball Device used to move the cursor around on a computer display screen. Consists of a mounting, usually a box, in which is set a ball. As the user spins the ball, the cursor moves at the speed and in the direction of the ball's motion. The housing is stationary, as opposed to the mobile mouse unit.

track ball

tracking Moving a cursor or predefined symbol across the surface of the visual display screen with a light pen, electronic pen, track ball, or mouse.

tracking

tracking symbol Small symbol on a video display screen that represents the position of the cursor.

tractor-fed printer Printer through which paper with holes along its edges is fed by sprocket wheels within the device

tractor-feed mechanism Pair of pin-studded belts that rotate in unison and pull paper, punched with marginal holes, into a printer.

transformation One of the modifications that can be made to the placement or size of an on-screen image. The three basic transformations are translation, scaling, and rotation.

translation Movement of an object along the x-, y-, and/or z-axes.

transparency For a graphics object or image, the attribute of letting an underlying image show through.

trash can

278

trash can A storage location on the desktop, used to discard folders, documents, drawings and application programs.

traverse adjustment A computer-aided mapping feature which automatically distributes corrections through any surveying traverse to eliminate the error of closure, and to yield an adjusted position for each traverse station.

tree A hierarchical arrangement of data into a structure similar to an upside-down tree.

triad (1) Any group of three, such as three bits, bytes, or characters. (2) In a color CRT, one set of red, green, and blue phosphors.

triangulate To subdivide a polygon into triangles to simplify rendering.

trichromatic Three-colored. In computer graphics, trichromatic generally refers to the three primary colors (red, green, and blue) combined to create all others.

trigger Button on a joystick.

triple click To press and release the mouse button three times rapidly in quick succession.

trochoid The curve made by any point on the edge of a circle rolling like a wheel.

true color (1) True color graphics systems are usually equipped with at least 24 bits per pixel; this translates to a total palette range of 16.7 million colors. (2) Color systems in which the color information in the image is used directly to create the output color rather than as an index to a table of colors in a palette.

T-switch An electrical switch that allows the user to change the connections between computing equipment just by turning the dial on a switch. T-switches are useful for sharing infrequently used or expensive peripheral devices, such as a laser printer.

turbo A trade name for hardware and software that implies high speed.

turnkey system Prepackaged, ready-to-use computer system containing all the hardware, software, training, and maintenance support needed to perform a given application. All the prepared system needs is the "turn of the key." For example, a turnkey desktop publishing system might consist of a CPU, monitor, hard disk, scanner, laser printer and appropriate software While easier to set up than off-the-shelf systems, equipment, training and support choices are sometimes limited.

turtle A robot that moves about on the floor, or a shape that moves about on the screen. Both types are used to demonstrated programming, and can draw a trail showing where they have been.

turtle graphics A graphics system first developed for the LOGO language. It consists of a turtle, which is displayed on the graphics screen and can be pointed and moved by simple commands. A variation of turtle graphics has been found to be useful for generating fractal curves.

TURTLE

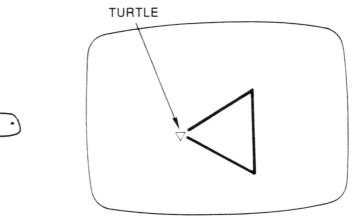

turtle graphics

tweaking In CAD, a modelling technique in which the user "tweaks" a control dial, causing a selected shape to elongate on the screen.

tweening See in-betweens.

two-dimensional graphics (2-D) A graphic image in two dimensions – height and width. The two-dimensional display is represented by two axes, x (horizontal) and y (vertical).

two-point perspective Perspective viewed when an object is observed from an angle. There are two vanishing points.

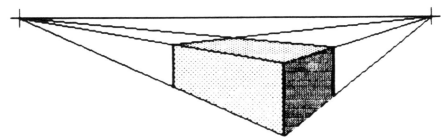

two-point perspective

typeface Collection of letters, numbers, and symbols that share a distinctive appearance (e.g., Helvetica, Times Roman, Bodoni, Schoolbook, Courier, and Palatino).

typeface family A group of typefaces that include the normal, bold, italic and bold-italic variations of the same design; a related group of type fonts.

type font Complete set of characters in a consistent and unique typeface.

typeover Ability of an impact printer to strike a character more than once to produce a boldface effect on the printed copy. See overstriking and shadow printing.

typeset quality Printer resolution of 1200 to 2540 dots per inch.

typesetting The production of camera-ready copy on a laser printer (low-quality typesetting) or an imagesetter (high-quality typesetting).

type size The size, in points, of a typeface.

type size

type style The weight (such as normal or bold) or posture (such as italic) of a font.

type table A file used by certain OCR programs that contains character shapes for a particular font. The program refers to the type table when recognizing that font.

typo In desktop publishing, a typesetting or clerical error in producing typed copy.

typography The science and art of designing typefaces and of composing printed works. It involves the selecting and using of typefaces for maximum effect. It also involves such matters as the composition of the page and the sizing of illustrations and other graphics.

typography

Uccello, Paolo (1397–1475) An Italian artist who first used perspective. He was the first to make drawings on a plane surface, like paper or canvas, which gave the impression of having depth, or a third dimension.

UCR See UnderColor Removal.

UltraPaint An Apple Macintosh graphics program that combines black-and-white painting, color painting, gray-scale image editing and object drawing. All basic paint tools are featured plus tools and special effects including blended fills, additive and subtractive lasso, marquee and wand selection, masking, three pattern/color airbrush, chalk, quill pen, auto tracing, editable brushes, patterns, 256 color palette and 1 degree rotation. Image manipulation includes contrast and brightness controls, charcoal, water droplet and smear. For drawing, all standard tools are provided plus Bezier curves and smooth polygons with complete editing control. WYSIWYG text and up to eight object-oriented layers per drawing. File formats supported include MacPaint, TIFF, MacDraw, and PICT.

undercolor removal (UCR) A technique for reducing the amount of magenta, yellow, and cyan in neutral areas by removing equal amounts of each and replacing them with the equivalent amount of black.

underline To format a selection of text so that the text is printed with a line slightly below it.

undersizing & oversizing Graphic editing tools for the systematic reduction or enlargement, respectively, of the areas in a layout.

undo Command that undoes the effect of the previous command and puts the text or graphics back the way it was. Some programs provide multiple undo levels, letting you take back commands you gave in the past.

union A method of combining two objects into one. The objects are "fused" into a single object.

Unisys A computer company formed in 1986 as a merger of the Burroughs Corporation and Sperry Corporation, both large mainframe manufacturers. Unisys continues to emphasize the product lines of both companies, and in addition, has introduced several new mainframe, minicomputer, and personal computer products.

UNIX An easy-to-use operating system developed by Ken Thompson, Dennis Ritchie and coworkers at Bell Laboratories. Since the UNIX operating system is very easy to use, its design concept had a great influence on operating systems for microcomputers. UNIX is widely used on a great variety of computers, from mainframes to microcomputers. It is a powerful operating system that has many high-level utility programs, and it is capable of running a number of jobs at once. It has many applications including office automation, network control, and control of numerically controlled machinery. Since it also has superior capabilities as a program development system, UNIX should become even more widely used in the future. UNIX exists in various forms and implementations.

update To modify a graphics file and make it reflect more recent information.

upgrade To apply an enhancement or other improvement to a hardware or software component of an existing graphics system.

upper case Capital letters. Contrast with lower case.

user Any person authorized to operate any aspect of a computer graphics system.

user

user interface See graphical user interface.

value The character of color or tone assessed on a scale from dark to light.

vanishing point In a perspective drawing, the place where parallel lines seem to come together.

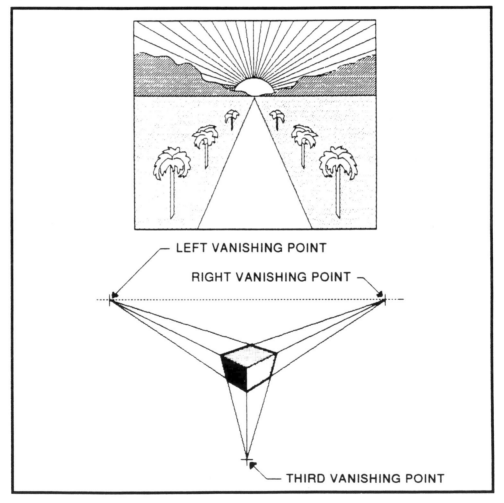

LEFT VANISHING POINT

RIGHT VANISHING POINT

THIRD VANISHING POINT

vanishing point

vantage point The position from which you view an object or scene.

VAX Designation for a family of 32-bit minicomputer systems manufactured by Digital Equipment Corporation. VAX machines were introduced in 1977 and range from desktop personal computers to large-scale mainframes.

VDT Acronym for Video Display Terminal, and input/output device consisting of a display screen and an input keyboard. Synonymous with CRT terminal.

VDU Acronym for Visual Display Unit, a peripheral device on which data are displayed on some type of screen.

vector (1) Type of cathode ray tube on which graphic data are represented by lines drawn from point to point rather than by illumination of a series of contiguous positions, as on a raster display device. (2) In plotting, an element of a line connecting two points. (3) In computer graphics, a line drawn in a certain direction from a starting point to an ending point.

vector font A font in which the characters are drawn in arrangements of line segments rather than arrangements of curves or bits.

vector graphics monitor A monitor that generates pictures by drawing numerous straight-line segments (vectors) on the screen.

vector image An image defined as a series of straight line vectors. The beginning and ending points of each line are stored and later adjusted as the image is sized.

vector processor A processor that performs simultaneous high-speed calculations on numerical elements. Vector processors are used extensively in systems that required intensive graphics operations.

Ventura Publisher A desktop publishing program for IBM PC, IBM PS/2 and Apple Macintosh computers from Ventura Software, Inc. The program provides typeset-quality desktop publishing. It formats files created with word processors, graphics programs, scanners or within the program itself. It is an excellent product for creating documents such as brochures, newsletters, or long structured documents like catalogs, technical manuals and books. It imports a wide variety of text and graphics files.

version Specific release of a software product of a specific hardware model. Usually numbered in ascending order. For example, DOS 5.0 is a later version of a disk operating system than is DOS 4.1 or DOS 3.3.

verso The left-side (even-numbered) page in a two-sided printing of a book or document. See facing pages.

vertex (1) Point where two sides of an angle meet. (2) Highest or lowest point on a graphed line. (3) The location at which vectors and polygon faces or edges intersect.

vertical Going up or down.

vertical axis The Y-axis in a Cartesian coordinate system.

vertical justification See leading.

vertical scrolling Ability of a system to move up and down through a page or more of data displayed on the video screen. See scrolling.

VGA Acronym for Video Graphics Array. An IBM high-resolution video display standard for its personal computers. VGA displays images at 640 pixels horizontally by 480 pixels vertically. This color bit mapped graphics display standard was introduced by IBM Corporation in 1987 with its PS/2 computers.

video Visual display, especially on a video display terminal.

video buffer The memory on a video adapter used to store the data waiting to be shown on the video display.

video digitizer Input device that converts the signal from a video camera into digital form and stores it in computer storage, where it can be analyzed or modified by the computer. See digitizer.

video disc An optical disc used to store video images and associated audio information.

video display page A portion of a computer's video buffer that holds one complete screen image.

video display terminal (VDT) Device entering information into a computer system and displaying it on a screen. A typewriterlike keyboard is used to enter information. See cathode ray tube, display, and screen.

video display terminal

video graphics Computer-produced animated pictures.

video graphics board A video display board that generates text and graphics and accepts video from a camera or video recorder.

video input camera Video camera that converts images (photographs, real-life situations, drawings) into dot-by-dot images in a computer's memory. The digitized images may be shown on a display screen or printed on paper by a graphics printer.

video monitor The device on which images generated by the computer's video adapter are displayed.

VideoPaint A powerful Apple Macintosh paint program. Its extensive features include over 40 sophisticated special effects – for example, spherization, blur, smudge, contour, Bezier curves, diffuse, dithering, fractals, custom shading, anti-aliasing brush and waterdrop tools, and a multi-layer painting environment. It has a strong three-dimensional modeling feature and includes wire frame creation and rendering with full control over light sources, shades and textures plus the ability to wrap images around three-dimensional models.

video RAM (VRAM) A special type of dynamic RAM (DRAM) used in high-speed video applications.

video signal Electronic signal containing information specifying the location and brightness of each point on a CRT screen, along with timing signals to place the image properly on the screen.

view (1) To display information on a computer display screen. (2) The display of a graphical image from a given perspective. (3) In CAD programs, an image of a three-dimensional graphics model as it would be seen from a particular viewpoint.

view

viewing pipeline The process by which picture data are translated from user input to the screen display.

viewport Process that allows a user to place any selected picture in a chosen location on a video display screen. Compare window.

287

view volume The space in which objects are seen to exist in a three-dimensional display.

vignette An irregular shape to a graphic image without square edges to frame it.

vignette

virtual image An image that has been copied into a computer's memory but that is too large to be displayed all at one time on the screen. Methods such as scrolling and panning are used to bring unseen portions of a virtual image into view.

visible page The image that is being displayed on the screen.

visual arts Arts appealing to the optical sense – painting, drawing, photography, etc.

visual display Visual representation of data, such as a picture or diagram drawn on a display screen or a diagram produced by a plotter or printer.

visual operating system An operating system that relies on icons, selected by a mouse, for giving commands to the computer.

visual page Visual representation consisting of one or more stored screen display files.

visual texture Surface variety that can be seen but not felt with the fingers.

visual programming A way for programmers to interact with software and the programs they construct. The term indicates a new dimension added to programs and software systems, namely the ability to gain different insights and new ways to deal with software through visual and graphical means. Although software can be very complex, visual programming can give one the means to cut through that complexity by providing ways to represent software clearly and concisely in both static and dynamic modes and in two or three dimensions, with color and highlighting.

visual thinking The art of problem solving with visual imagery.

volume Any three-dimensional quantity that is bounded or enclosed, whether solid or void.

von Kock snowflake In 1904, Helge von Kock (1870-1924) described a curve which is now called the von Kock snowflake. Construction of the curve begins with two shapes, an initiator and a generator. The generator is an oriented broken line made up of N equal sides of length R. Thus each stage of the construction begins with a broken line and consists in replacing each straight interval with a copy of the generator, reduced and displaced so as to have the same end points as those of the interval line being replaced. Because of the construction process, the curve exhibits the property of limited self-similarity and is a fractal. The fractal dimension of the von Kock snowflake is 1.2618.

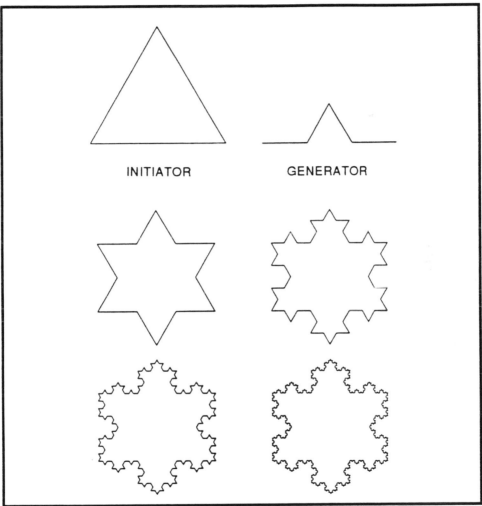

INITIATOR   GENERATOR

von Kock snowflake

voxel Short for volume element. Voxels are three-dimensional elements that describe the data in a volumetric structure. It can be thought of as a "solid pixel."

Wallis filter An image procesing enhancement technique.

warm Referring to color images, ones that have a reddish tint. Those that are more blue are referred to as cool.

warping The transformation of an image in a complex manner that may result in the image being twisted and enlarged in some areas and reduced in others.

warping

Water Color A raster-based paint program designed to emulate the watercolor process operating in MS DOS. The program emulates standard artist tools. Users can mix colors and water and use either nylon or natural bristle brushes as they would on a real canvas. Layering techniques allow objects to be quickly added or deleted.

weight The variation in the heaviness of a typeface.

wheel graph Another name for pie chart.

whitespace (1) A character that does not result in a printed number, letter, or symbol, e.g., space or tab. (2) The portion of the page not printed. A good page design involves the use of white space to balance the areas that receives text and graphics. (3) An element of graphic design.

widow Last line of a paragraph sitting alone at the top of a page of text. Considered undesirable in all forms of printing. Compare with orphan.

window Portion of the video display area dedicated to some specific purpose. Special software allows the screen to be divided into multiple windows that can be moved around and made bigger or smaller. Windows allow the user to treat the computer display screen like a desktop where various files can remain open simultaneously.

window

Windows A graphics-based operating environment for IBM-compatible microcomputers from Microsoft Corporation. It runs in conjunction with DOS. Some of the graphical user interface features include pull-down menus, multiple typefaces, desk accessories, and the capability of moving text and graphics from one program to another via a clipboard.

windows environment Any operating system or program that provides multiple windows on screen. Microsoft Windows, OS/2 Presentation Manager and Apple Macintosh Finder are examples of windows environments.

windows program A program written to run under Microsoft Windows.

window-to-viewport mapping The transformation of primitives from the world coordinate system to the device coordinate system.

windowing Act of displaying two or more files or disparate portions of the same file on the screen simultaneously.

windowing software Programs that enable users to work with multiple on-screen windows.

wire chart The primary end-product of a CAD/CAM wiring diagram system, which generates it automatically. A wire chart lists all devices, connections, and properties in a wiring diagram indicating physical locations of devices and connections, as well as the optimum wiring order for each connection to be made.

wireframe graphics A computer-aided design technique for displaying a three-dimensional object on the CRT screen as a series of lines outlining its surface. The skeletal form of an image created by a vector graphics display.

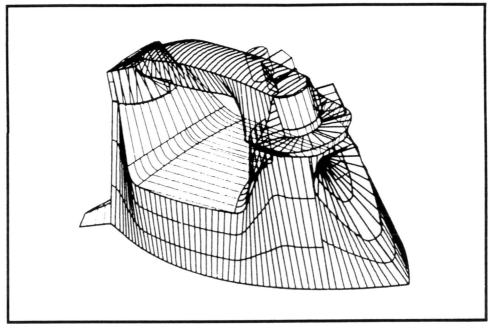

wire frame graphics

wiring diagram (1) Graphics representation of all circuits and device elements of an electrical system and its associated apparatus or any clearly defined functional portion of that system. A wiring diagram may contain not only wiring system components and wires but also nongraphic information such as wire number, wire size, color, function, component label, pin number, etc. (2) Illustration of device elements and their interconnectivity as distinguished from their physical arrangement. (3) Drawings that show how to hook things up. Wiring diagrams can be constructed, annotated, and documented on a CAD system.

WMF Acronym for Windows Metafile Format. A common graphics file format for applications that run under Microsoft Windows.

WordPerfect A full-featured word processing program for IBM-compatible microcomputers, Apple Macintosh, and other computers. It was introduced in 1980 by WordPerfect Corporation. Features include on-screen columns, text boxes, styles, borders, graphics drawing/editing, sort, merge, table of contents/index generation, line numbering, spelling checker and on-line thesaurus. Imports and exports MacWrite documents, as well as WordPerfect documents that were created on many different computers.

word processing (WP) Technique for electronically storing, editing, and manipulating text by using an electronic keyboard, computer, and printer. The text is recorded on a magnetic medium, usually floppy disks. The final output is on paper. Words and letters are manipulated electronically, making it easy to copy and edit text. Popular word processing programs are Microsoft Word, WordPerfect, DisplayWrite, Professional Write, WordStar and FullWrite Professional.

WordStar The first full-featured word processing program for IBM-compatible microcomputers. It was introduced in 1978 by WordStar International. WordStar gave sophisticated word processing capabilities to personal computer users at significantly less cost than the dedicated word processing machines of the time. Several different versions of WordStar are available today.

word wrap Feature that automatically moves a word to the beginning of the next line if it will not fit at the end of the original line. Feature found in word processing and page layout programs.

working drawing In building design, a detailed layout of a component with complete dimensions and notes, approved for production. It can be generated by a CAD/CAM system.

workstation Configuration of computer equipment designed for use by one person at a time. This may have a terminal connected to a computer, or it may be a stand-alone system with local processing capability. Examples of workstations are a stand-alone graphics system, and a word processing system.

world coordinates The coordinate system that is scaled so that user-defined objects can be represented in units appropriate to the application, such as inches, meters, and miles. Each object in a picture is first described in its own model coordinates, and all are then mapped into world coordinates.

world space The three-dimensional coordinate space where objects interact to make scenes.

WPG A WordPerfect graphics file format.

wraparound type Type that wraps around a graphic image in a body of text.

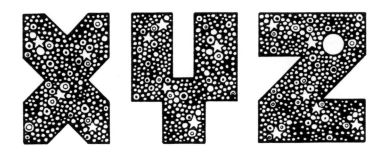

X axis On a coordinate plane, the horizontal axis. Contrast with Y axis and Z axis.

xerography A copying system that depends on an image formed from electrostatic charges. Powdered ink is attracted to the charged parts of a surface and then fused onto paper. The method is the basis of most type of office copiers and also of laser printers.

X-height The height of lowercase letters without ascenders and descenders.

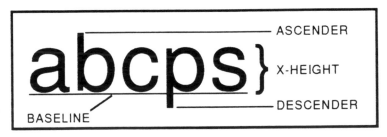

X-height

X-Windows A graphical user interface for UNIX, developed at MIT, that many firms have made a standard. Essentially a graphics display server, X-Windows is the opposite of most client server systems where the workstation is the client and the larger machine is the server. X-Windows depends upon the power of the server to support the interface, while the back-end or client system provides data processing and manipulation.

X-Y chart Form that allows plotting of one data series against another, without a time axis. Often used to determine if there is a correlation between two series, with the direction, slope, and curvature of the line showing the relationship.

X-Y matrix A group of rows and columns. Used as a reference framework for two-dimensional structures, such as two-dimensional graphics images, charts, tables, mathematical graphs and plots, digitizer tablets, digital plotters and display screens.

X-Y plotter Output device that draws points, lines, or curves on a sheet of paper based on X and Y coordinates from a computer. See plotter.

X-Y-Z coordinate system A three-dimensional system of Cartesian coordinates that includes a third (Z) axis running perpendicular to the horizontal (X) and vertical (Y) axis.

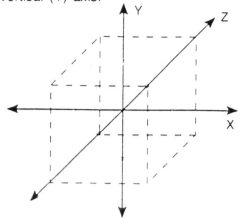

X-Y-Z coordinate system

Y axis On a coordinate plane, the vertical axis. Contrast with X axis and Z axis.

yellow One of the three subtractive primary colors.

YIQ A color model designed for the Macintosh II microcomputer. It stresses luminance as a component of color.

yon plane The back clipping plane that defines a finite view volume. Graphic entities straddling this boundary are clipped in the Z-axis.

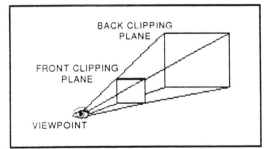

yon plane

Zapf Chancery A typeface developed by Hermann Zapf, a German typeface designer and owned by the International Typeface Corporation (ITC). The typeface is included as a built-in font with many PostScript laser printers.

abcdefghijklmnopqrstuvwxyz
ABCDEFGHIJKLMNOPQRSTUVWXYZ
1234567890 .,;:"&!?$

Zapf Chancery

Zapf Dingbats A set of decorative symbols developed by Hermann Zapf, a German typeface designer. Zapf Dingbats are used for decorative purposes in a document. The typeface is included as a built-in font with many PostScript laser printers.

☞ ☛ ☞ ☚ ☛ ✂ ✄ ☎ ✆ ∞ ✇ ✎

✐ ❻ ❾ 6 9 ⍟ © ❨ ❩ ✔ ✓ ■

□ ▼ ▽ ✕ ✖ ❭ ❭ ◖ ◗ ∗ ∗ ✳

✻ ✼ ✦ ✸ ✶ ✴ ✳ ✷ ✽ ✻ ✲ ✺

Zapf Dingbats

Z axis On a coordinate plane, the axis that represents depth. Contrast with X axis and Y axis.

z-clipping Clipping of a three-dimensional object in the depth dimension in three-dimensional graphics.

zoom To view an enlarged (zoom in) or reduced (zoom out) portion of a page on screen.

zoom box A box symbol that appears in the right corner of some program windows. Clicking in the zoom box causes the window to expand to fill the entire screen or to contract to a smaller size. Clicking it again returns the window to its original size.

zooming Changing of a view on a graphics display by either moving in on successively smaller portions of the currently visible picture or moving out until the window encloses the entire scene. Capability that proportionally enlarges or reduces a figure displayed on a visual display screen. See image enhancement.

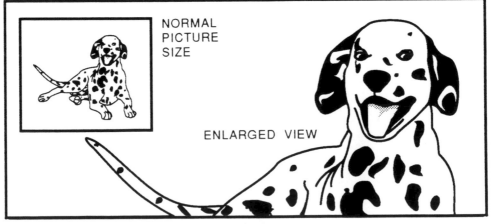

zooming

0 The numeral zero. The slash is used to distinguish it from a capital O.

1.2 M Refers to 1.2 megabytes of storage on a high-density (HD) 5.25 inch floppy disk

1-2-3 See Lotus 1-2-3.

1.4 M Refers to 1.4 megabytes of storage on a high-density (HD) 3.5 inch floppy disk.

2-D graphics A graphic image in two dimensions--height and width.

2-D graphics

2 1/2-D An enhancement to a two-dimensional system in which priority values are assigned to displayed objects, allowing them to be overlapped on the screen to produce an effect like pieces of paper on a desk, each partially obscuring the one below.

3-D graphics A graphic image in three dimensions--height, width, and depth. A screen picture which has the illusion of being solid. The simplest 3-D picture is called a wire-frame drawing. All the lines which make up the picture are shown, even if they would be hidden if the object really were solid.

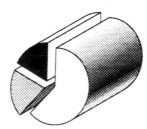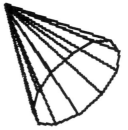

3-D graphics

3.5-inch disk A floppy disk, called a microfloppy, encased in a plastic housing.

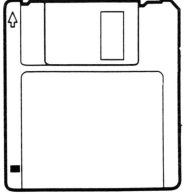

3.5-inch disk

4GL Short for fourth-generation language. A user-oriented language that makes it possible to develop programs with fewer commands than those needed for older procedural languages. An example of this type of language is Structured Query Language (SQL).

5.25-inch disk A flexible piece of mylar encased in a protective covering that records data. Also called a floppy or minifloppy disk.

7-bit track An older tape recording scheme that places data on seven separate parallel tracks on reels of 1/2 inch magnetic tape.

8-bit color Refers to systems that allocate 8 bits of information for each pixel (spot) in the image. This provides 256 possible colors or levels of gray.

8-bit microcomputer A microcomputer that uses a central processing unit with an 8-bit data bus and processes one byte (8-bits) of information at a time.

9-bit track A tape recording scheme that places data on nine separate parallel tracks on reels of 1/2 inch magnetic tape.

16-bit microcomputer A computer that works with information in groups of two bytes (16-bits) at a time.

24-bit color Refers to systems that allocate 24 bits of data to each pixel (spot) in the image. Usually, the bits are allocated as 8 bits each for the three additive primary colors (red, green, and blue). That arrangement provides over 16 million color possibilities.

30 percent rule A rule for determining the positioning of points and Beizer control handles. The distance from a Bezier control handle to its point should be approximately 30 percent of the length of its segment.

32-bit microcomputer A computer that works with information in groups of 32-bits at a time.

80-20 rule An empirical rule related to data usage in large databases that states that 80% of the accesses to a database will deal with only 20% of the data.

90-10 rule An empirical rule for very large databases that states that in order to find the data relevant to a query, nine times as much data as is needed to answer the query must be brought into main memory for processing.

101 key keyboard A standard keyboard for newer IBM personal computers.

286 See 80286.

287 See 80287.

360 K Refers to 360 kilobytes of storage on a 5.25-inch floppy disk

386 See 80386.

386DX See 80386DX.

386SX See 80386SX.

387 See 80387.

486 See 80486.

720K Refers to 720 kilobytes of storage on a 3.5-inch floppy disk.

303x A series of mainframes introduced by IBM Corporation in 1977: 3031, 3032 and 3033.

308x A series of large-scale mainframes introduced by IBM Corporation in 1980: 3081 and 3084.

309x A series of large-scale mainframes introduced by IBM Corporation in 1986.

3270 A terminal used with IBM mainframes.

3770 A terminal used with IBM mainframes.

4004 The first microprocessor manufactured by Intel Corporation.

43xx A series of medium-scale mainframes introduced by IBM Corporation in 1979: 4300, 4321, 4331, 4341, 4361 and 4381.

5100 A desktop computer introduced by IBM Corporation in 1974.

6502 An 8-bit microprocessor manufactured by MOS Technology; made popular in many early home computers such as the Apple II, Commodore 64 and Atari 800 series computers.

6800 An 8-bit microprocessor manufactured by Motorola Corporation. It was the precursor of the popular 68000 family of microprocessors.

8048 A single-chip microcomputer.

8080 An 8-bit microprocessor manufactured by Intel Corporation. It was introduced in 1974 and influenced the design of several future microprocessors.

8086 A 16-bit microprocessor manufactured by Intel Corporation; introduced in 1978. This chip was the forerunner of Intel's 80x86 line of microprocessors. The 8088 used in many PC compatibles is a slightly less capable version of this chip. Produced under license by other manufacturers.

8087 A math coprocessor manufactured by Intel Corporation; designed to be used with 8086 and 8088 microprocessors.

8088 A 16-bit microprocessor developed by Intel Corporation. This microprocessor was used in the original IBM PC and IBM PC XT computers, as well as millions of PC compatibles. It is now considered obsolete, although it continues to be used in some portable computers. Produced under license by other manufacturers.

8100 A minicomputer introduced by IBM Corporation in 1978.

8514 A high-resolution display system from the IBM Corporation. Introduced as the high-end offering for IBM PS/2 models to be used for desktop publishing, computer-aided design, and other uses requiring many colors and high resolution.

9370 A series of entry-level mainframes introduced by IBM Corporation in 1986.

21064 A Reduced Instruction Set Computing (RISC) chip from Digital Equipment Corporation. This 150 MHz microprocessor is said to perform up to 300 million instructions per second. Introduced in 1992.

65816 A 16-bit microprocessor manufactured by Western Digital Design; it can emulate the 6502 microprocessor.

680x0 Refers to Motorola Corporation family of microprocessors: 68000, 68010, 68020, 68030, and 68040.

68000 A 16-bit microprocessor manufactured by Motorola Corporation; introduced in 1979. The 68000 family of microprocessors is used in several popular microcomputers, including the Apple Macintosh, Commodore Amiga and Atari ST. Other more powerful versions, including the 68020, 68030 and 68040 have been successfully introduced in more recent versions of these and other computers, and have taken the 68000 line into the 32-bit world.

68020 A 32-bit microprocessor manufactured by Motorola Corporation; introduced in 1984.

68030 A 32-bit microprocessor manufactured by Motorola Corporation; introduced in 1987.

68040 A 32-bit microprocessor manufactured by Motorola Corporation; announced in 1987.

68881 A math coprocessor manufactured by Motorola Corporation; designed to be used with 68000 and 68020 microprocessors.

68882 A math coprocessor manufactured by Motorola Corporation; designed to be used with the 68030 microprocessor.

80x86 Refers to Intel Corporation's family of microprocessors: 80286, 80386, and 80486.

80x87 Refers to Intel Corporation's family of math coprocessors: 80287, 80387, and 80387SX.

80286 A 16-bit microprocessor manufactured by Intel Corporation; introduced in 1982 and used in the IBM Personal Computer AT computer and compatibles. Manufactured by several other companies now as well.

80287 A math coprocessor manufactured by Intel Corporation; designed for use with 80286 and 80386 microprocessors.

80386 A 32-bit microprocessor manufactured by Intel Corporation. There are two versions of this microprocessor: the 80386SX and the 80386DX.

80386DX A 32-bit microprocessor manufactured by Intel Corporation. It was introduced in 1985.

80386SX A microprocessor manufactured by Intel Corporation. It was introduced in 1988 as a low-cost alternative to the 80386DX. The 80386SX is basically an 80386DX microprocessor limited by a 16-bit data bus. The 80386SX is a slower speed version of the 80386 with the same flexibility.

80387 A math coprocessor manufactured by Intel Corporation; designed for use with the 80386DX microprocessor.

80387SX A math coprocessor manufactured by Intel Corporation; designed for use with the 80386SX microprocessor.

80486 A 32-bit super microprocessor manufactured by Intel Corporation. It was introduced in 1989 and has the built-in equivalent of an 80387 math coprocessor. The 80486 is approximately 50% to 30% faster than the 80386, depending on the application.

80860 A 64-bit RISC-based microprocessor from Intel Corporation.

82385 A cache controller chip that governs cache memory in fast personal computers using the Intel 80386 and 80486 microprocessors; developed by Intel Corporation.

88000 A family of 32-bit RISC microprocessors introduced by Motorola, Inc. in 1988.

PICTURE AND PHOTOGRAPH CREDITS

Page Number

Cover Art - A computer created version of "Stormy Sea Off Kanagawa," an engraving by Katsushika Hokusai (1760-1849). Hokusai was a painter and engraver of extraordinary power and versatility, a giant by any standard. He was fascinated by eddies and whorls of every kind, as exemplified by the cover art.

ABOUT
THE
AUTHOR

Donald D Spencer is an internationally known computer science educator and author. He received his Ph.D. degree in computer science and has worked in the computer field since 1959. Dr. Spencer is the author of over 160 computer science books published by 20 different textbook publishers. Several of his books have been translated into German, Hungarian, French, Italian, Spanish, Japanese and other languages. He has worked on some 25 different mainframe computer systems and 20 different microcomputer systems, and has been involved in a number of pioneering projects.

Dr. Spencer has taught computer science in college and industry, and has held computer related positions in several industrial organizations. He has spoken at many conferences and seminars on educational computing. Dr. Spencer has made frequent lectures about computers to students and teachers in elementary schools, secondary schools and colleges. He is a past chairman of the National ACM Committee on Secondary School Programs. Dr. Spencer is currently a member of several school and college committees on computer science education.

He is a member of several educational and professional societies including the Association for Computing Machinery (ACM), the National Council of Teachers of Mathematics (NCTM), the Institute for Electrical and Electronics Engineers (IEEE), the International Society of Technology in Education (ISTE), the Mathematical Association of America (MAA), and the National Service Robot Association (NSRA). Several million copies of his books have been used by students, teachers, professionals, and general audience readers all over the world.

305